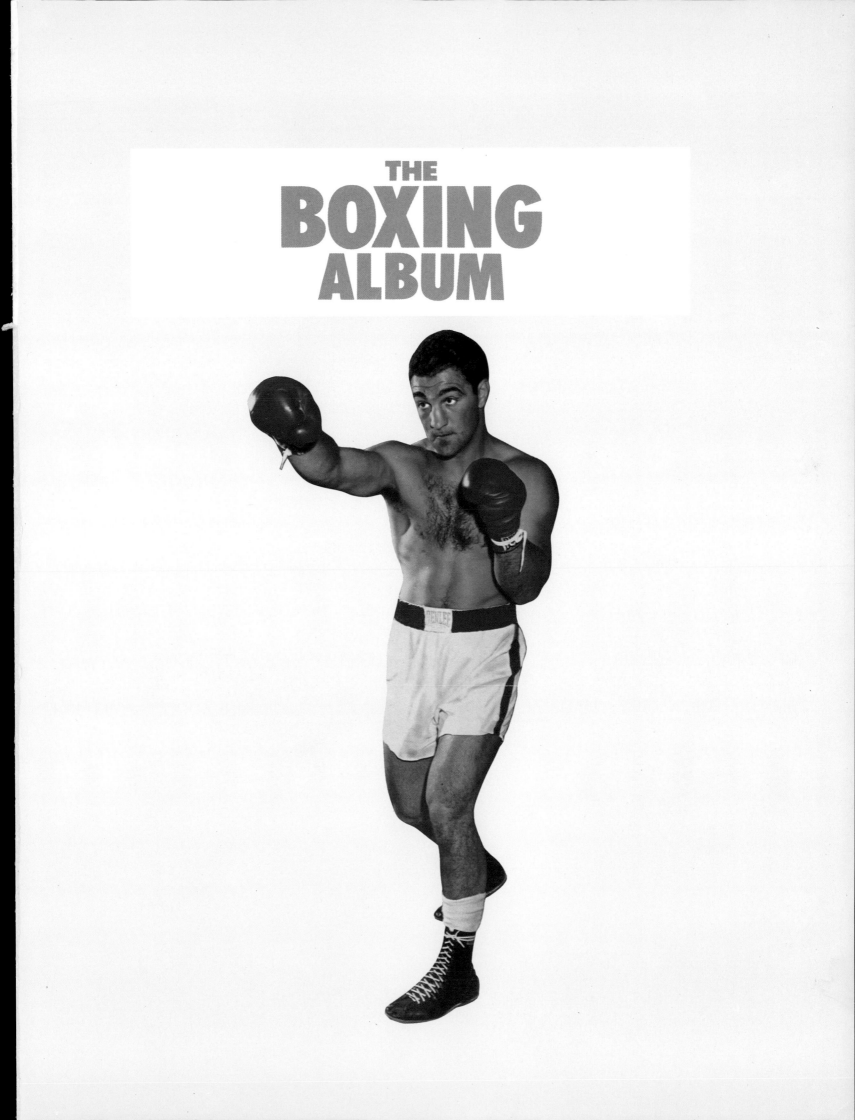

THE
BOXING
ALBUM

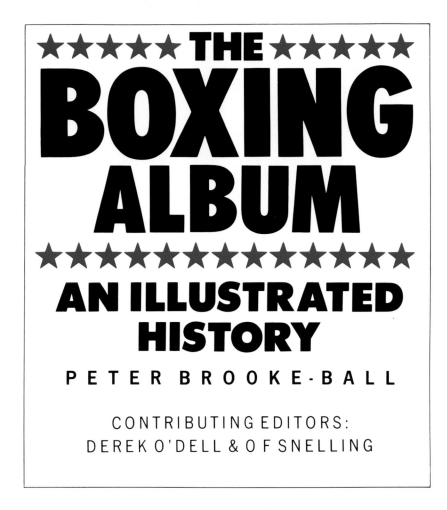

THE
BOXING
ALBUM

AN ILLUSTRATED
HISTORY

PETER BROOKE-BALL

CONTRIBUTING EDITORS:
DEREK O'DELL & O F SNELLING

SMITHMARK

© 1995 Anness Publishing Limited

This revised and updated edition first published
in the United States in 1995 by
Smithmark Publishers
a division of U.S. Media Holdings, Inc.
16 East 32nd Street
New York
New York 10016

SMITHMARK books are available for bulk purchase
for sales promotion and premium use.
For details write or call the manager of special sales,
SMITHMARK Publishers, 16 East 32nd Street,
New York, NY 10016; (212) 532-6600.

Produced by Anness Publishing Limited
Boundary Row Studios
1 Boundary Row
London SE1 8HP

ISBN 0 8317 4810 9

Publisher: Joanna Lorenz
Project Editors: Bobby Hugs and Vicky Thomson
Art Director: Peter Bridgewater
Designer: Peter Laws

Typeset by MC Typeset Ltd, Rochester, Kent
Printed and bound in China

★

CONTENTS

INTRODUCTION

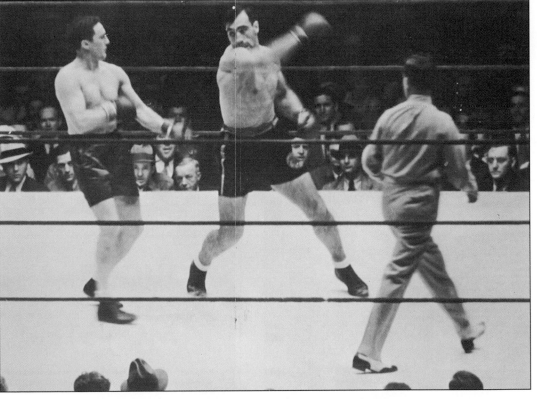

Above: Max Baer (left) in action against the giant Italian world champion Primo Carnera on June 14 1945. Many still look back to the 1920s, 30s and 40s as the heart of boxing's history. The sport was not so highly organized, and the fighters themselves risked greater injury for lower rewards, but there were fewer pointless matches, less hype and hot air, and there was an honest endeavour and grittiness that is sometimes missing today.

Left: Two of the greatest, Thomas Hearns and 'Sugar' Ray Leonard, meet in Las Vegas in 1989 in what was a truly classic encounter. The fight ended in a draw.

Right: Three separate fights are portrayed in this red and black decoration found on a Greek *cylix* (chalice) which is kept in the British Museum. In the top, left, depiction, two boxers, wearing *himantes*, are sparring. The figure to the left is attempting to parry a blow prior to delivering a right uppercut. The two grappling figures appear to have broken the rules by wrestling and are being brought to heel by the referee who holds a forked stick, the symbol of his authority. In the bottom section, two fighters are flailing at each other with open hands under the keen eye of the referee, while the figure to the right prepares a thong prior to wrapping it around his hands.

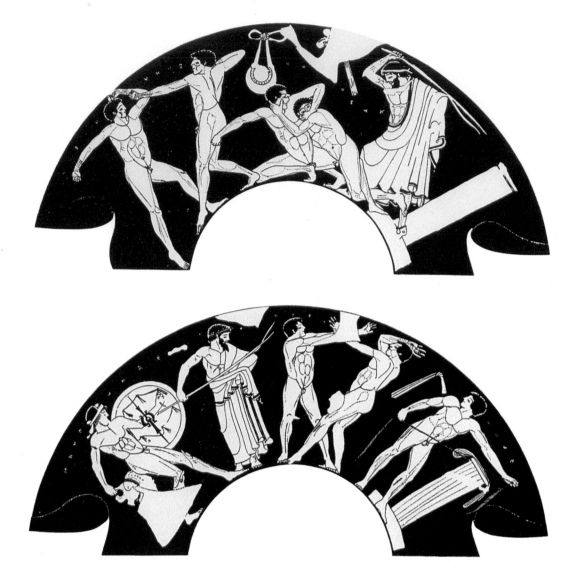

Until the British resurrected the sport in the early eighteenth century, boxing had remained dormant since the fall of the Roman Empire. Needless to say men, more often than not fortified with ale, had settled matters of honour with fisticuffs in the interim, but not according to any recognized set of rules.

The origins of boxing date back to ancient Greece: Homer mentions a form of organized boxing in the *Iliad*. The honour of 'inventing' the sport, however, goes to the Greek king Theseus, who is thought to have introduced boxing as an entertainment some time before the fifth century BC.

Over the years boxers evolved ways of protecting themselves and, as a consequence, bouts grew longer. They bound their hands with soft leather thongs (*himantes*) not so that they could deliver more punishing blows, nor indeed to soften blows, but so that their knuckles, thumbs and forearms were protected from fractures and grazes.

The rules in ancient Greek boxing were few and far between and mostly relied on traditional codes of honour. For example, punches to any part of the body were permitted but grappling and wrestling were not considered sportsmanlike. There were no rings as such in early forms of boxing, simply fighting areas defined by spectators. This meant that it was difficult for an attacking boxer to pin his man down in a corner, as the besieged fighter could always back away. Ring-craft was virtually non-existent, and the two boxers invariably stood with their feet anchored to one spot as they swung blows at each other. The concept of having 'rounds' did not occur to the Greeks, so the two men continued to slug each other until one surrendered or was knocked senseless.

Boxing was first included in the ancient Olympic Games at the twenty-third Olympiad in 688 BC. There were no weight divisions, so small men stood little chance when exchanging blows with the brawny hulks who invariably ended up as the champions.

Left: This bronze statue in the Museo della Terme in Rome shows a Greek fighter fully prepared for combat. The Greeks fought naked but to strict codes of honour, so this hero could at least expect his manhood to remain intact at the end of the contest. His hands and forearms are bound with leather thongs, *himantes*, and stout *sphairai* (which were probably made of hardened leather and could inflict considerable damage) cover his knuckles. The sculptor obviously had an eye for accuracy as the boxer has perhaps the first recorded cauliflower ear.

Below: This ancient Greek wall-painting depicts two young boys in training for pugilism. Interestingly, the boy on the right seems to be bare-fisted, while the boy on the left has his hands wrapped.

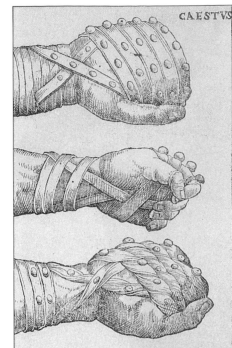

CAESTVS

Left: The introduction of the *caestus* by the Romans began the decline of ancient boxing, which thereafter became a gladiatorial sport in which men fought to the death for the amusement of spectators. The *caesti* illustrated here may not be wholly accurate representations of what the weapons actually looked like, as they first appeared as wood engravings in *De Arte Gymnastica*, a book by Hieronymus Mercurialis which was not published until 1573. They do, however, give an impression of how the gruesome implements were worn and what they were fashioned from. Made from leather thongs encrusted with metal beads, the *caestus* was heavy and lethal. The bottom illustration shows twisted thongs which presumably added more cutting power.

Right: This somewhat romantic impression of gladiators fighting in ancient Rome is also taken from a wood-engraved illustration found in *De Arte Gymnastica*. The men wear *caesti*, but both appear to be physically unscathed. In truth, such a contest would have been a bloody affair and one solid punch would have been sufficient to kill or severely maim an opponent. Also missing from the drawing are ranks of spectators baying for blood. It could be that the illustration is supposed to represent fighters in training, but it is highly unlikely that professional gladiators would risk a sparring session while wearing deadly *caesti*.

PVGILES

Left: The decoration on this sixth-century BC vase shows pugilists going hard at each other with *caesti* on their fists.

One bruiser by the name of Milo is said to have won the boxing competition at four consecutive Games. Seventy-two years after boxing was introduced to the Olympics, a junior division for boys was included, and was no doubt used by ambitious youngsters as a stepping stone to gain entry to the senior competition four years later. Contrary to popular belief, Greek athletes at the Olympics were not amateurs but hardened professionals. Sure enough, the victor of a competition was awarded his wreath of bay leaves, but he was also given a prize of 500 drachmas and was entitled to free food for life.

During the latter days of the ancient Olympics, Romans and other foreigners were allowed to take part and so boxing was taken to Rome. By this time, boxers had given up soft wrappings and had taken to wearing hard and sharp *himantes* which were designed to inflict wounds as well as to protect. The ancient Romans, with their notorious lust for blood, were not convinced that the new, improved *himantes* were sufficiently lethal, so they devised the *caestus*.

The *caestus* was a weapon worn by professional gladiators and comprised a binding studded with stones or sharpened spikes of metal. The men who wore these fought for their lives in the circus, fully aware that one blow to the temple would be sufficient to kill. There were no rules in gladiatorial boxing and the sport degenerated into bloody combat, the victor being the one who slaughtered his opponent before he himself was dispatched. Fighters did not know the meaning of self-defence – any boxer who attempted to protect himself would certainly get the thumbs down – and the hapless men were simply trained to absorb punishment and to hit before being hit. The boxing skills which are recognized today, and which the Greeks may have developed before they were over-run, were never given a chance to evolve by the Romans. Gladiators continued to fight in arenas for the amusement of bloodthirsty spectators until the fall of the Roman Empire in the fifth century AD. And when the Empire fell, the sport of boxing, if sport is the right word, disappeared with it.

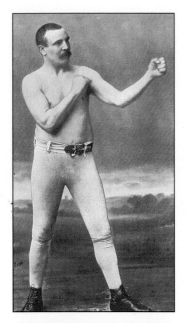   

THE
CHAMPIONS

On these two pages are shown a host of champions and nearly-men from the 1890s and 1900s – the golden age of the fight game, when bare-fisted sluggers gave way to the modern giants. Smaller pictures: top rank, left to right: Jim Fell; Joe McAuliffe; Frank Craig; Mike Donovan; 'Denver' Ed Smith. Middle rank: Jim Daly; Joe Goss; Jack Welch; Jack Ashton; John Donaldson. Bottom rank: Samuel Blakelock; Captain J C Dailey; William Sheriff; Frank Herald; 'Sparrow' Golden. Above left: Jimmy Carney. Above right: George Godfrey. Right: Jimmy Carroll.

Above: James Figg's card of 1719, which was engraved for him by his friend, the great English painter William Hogarth. This was the first advertisement for the 'Noble Science of Defence'. In addition to boxing, Figg also taught his clients how to use the sword and the quarterstaff.

Right: John (Jack) Broughton (1704–1789) is regarded as the 'Father of Boxing'. He established a boxing school and arena near the Haymarket in London, and he encouraged his pupils to wear gloves so that they would not inflict too much damage on each other. After one of his defeated opponents, George Stevenson, died, Broughton introduced a set of rules which remained in force for the best part of a century. He became a Yeoman of the Guard at the Tower of London and there is a memorial to him in Westminster Abbey.

THE EARLY CHAMPIONS

An Oxfordshire-born Englishman by the name of James Figg is credited with the rebirth of boxing, when, in 1719, he advertised a boxing exhibition at his booth at Southwark Fair in London. Figg was better known at the time as a cudgel-fighter and swordsman but he nevertheless claimed to be boxing's first champion and he went on to open his celebrated amphitheatre off the Tottenham Court Road in what is now the West End of London. One of Figg's major achievements was to attract the attention of England's gentry. He was lucky enough to be a close friend of the painter William Hogarth who not only completed a portrait of the fighter but also produced illustrated publicity leaflets for him. So, as well as being the first champion, Figg also became the first promoter, not just for himself but for everyone involved.

Figg had many fistic encounters at his amphitheatre, where the arena was surrounded by wooden planks, and he even attracted international opposition. One of his most famous fights was against a Venetian gondolier who nearly got the better of Figg before eventually being flattened by a body blow. Figg retired undefeated in 1734 and one of his pupils, George Taylor, assumed the title of champion. In 1740 Taylor was beaten by Jack Broughton, who immediately began to revolutionize the art of boxing. Three years after beating Taylor, Broughton built his own amphitheatre, complete with a raised stage, in Hanway Street and drafted a set of rules which transformed the sport. Until Broughton's Rules were published, there were virtually no codes of conduct and a boxer was consequently allowed to use any tactic he wished.

Broughton remained champion until 1750 when he was beaten by Jack Slack, a Norwich butcher, who

Right: Daniel Mendoza (1763– 1836) was a clever man and the most skilful boxer of his era. He managed his own affairs and is thought to be the first person to introduce a 'gate' at which spectators had to pay in order to see a contest. The first Jewish champion, he introduced new defensive techniques to boxing and he had a great influence on subsequent generations of fighters.

MENDOZA.

Above: John Smith, called 'Buckhorse', was a familiar figure in the London rings during the middle of the eighteenth century. His ugliness was only in part due to bare-knuckle fighting as he was born with a misshapen face. He had a reputation for being an outstandingly brave and powerful fighter.

became known as the 'Knight of the Cleaver'. However Broughton was hailed as the 'Father of Boxing' and during his reign he was much favoured by the aristocracy, especially the Duke of Cumberland. In fact he was so adored by men from all walks of life that when he died at the age of eighty-five a special memorial stone was laid for him in no less a place than Westminster Abbey.

Jack Slack and his contemporaries did little for boxing and the sport lost favour and reputation, not only with the public, but with wealthy patrons as well. Slack himself was at first seen to be a brave and able fighter; but he later resorted to using unfair, open-fisted 'chops' and he frequently bribed opponents to lose. He was not averse to taking bribes himself and when he lost the title to Bill 'The Nailer' Stevens in

1760, his backer, the powerful Duke of Cumberland, suspecting that he had accepted payment, turned his back on boxing for good. Equally disillusioned, the public shunned fights while the boxers determined the championship among themselves based on who could pay the biggest bribes.

A new era of bare-knuckle fighting began with the arrival on the pugilist scene of a Spanish-English Jew by the name of Daniel Mendoza who became so famous when he beat Sam 'Butcher' Martin in 1787 that he pronounced himself champion. However it was not until he had got the better of Bill Warr in seventeen minutes on Bexley Heath in 1794 that he was universally acknowledged as undisputed champion of England. Mendoza was unusually intelligent for a boxer of the time, and he cultivated the art of

Right: 'Gentleman' John Jackson (1769–1845) was a canny boxer and was given his nickname because of his good manners and dandy's clothes. However when he wrested the championship from Mendoza in 1795, he is supposed to have held his opponent's head by the hair as he punched him into oblivion. Jackson had friends in high places and taught Lord Byron, among others, to box at his school in Old Bond Street, London.

Above: Richard Humphries beat Daniel Mendoza twice, in 1787 and 1788, before the latter became champion. However Mendoza avenged those defeats in 1789 and 1790, and, after the fourth fight, Humphries decided that he had had enough and retired.

defence which had largely been ignored in favour of developing strength and endurance. Mendoza's tactics were admired by many but not by all; some, unused to this new and artful style, proclaimed him a coward as he cannily moved around the ring to gain an advantage. Mendoza's strategy was, however, adopted by a new generation of boxers, most particularly in Ireland, which he toured and where he eventually established a boxing school. Mendoza lost his crown to 'Gentleman' John Jackson in 1795 (in what was by every account a not very gentlemanly fight) and retired to write his *Memoirs*. He returned to the ring eleven years later, aged fifty-seven, but gave up for good after losing to Tom Owen.

Like Mendoza, 'Gentleman' John Jackson, so-called because he dressed in dandy's clothes and was

Above: 'Jem' Belcher (1781–1811) beat many of the best boxers of his day but ironically is most remembered for the fights he lost – especially those against Tom Cribb. Called the 'Napoleon of the Ring' because of his clever strategies, he lost an eye while playing rackets in 1803 and relinquished his title to Henry 'Game Chicken' Pearce in 1805. He is thought to have been the first person to place his 'colours' on the corner post of a ring.

Right: Thomas Cribb (1781–1848) was a comparatively slow boxer but sturdy and determined for all that. His greatest bouts were against Tom Molineaux whom he fought twice, in 1810 and 1811, winning both times. He retired to run a public house and such was his popularity that when he died a memorial was erected to him by public subscription in Woolwich Churchyard.

well-spoken, was a 'scientific' boxer who heavily relied on nimble footwork for his victories. Like several champions before him he ran a boxing school; it was situated at no. 13 Old Bond Street, London, and among his pupils was Lord Byron who dubbed him the 'Emperor of Pugilism'.

One of the most well-liked and respected boxers at the turn of the century was John ('Jem') Belcher who was the grandson of Jack Slack, the infamous former champion. He reigned supreme from 1800 to 1803 when he lost an eye while playing rackets. He retired for a time but came back two years later and fought Henry Pearce who beat him in thirteen rounds. He boxed two more contests, both against Tom Cribb, but lost on each occasion and eighteen months later died at the tender age of thirty.

One of the most extraordinary characters ever to box was John Gully, who came from a well-to-do

family but had been thrown into a debtors' prison as a result of a business venture that failed. In those days there was little hope of ever getting out of a debtors' jail, but Gully had earned a reputation as a competent amateur fighter and the reigning champion, Henry Pearce, entered the prison to spar with him. Gully, by all accounts, got the better of the champion and the news spread far and wide. In due course, Gully's debts were paid by a benevolent sportsman on the condition that he would fight Pearce for the championship of England.

The two met on October 8 1805 at Hailsham in Sussex. After sixty-four rounds Gully was beaten, but not before putting up an impressive show. So much so that when Pearce retired he declared Gully to be his successor. Not everybody was satisfied with this conclusion, so Gully was obliged to fight the 'Lancashire Giant', Bob Gregson. After Gregson had

Right: The first fight between 'Jem' Belcher and Tom Cribb at Moulsey Hurst on April 8 1807. Belcher had the better of the fight, but had to retire with shattered hands. 'What did I tell you?', cried a bloody Cribb as Belcher left, unable to throw another punch: 'I said that my head would break his hands to pieces!'

Below: The magnificent early champion, Henry 'Game Chicken' Pearce.

HEN⁻ PEARCE
FROM AN OLD ENGRAVING.

Left: Tom Molineaux (1784–1818) followed Bill Richmond to England, landing in 1809. Like Richmond, his family had been slaves and he found fame and fortune in Britain. He is best remembered for his two fights against Tom Cribb. He nearly won the first, and had it not been for some trickery by Cribb's seconds he might have become champion. In their second encounter, however, the American's jaw was broken and he was soundly beaten. As can be seen, right, the action against Cribb was fast and furious, and this was not one of the highlights of Molineaux's great career.

SHUREY'S EDITION.
ONE PENNY.
FAMOUS FIGHTS
PAST AND PRESENT.
EDITED BY HAROLD FURNISS

Vol. III.—No. 31.   TOM CRIBB'S SECOND BATTLE WITH MOLINEAUX.

Above: James ('Jem') Ward was a distinguished boxer, but his character was more dubious. His reign as champion came during a period when boxing was part of the underworld, and notorious for 'fixes' and out-of-ring violence. He was the first champion ever to regain his crown, when he beat Simon Byrne in 1831.

Right: Irishman Simon Byrne, 'The Emerald Gem', shows his class against Phillip Sampson, 'The Birmingham Youth', in 1829. Sampson was no match for Byrne, and despite being physically carried to the scratch by his seconds on numerous occasions, he eventually gave way to the slaughter after one hundred and four minutes.

been soundly beaten twice, in 1807 and 1808, Gully was acknowledged as the genuine champion; but after the second contest he vowed that he would never fight in the ring again. Among those who pleaded with him to change his mind was the Duke of York, but Gully's resolution stayed firm and he went on to amass a great fortune. He established a racing stable and two of his horses won the Derby. He also acquired land and coal mines and in 1832 was elected a Member of Parliament. He died a wealthy and successful man in 1863 at the age of eighty.

After Gully had retired in 1808 Tom Cribb laid claim to the crown and challenged the one-eyed 'Jem' Belcher for the championship in their second encounter. He won the contest in thirty-one rounds in 1809 and successfully defended his title in two epic encounters against the black American, Tom Molineaux. Cribb did not fight professionally again after his second bout with Molineaux in 1811, but continued to hold the title until 1822, when he named Tom Spring as his successor.

Spring proved to be a worthy champion and remained undefeated upon his retirement in 1824 after two classic fights against the Irish champion, Jack Langan. Tom Cannon claimed the title after Spring, but his reign was short-lived and he was beaten by 'Jem' Ward in 1825. Ward was a shady character and is known to have bet money on himself to lose. However he became the first man to regain the championship title after losing it. He was defeated by Peter 'Young Rump Steak' Crawley in 1827, but became champion again four years later when he beat the Irishman, Simon Byrne. In 1831 Ward was presented with a Championship Belt, the first awarded.

Above: James 'Deaf 'Un' Burke
was born in 1809 and died in
1845. He was well-liked, though a
rogue of the first water. He was a
successful fighter, and worked
his way up to become champion
in 1833. In that year he had his
most famous fight – one of the
most brutal recorded in the
history of the sport. He fought
Simon Byrne at a place called
No-Man's-Land in Hertfordshire,
and the two men went at it for
ninety-nine rounds which lasted
one hundred and eighty-six
minutes: Byrne died two days
later of his injuries.

THE FIGHT BETWEEN DEAF BURKE AND BILL FITZMAURICE.
Vol. II.—No. 21.

James Burke, known as the 'Deaf 'Un', called himself champion after Ward's retirement but Simon Byrne disputed his claim. To settle the issue, Burke and Byrne fought a bitter battle in 1833 that lasted three hours, six minutes for a total of ninety-nine rounds. Burke won the undisputed title, while the unfortunate Byrne was carried off, and died of his injuries soon after. Burke was forced to flee to America because of the ensuing furore and there he fought an old enemy, Samuel O'Rourke, in New Orleans. O'Rourke was a mobster and hoodlum and

**Above: Burke in action against
Bill Fitzmaurice. Burke
eventually triumphed after one
hundred and sixty-six rounds
which lasted two minutes under
three hours. Fitzmaurice may
have been hampered in his
challenge by the absence of his
manager, Charlie Gibletts, who
was in prison at the time, having
been caught body-snatching in
Bishop's Stortford.**

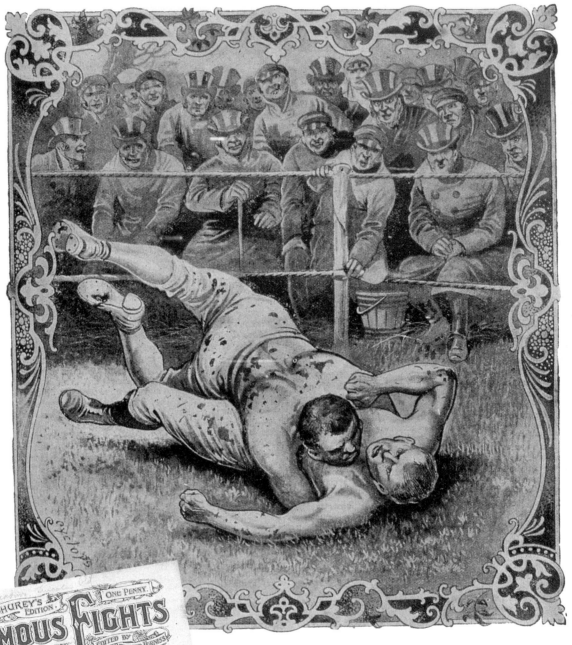

Left: The fight between Ben Caunt and John Leechman, 'Brassey of Bradford', on October 26 1840 at Six Mile Bottom, between Newmarket and Cambridge. The fight was attended by many of the sporting nobility, including the Duke of Beaufort, the Marquis of Worcester, the Marquis of Exeter, and Lord George Bentinck: it was just as well that a group of special constables sent to hunt out and stop the battle were guilefully diverted to another county. Caunt downed his man for good in the one-hundredth round.

Above: William Abednego Thompson, called 'Bendigo' in fight circles, was one of the most remarkable ring characters of these early days. In this fight he beat 'Young' Langan in one hour thirty-three minutes, after spending most of the preliminary stages shamming that he was too hurt to continue. Langan relaxed in anticipation of victory, and, with his defences down, 'Bendigo' was able to land a winning blow. He proceeded to take the championship from Caunt shortly afterwards.

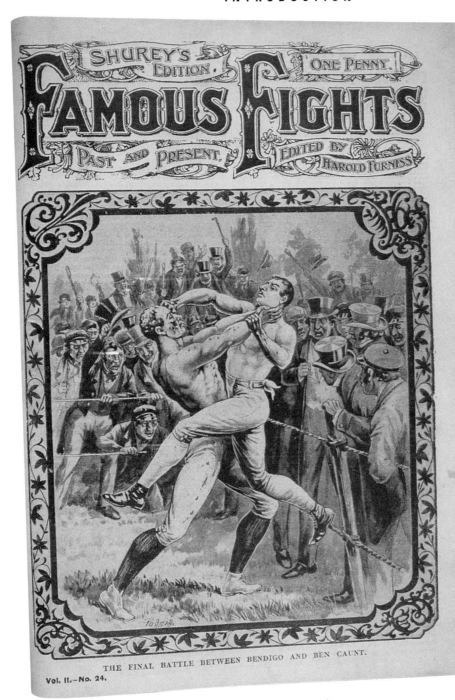

THE FINAL BATTLE BETWEEN BENDIGO AND BEN CAUNT.

Vol. II.—No. 24.

Above and left: William 'Bendigo' Thompson (1811–1880) was a fiery character who was in perpetual trouble with the law. He first won the championship from Ben Caunt in 1835, then lost it to the same man in 1838. 'Bendigo' got the better of James Burke in 1839, and regained the championship title in a third bloody battle against Caunt in 1845. In later years 'Bendigo' gave up his former ways and became a preacher. The town of Bendigo in Australia is named after him and a play has been written about his extraordinary life. The scene, left, is from 'Bendigo's' last fight against Caunt.

his cronies broke up the fight in the third round when they saw that their boss was losing. Burke escaped and went to New York where he had one fight before returning to England. In 1839, Burke fought William 'Bendigo' Thompson (a fighter who had won and lost the championship title in the intervening years), but was disqualified for head-butting.

Thompson was a curious man. He was one of triplets who were nicknamed Shadrach, Meshach and Abednego, the last being corrupted to 'Bendigo'. Short and stocky, he was not the cleanest of fighters but he was nevertheless brave and resourceful. Before beating Burke, he had had two notorious en-

counters with Ben Caunt for the championship, and each man had won one contest when the other was disqualified for fouling. When they met for the third time, in 1845, a ferocious struggle took place with both men employing nasty tactics. 'Bendigo' eventually got the better of his old adversary in ninety-three rounds after Caunt broke the rules by going down without being struck. 'Bendigo's' last fight was in 1850 against Tom Paddock, who was disqualified when he struck the champion while he was down. 'Bendigo' retired after his fight with Paddock and during one of his frequent later spells in prison he had a mystical revelation. He consequently became an evangelist and travelled the world preaching.

Above: Bill Richmond (1763–1829) was the son of an American slave who learned his boxing skills while sparring against British soldiers stationed in the United States. He was brought to England by the Duke of Northumberland and had several impressive victories before being knocked out by Tom Cribb. He was the first black boxer to rise to prominence and he continued to fight until he was fifty-six, at which age he knocked out Jack Carter.

Right: Tom Sayers (1826–1865) is one of the most famous of all bare-knuckle fighters. Small and light, he was only ever beaten once, by Nat Langham. His 1860 fight against the American, John C Heenan, ranks among the greatest of all time, despite the fact that it ended in a draw. Nicknamed 'Peerless' because of his skill, he was buried at London's famous Highgate cemetery.

THE FIRST CHAMPIONS IN THE UNITED STATES

By the middle of the nineteenth century, boxing had taken root in America. Many English and Irish fighters had toured the country giving exhibition bouts, and several Americans, most notably the ex-slaves Bill Richmond and Tom Molineaux, had come to fight in England. A New Yorker by the name of Jacob Hyer is considered the 'Father of the American Ring'. He was the first American to fight professionally and his match against Tom Beasley in 1816 was the first to be fought to British Prize Ring Rules. In 1849 Hyer's son, Tom, became the first heavyweight champion of America when he beat 'Yankee' Sullivan, an Irish émigré. After Tom Hyer retired, another Irish-American, John Morissey, beat 'Yankee' Sullivan and the up-and-coming John C Heenan to claim the American title. Then Morissey retired and Heenan had nobody to fight. A suggestion was put forward that he challenge the reigning British champion,

Tom Sayers, to determine who would be the undisputed champion of the world.

Sayers, a bricklayer by trade, had clinched the British title by knocking out Tom Paddock in 1858. He was a small man and weighed little more than 150 pounds, but by the time he met Heenan, the 'Benecia Boy', in 1860, he had a formidable reputation for beating men far larger than himself. His one defeat had been in 1853 at the hands of Nat Langham.

In one of the most memorable fights in boxing history, the first international contest for a world title ended in a draw. Sayers did not fight again, and on his retirement Heenan assumed the crown of world champion. The two, in fact, became close friends and when Heenan went to England in 1863 to fight Tom King, Sayers acted as his second. Heenan lost that contest and both he and King retired shortly afterwards.

Above, left, and bottom: John C Heenan (1833–1873) came over to England in 1860 to fight Tom Sayers to decide who would be champion of the world. The fight was called a draw after crowd interference, with Heenan having to break away through the mob (bottom), but Heenan had had the English hero on the ropes. To look at Heenan's face on the day after the fight (above), there is no doubt that Sayers scored some good hits, too. Perhaps surprisingly, Heenan and Sayers became friends and they later fought exhibition matches together. Heenan returned to England in 1863 and lost to Tom King. He never fought again.

Right: This engraving, which was originally reproduced in a newspaper of the time, illustrates the procession at Tom Sayers' funeral in 1865.

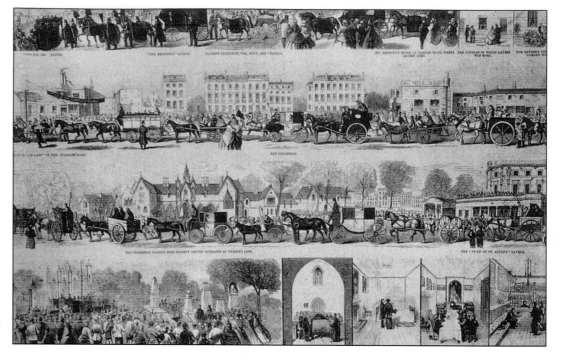

Above: Peter Jackson was a talented boxer who bridged two eras, fighting both with and without gloves. He started his career in 1882 while in Australia and travelled to America in 1888. John L Sullivan refused to fight him because of his colour, but he fought a closely-contested sixty-one-round draw with James J Corbett in 1891.

Right: Jackson fights Corbett on May 21 1891 at the California Athletic Club: the men are wearing gloves, and a new age has begun.

Left and below: 'Jem' Mace could lay claim to being the last of the great bare-knuckle fighters: after him came Sullivan, and a new generation. In a tribute to him, *Famous Fights* proclaimed: 'In his prime Mace was one of the finest-looking athletes, and *the* most finished boxer we ever saw in the Prize Ring. Indeed, we think it is not too much to say that amongst the Champions of England, of whom he was the last, there was not one superior to him in science or Ring-craft.' He is pictured, below, at his peak, on the cover of the magazine.

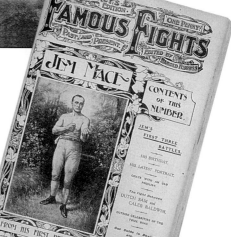

THE LATE NINETEENTH CENTURY

With the passing of the great Sayers and Heenan, boxing fell into some disarray, especially in England where it began to lose favour with the public. This was due, in no small part, to the preachings of the influential clergy who were united in their battle against fist-fighting. Jem Mace, who had once beaten Tom King, was acclaimed as the world champion but, like so many English boxers, he spent much of his time in the United States.

Mace's last fight, a draw, was against an American called Joe Coburn on November 30 1871. Coburn had laid claim to the American title in 1863 on beating another Irishman, Mike McCool. Five years later, however, McCool claimed the title when Coburn was arrested by the police just before their return bout was due to begin. An Englishman, Tom Allen, who had fled the victimization back in his own country, went on to defeat McCool in 1873. Joe Goss, another Englishman who had crossed the Atlantic, got the better of Allen in 1876, but lost to Paddy Ryan in an eighty-seven-round contest in 1880. Ryan's reign as American champion was brief and he got his come-uppance against no less a personage than the mighty John L Sullivan. With the coming of Sullivan was born a new breed of fighters, who were to become the first generation of the modern game.

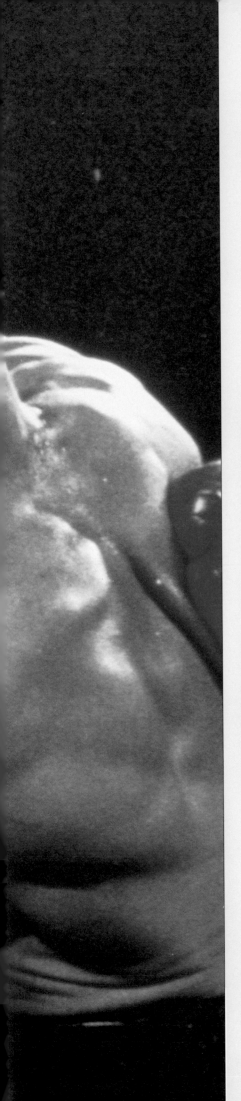

GREAT CHAMPIONS OF THE GLOVED ERA

Above: The Cuban crowd goes wild in Havana on April 5 1915, as Jess Willard stands above the felled Jack Johnson. It is the twenty-sixth round of their heavyweight title bout, and Willard is about to don the crown he was to wear for the next four years.

Left: Discounting the legendary Bob Fitzsimmons, who was born in England but moved to New Zealand as a child, Britain has seldom come close to even contesting the heavyweight championship in the twentieth century. In this rare British title challenge, Frank Bruno briefly raised his countryman's hopes in February 1989, but after shaking Mike Tyson in the first round, he was stopped in the fifth.

JOHN L SULLIVAN

John L Sullivan will forever be remembered as the first man to become officially recognized as the heavyweight champion of the world, although he claimed the title while boxing to Prize Ring Rules.

He was born of Irish parents in Boston, and as a teenager won a reputation for being something of a braggart, challenging all-comers to take him on and showing off his immense strength by lifting full beer barrels over his head. Not surprisingly, he was dubbed the 'Boston Strong Boy'.

Paddy Ryan, the reigning American champion, refused to fight Sullivan in 1880 so the 'Boston Strong Boy' went on a nation-wide tour, offering fifty dollars to anyone who could last four rounds with him in a ring (on a subsequent tour the challenge went up to $1,000 to anybody who could last four rounds). Nobody succeeded in taking money from him and in 1882 Ryan at last agreed to a fight. The contest took place at Mississippi City on February 7 1882, and Ryan was knocked out in nine rounds that lasted just under eleven minutes.

After his fight with Ryan, Sullivan claimed that he was both American and world champion but others disagreed, including Charlie Mitchell, the British champion. Mitchell and Sullivan first met in New York in 1883 and the Englishman went down in the third round. However, the fight never came to a completely satisfying conclusion, because the police burst in and broke it up. Another man left unhappy by Sullivan's claims was Jake Kilrain, who had challenged the 'Boston Strong Boy' to a contest but had been rejected. This refusal to fight prompted Richard K Fox, owner of the prestigious *Police Gazette*, to pronounce Kilrain champion. In 1887, outraged at Fox's impertinence, Boston businessmen clubbed together and gave Sullivan a $10,000 gold belt, inlaid with 397 diamonds, as

BORN ROXBURY, MASSACHUSETTS, OCTOBER 15 1858 **TURNED PROFESSIONAL** 1878 **WORLD HEAVYWEIGHT CHAMPION** (PRIZE RING RULES) 1882–1892 **TOTAL PROFESSIONAL FIGHTS** WON 38, LOST 1, DREW 3 **DIED** ABINGDON, MASSACHUSETTS, 1918

a token of the fact that, in their eyes, he was the genuine world champion.

A year after gaining his magnificent belt, Sullivan travelled to France where he encountered Mitchell for a second time. This bout lasted for thirty-nine rounds, but was abandoned as a draw because the foul weather made the conditions atrocious in the field where the ring was pitched. Sullivan was on top when the contest was stopped and the Englishman could count himself lucky that the weather came to his rescue.

After returning to the United States, Sullivan finally agreed to face Jake Kilrain. Their epic contest at Richburg, Mississippi, in 1889 lasted more than two hours before Kilrain succumbed in the seventy-fifth round. This was the last heavyweight contest to be fought under Prize Ring Rules and after it Sullivan claimed, with few arguments this time, that he was the undisputed world champion.

After the Kilrain contest Sullivan became something of a drunkard, but returned to the ring in 1892 to fight James J Corbett under Queensberry Rules in New Orleans. Hopelessly out of condition, Sullivan found himself out-boxed by the athletic young Californian and he was knocked out in twenty-one rounds.

Before his battle with Corbett, Sullivan had appeared in a play, *Honest Hearts and Willing Hands*, and he resumed his career on the stage afterwards, earning nearly $1 million by the time he retired in 1915. He also became a reformed character, and toured the land preaching against the evils of drink.

Sullivan steadfastly refused to fight black boxers throughout his career and thus avoided meeting the likes of Peter Jackson. Nevertheless, he became one of America's greatest and most fêted sporting heroes. He was never a subtle boxer but relied on brute strength and a formidable right hand to floor opponents.

Left: Sullivan is credited with creating the unified world heavyweight championship crown by eliminating all of the other contenders over a seven-year period. In 1882 he beat Paddy Ryan, the American champion; in 1883 he defeated Charlie Mitchell, champion of England; and in 1889 he finally met and fought the other great American pretender Kilrain (see below) in an epic encounter – the last bare-fist championship fight – which left Sullivan the undisputed king of the ring. He was 5 feet 10½ inches tall, and his top fighting weight was 190 pounds. He lost the crown to Corbett in 1892, and fought his last bout against Tom Sharkey in 1896.

Above: Jake Kilrain, of Baltimore, was controversially declared champion of the world in 1887 when Sullivan refused a match with him. The two men eventually met on July 8 1889 to resolve the championship. After a seventy-five round bout that lasted two hours, sixteen minutes, and twenty-three seconds, Sullivan emerged the victor on a knock-out.

BOB FITZSIMMONS

BORN HELSTON, CORNWALL. DATE GIVEN VARIOUSLY AS JUNE 4 1862, JUNE 14 1862, MAY 26 1862, AND MAY 26 1863 **TURNED PROFESSIONAL** IN AUSTRALIA BETWEEN 1883–1888 **WORLD MIDDLEWEIGHT CHAMPION** 1891 **WORLD LIGHT-HEAVYWEIGHT CHAMPION** 1903–1905 **WORLD HEAVYWEIGHT CHAMPION** 1897–1899 **WORLD CHAMPIONSHIP FIGHTS** (HEAVYWEIGHT) WON 1, LOST 2; (MIDDLEWEIGHT) WON 2 (LIGHT-HEAVYWEIGHT) WON 1, LOST 1 **DIED** CHICAGO, OCTOBER 22 1917

Bob Fitzsimmons remains dear to British hearts as he is, incredibly, the only world heavy-weight champion of the modern era to have been born in England. When he was just nine years old, however, his Cornish parents emigrated to New Zealand and he was brought up in the town of Timaru where his father set up in business as a blacksmith.

As soon as he was able, the young Fitzsimmons helped his father in the smithy, which is where he developed the massively impressive arm and chest muscles that were to prove so telling in later years. In 1880 the famous bare-knuckle fighter, 'Jem' Mace, travelled to New Zealand and organized a competition, which was duly won by the apprentice blacksmith. Mace recognized in Fitzsimmons a natural talent and encouraged him to take up a career as a professional.

Fitzsimmons furthered his boxing career in Australia where he remained for ten years before setting sail for California in 1890. Fighting as a middleweight, he gained two quick successes in America before challenging Jack Dempsey, dubbed the 'Nonpareil' (because he was reckoned to be unbeatable), for the world title. The American pundits did not take the little-known Fitzsimmons seriously as a genuine contender. His torso and arms looked powerful enough, but his frail legs and receding hairline made him appear to be something of a joke. They were proved badly wrong when Fitzsimmons knocked out Dempsey in thirteen rounds.

After successfully defending his middleweight title against Dan Creedon in 1894, Fitzsimmons began to take on heavyweights whom he felled with remarkable regularity. After embracing American citizenship, he finally had a chance to challenge James J Corbett for the heavyweight crown in Carson City, Nevada, on

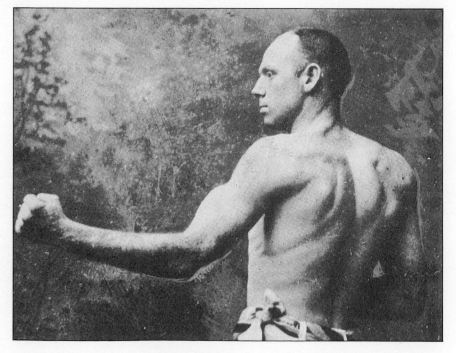

Right: Bob Fitzsimmons still rates as one of the most unlikely-looking fighters ever to have taken to the ring. He was 5 feet 11¾ inches tall, but weighed only 165 pounds: his legs could best be described as skinny, but the gangling form was topped by a stupendously strong torso, developed by years of working in his father's smithy. His weight allowed him to fight at middleweight, while his strength and courage made him more than a match for the heavier men of the day in the top division. He became the first boxer ever to win championships in three divisions when, towards the end of his career, he captured the newly-created light-heavyweight crown.

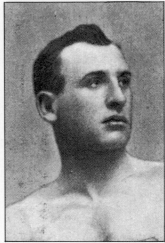

Above: Dan Creedon was born in New Zealand in 1868: he won the Australian middleweight championship before heading for America. His success there won him a fight with Fitzsimmons for the world middleweight championship. This took place on September 26 1894 at the New Orleans Olympic Club for a purse of $5,000. The fight lasted only four minutes before Fitzsimmons whipped three quick lefts into Creedon's handsome nose, despatching the pretender to the canvas and ending the bout.

Left: In a posed publicity shot, Fitzsimmons demonstrates his left-hook on Bob Armstrong.

March 14 1897. Like many before him, 'Gentleman Jim' Corbett thought Fitzsimmons to be over-rated. His confidence seemed well-founded as he was twenty pounds heavier, and the younger man by four years. Corbett did indeed get the better of the early rounds, but gradually began to flag and was caught by a stunning blow to the solar plexus in the fourteenth. Unable to catch his breath and get up, the champion was counted out.

In 1899, Fitzsimmons lost his heavyweight crown at the first defence. James J Jeffries was thirteen years younger and weighed some sixty pounds more than the ageing champion, who broke several bones in his hands attempting to flatten the Californian giant. With incapacitated fists, and completely unable to retaliate against the onslaught, the gallant Fitzsimmons was knocked out in the eleventh round. In a return match three years later, Jeffries confirmed his superiority over Fitzsimmons, who was by this time well past his best, and he overwhelmed the smaller man in eight rounds.

The loss of the heavyweight title did not mean the end for Fitzsimmons, however, and in 1903 he outpointed George Gardner to become world champion of the new light-heavyweight division, thus becoming the first man in history to win three world titles.

Fitzsimmons lost the light-heavyweight title to 'Philadelphia' Jack O'Brien in 1905 but steadfastly refused to give up boxing: he continued to fight until January 29 1914.

Like John J Sullivan before him, Fitzsimmons found acting, or at least appearing in vaudeville shows, a lucrative sideline to boxing. He toured with his own show for a while, but was severely lampooned by critics who wanted to see him fight for real and not in staged acts.

JAMES J CORBETT

James J Corbett's place in boxing history is assured, as he was the first man to win the world heavyweight championship under the Marquess of Queensberry Rules which, amongst other things, demanded that gloves be worn by combatants. He is also remembered because he was one of the first gloved boxers to use his brains as well as his fists; until he introduced a new artistry and skill into boxing, fighters, with rare exceptions such as Mendoza, usually resorted to brawling. Corbett developed his style because he did not possess a particularly telling punch, so he adopted what was in those days an unconventional strategy in which he used his feet to avoid being trapped in the corners. He also stuck out as something of an oddity in the aggressive world of boxing in that he dressed flamboyantly, was quietly spoken, and was unusually well-mannered. He was dubbed 'Gentleman Jim', a not entirely complimentary nickname, by a boxing public that at the time preferred their heroes to be bruising, brawny hulks.

Corbett enjoyed a highly successful amateur boxing career while earning his keep as a San Francisco bank clerk. He turned professional in 1884 with the express intention of ultimately challenging John L Sullivan for the heavyweight title. First, however, he had to prove his mettle by overcoming a local adversary, Joe Choynski. In 1889, Corbett and Choynski had three epic battles under Prize Ring Rules. The first was declared a no contest but the second, which took place on a barge away from the suspicious eyes of the police, resulted in Corbett knocking out Choynski in the twenty-seventh round. After winning the third fight in four rounds, 'Gentleman Jim' challenged the West Indian, Peter Jackson, whom Sullivan had refused to fight because he was black. In 1891, Corbett and Jackson fought

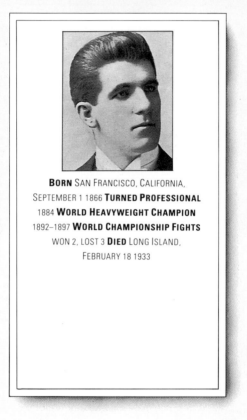

BORN SAN FRANCISCO, CALIFORNIA, SEPTEMBER 1 1866 **TURNED PROFESSIONAL** 1884 **WORLD HEAVYWEIGHT CHAMPION** 1892–1897 **WORLD CHAMPIONSHIP FIGHTS** WON 2, LOST 3 **DIED** LONG ISLAND, FEBRUARY 18 1933

each other for sixty-one rounds, after which both men were exhausted: the fight was declared a no-contest.

The following year Corbett and Sullivan finally met in a New Orleans ring, both wearing five-ounce gloves in accordance with the Queensberry Rules. Sullivan, weighing some forty pounds more than Corbett, was the clear favourite, but the younger man never allowed the 'Boston Strong Boy' to land a heavy punch on him. Instead he gradually wore down the out-of-condition champion by moving around the ring, and in the twenty-first round he unleashed a flurry of blows that knocked Sullivan out.

In 1894, Corbett successfully defended his heavyweight title by knocking out Charlie Mitchell, an Englishman who had unwisely baited the champion, in three rounds. Three years elapsed before he again stepped into a ring and this time his challenger was the ungainly middleweight Bob Fitzsimmons. Corbett under-estimated Fitzsimmons and after winning the early rounds, he began to wane. In the fourteenth round he was floored by a punch to the solar plexus and relinquished his championship title.

Three years after losing the heavyweight crown, which by this time belonged to James J Jeffries, Corbett challenged for it once more. After leading on points, for once in his life he allowed himself to be trapped on the ropes, and Jeffries knocked him out in the twenty-third round. In 1903, he again fought Jeffries for the championship but, at the age of thirty-seven, the task was too much for him and the bout was over in ten rounds.

'Gentleman Jim's' skills were copied and admired by subsequent generations of boxers but the American public never really forgave him for beating their supreme hero, John L Sullivan, and he was never universally popular as a boxer.

Left: Corbett was on the spot in America and ready to challenge for the heavyweight championship while Fitzsimmons was still in Australia. Thus it was Corbett who took the crown from Sullivan. Below: Corbett's great rival Joe Choynski.

Above: Corbett, though not a popular figure, was the darling of the media, and dressed the part. He was the first boxer to acknowledge the role of the heavyweight champion in popular culture by creating an 'image' for himself outside the ring, and he traded on this by building a career on the stage.

Left: The magnificent heavyweight James J Jeffries started in boxing as Corbett's sparring partner, when the latter was in training for his title defence against Fitzsimmons (a fight he was to lose). Ironically, Jeffries, having learnt much from Corbett and turned professional, proved to be Fitzsimmons' first challenger, when, on March 17 1897, the champion eventually decided it was time to defend for the first time a title that he had by then held for over three years. The unfancied Jeffries shocked the boxing world by knocking Fitzsimmons out in the eleventh round, and he proceeded to hold the title until August 1904, when he retired undefeated. His successful defences included a classic bout against Tom Sharkey (by all accounts one of the great fights of all time), a return against Fitzsimmons, and two wins over his old mentor, and now rival, James J Corbett, on May 11 1900 and August 14 1903.

JACK JOHNSON

The title of the most controversial boxer of all time must go to Jack Johnson, the son of a bare-knuckle fighter, who challenged and overcame the supposed superiority of the white man and became the first black heavyweight champion of the world.

Johnson ran away from home when he was twelve and took up work in a racing stables. When he was nineteen, he returned to his home in Galveston and won a fight in a boxing booth at a local fair. This victory was enough to persuade him that it was time to turn professional.

Subsidizing his meagre takings in the ring with occasional work as a painter and decorator, Johnson steadily built up an impressive reputation, and during the next eleven years he disposed of several men who had hopes of the world title. In fact he became so successful that many of the top white fighters ran scared, drawing the so-called 'colour line' and refusing to fight him. Johnson became so incensed that when the reigning world heavyweight champion, the Canadian Tommy Burns, went on a world tour in 1908, he followed in hot pursuit. Burns eventually relented to Johnson's pressure and they fought for the world crown in Sydney, Australia, on Boxing Day 1908.

Johnson relished his opportunity and toyed with the smaller Canadian, taunting him throughout the fight. The police had to declare a halt to the contest in the fourteenth round and Johnson was pronounced the winner, and champion of the world.

Johnson's victory was not well-received in America, and to add fuel to the fire his arrogant behaviour, coupled with the fact that he flirted with white women, made him one of the most unpopular personalities in the country. White America searched for a champion who could dethrone the upstart and Stanley Ketchel, the world middleweight champion, was put forward.

BORN GALVESTON, MARCH 31 1878 **TURNED PROFESSIONAL** 1897 **WORLD HEAVYWEIGHT CHAMPION** 1908–1915 **WORLD CHAMPIONSHIP FIGHTS** WON 6, LOST 1, DREW 1 **DIED** RALEIGH, NORTH CAROLINA, JUNE 10 1946

The 'White Hope' and Johnson are supposed to have come to an agreement that the fight should go the distance so that a lucrative rematch would be assured. The two faced each other in October 1909 in Colma, California, and Ketchel succeeded in putting Johnson on the canvas in the twelfth round. That was enough for Johnson and he smacked Ketchel so hard a few seconds later that, so one version goes, two of the white man's teeth were embedded in Johnson's glove.

The venerable James J Jeffries was brought out of retirement to take on Johnson in 1910, but the referee was obliged to stop the fight in the fifteenth round to prevent the ageing challenger from receiving permanent damage. After one more successful defence against Jim Flynn, in 1912, Johnson fled the United States after he was accused of 'transporting a white woman for immoral purposes' to avoid a one-year prison sentence. He fought two fights in Paris during his exile years and was then persuaded to face Jess Willard. Havana, Cuba, was chosen as the location for the Johnson versus Willard fight as no promoter in the United States dared to stage the contest on home soil. The bout took place on April 5 1915, and the huge cowboy from Kansas knocked out the thirty-seven-year-old Johnson in the twenty-sixth round.

After his defeat, Johnson returned to the United States to serve his prison sentence and he continued to box in exhibitions until he was in his mid-sixties. He died in a car accident at the age of sixty-eight.

Johnson is reckoned by many to be the best heavyweight that ever lived. He developed his defensive skills to a fine degree during the years when he was shunned by the best white boxers, and one of his techniques was to fend off punches with an open left glove before delivering a lethal right upper-cut.

Above: Perennially controversial, Johnson enjoyed nothing more than dressing the part of the gentleman to annoy his racist detractors.

Above: To its shame, the boxing community closed ranks against Johnson, unable to come to terms with the concept of a black champion. Once he had won the championship from Burns, a blatant publicity campaign was launched to find a white man to take it off him. One such, seen here on the canvas, was Stanley Ketchel, who was a victim of Johnson's duplicity, as well as his fists. The story is that the two fighters agreed to go the distance to ensure a lucrative rematch, but that Johnson, having been knocked down by Ketchel, changed his mind and despatched him.

Left: As well as fighting on into his sixties, Johnson also helped fine boxers like Abe Simon.

TOMMY BURNS

A French-Canadian, Tommy Burns is on record as being the shortest man ever to hold the world heavyweight title. He stood just five feet seven inches tall and was never more than a light-heavyweight: yet, with his swift movements and long reach, he beat men far taller and heavier than himself with apparent ease.

When James J Jeffries retired and relinquished his world heavyweight crown in 1905, he arranged a fight between Jack Root and Marvin Hart to decide who should claim the vacant title. Hart won, but his reign was short, as the little-known Burns wrested it from him on February 23 the following year, winning the twenty-round contest on points. However, Burns still did not feel he was getting the recognition he deserved, so he systematically set out to prove his worth. His first defence was in Los Angeles on October 2 1906 against Jim Flynn, whom he knocked out in twelve rounds.

BORN CHESLEY, ONTARIO, JUNE 17 1881 **TURNED PROFESSIONAL** 1900 **WORLD HEAVYWEIGHT CHAMPION** 1906–1908 **WORLD CHAMPIONSHIP FIGHTS** WON 12, LOST 1, DREW 1 **DIED** VANCOUVER, MAY 10 1955

This was followed by two battles against 'Philadelphia' Jack O'Brien, also in Los Angeles; the first fight was a twenty-round draw, but Burns won the second on points.

After knocking out Bill Squires in the first round of a bout held during the summer of 1907, Burns travelled to London, England, where he faced the British champion, Gunner Moir, at the National Sporting Club. Moir proved to be no match for the world champion and was knocked out in ten rounds. Staying in London, Burns then had a simple four-round victory over Jack Palmer at the Wonderland arena. To complete a successful tour of Europe, Burns had easy wins over challengers in Dublin and Paris before setting sail for Australia to look for some rich purses.

While he was making this series of comparatively easy defences, Burns was well-aware that there was only one person who could seriously threaten him,

Right: Marvin Hart has the distinction of being the least well-recognized of all the heavyweight champions. His rule started in controversy, when Jeffries decided to retire and, according to some sources (Jeffries himself later denied this), took it on himself to nominate two boxers – Hart and Jack Root – to fight for the succession. Although Hart won the bout, on July 3 1905, and was duly crowned by Jeffries, others thought that better boxers had been ignored. The matter was resolved a few months later when Tommy Burns outpointed Hart in twenty rounds. Burns proceeded to gain outright recognition by defeating all the serious contenders in quick succession.

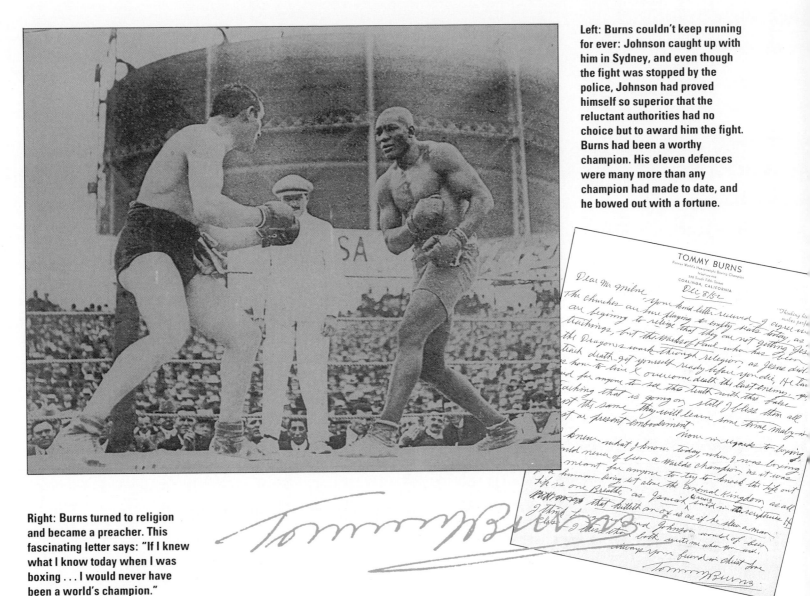

Left: Burns couldn't keep running for ever: Johnson caught up with him in Sydney, and even though the fight was stopped by the police, Johnson had proved himself so superior that the reluctant authorities had no choice but to award him the fight. Burns had been a worthy champion. His eleven defences were many more than any champion had made to date, and he bowed out with a fortune.

Right: Burns turned to religion and became a preacher. This fascinating letter says: "If I knew what I know today when I was boxing . . . I would never have been a world's champion."

and that was the mighty Jack Johnson. The Canadian was man enough to admit that he stood little chance against the 'Galveston Giant', but he insisted that he wanted to cash in on his title while he still could. The huge American saw it differently, and claimed that Burns was scared to fight. He followed him to Australia, baying for blood.

Realizing that he would have to confront Johnson sooner rather than later, Burns made two quick and conclusive defences of his crown against lesser opponents in the August and September of 1908, and only then agreed to a showdown with Johnson. A huge arena was especially constructed in Sydney for the fight which was scheduled for Boxing Day. When they finally met in the ring, Burns was dwarfed by Johnson, who stood six and a half inches taller and weighed twenty pounds more. He put up a courageous fight but was regarded as a plaything by

Johnson, who taunted him with verbal abuse as well as stinging punches. In the fourteenth round, the police decided to intervene and stop the fight, which was inevitably awarded to Johnson.

Soon after losing to Johnson, Burns gave up boxing for a while to concentrate on managing and promoting, but in 1920 he came out of retirement to challenge the Englishman Joe Beckett, who was British and Commonwealth champion. Aged thirty-nine, his years were against him, and he was stopped by Beckett in seven rounds.

Burns was a shrewd businessman as well as a wily and cunning boxer. He had a hand in promoting many of his own championship fights and he always insisted on seeing his purse money before he got into the ring with an opponent. He invested his considerable fortune wisely and became a wealthy man before being ordained a preacher in 1948.

JIM DRISCOLL

'Peerless' Jim Driscoll ranks as one of the greatest and cleverest boxers never to have been internationally recognized as a world champion. He won every other important title available to him and was only denied the world championship crown because of the ludicrous New York State Frawley Law.

Driscoll was born and brought up in the Welsh city of Cardiff. As a boy he worked in a local newspaper office and legend has it that he used to spar with all-comers protected only by strips of paper wrapped around his hands. He became British featherweight champion in 1907 after knocking out Joe Bowker in the seventeenth round of a contest held at the National Sporting Club, London. It was a title he never lost and he only relinquished it when he retired in 1913. In 1909 he went after Abe Attell, the featherweight world champion, but the wily American insisted that they meet in New York State in a 'no-decision' bout.

At the time boxing in New York was governed by the notorious Frawley Law which permitted boxing, but only on the condition that no decision was made at the end of the fight. This meant that all matches were effectively exhibition bouts and the only way a man could win was to knock out an opponent. Members of the press in attendance could give their verdicts on a fight but their decisions held no sway with the ruling bodies. Champions took advantage of this law and readily defended their titles in New York, safe in the knowledge that all they had to do to retain their crowns was to stay upright through the scheduled number of rounds.

Driscoll had just about everything a boxer requires, but he was not renowned for his punching power. Throughout their ten-round fight, he comprehensively out-boxed Attell, who frequently missed his target altogether. However Attell survived, and

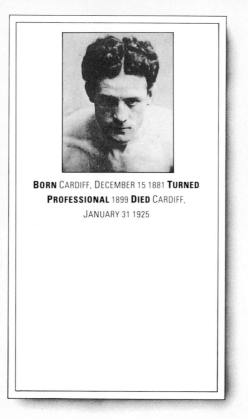

BORN CARDIFF, DECEMBER 15 1881 **TURNED PROFESSIONAL** 1899 **DIED** CARDIFF, JANUARY 31 1925

therefore retained his title. The press gave a unanimous verdict in Driscoll's favour but it was not enough to make him champion. But back in Britain, and particularly in Wales, he was regarded as the uncrowned champion of the world.

Returning home across the Atlantic, Driscoll won the first featherweight Lonsdale Belt match on stopping Seaman Hayes in six rounds. He went on to make the treasured belt his own property by humbling Spike Robson in two subsequent contests. Driscoll's darkest day came in December 1910 when he was pitted against fellow Welshman Freddy Welsh in Cardiff. The fight for the British lightweight title turned dirty and Driscoll lost his temper, butting Welsh in the tenth round and earning a disqualification.

In June 1912 Driscoll knocked out the Frenchman, Jean Poesy, in twelve rounds at the National Sporting Club, and became European featherweight champion. He successfully defended his new title in a twenty-round draw against Owen Moran and retired from the ring in 1913.

During World War One he became an army physical education instructor, but, short of cash, decided to make a comeback when the war ended. He had two wins before meeting the Frenchman, Charles Ledoux, at his favourite venue, the National Sporting Club. Driscoll had the best of the early rounds but in the sixteenth was caught by a flurry of blows from the hard-hitting Frenchman and was forced to retire.

Driscoll earned the nickname 'Peerless' because of his mastery in the ring. He was technically superb, particularly in defence, and Ledoux, who was eleven years his junior, had the grace to pay him a tribute after his victory. Driscoll was, in fact, already a sick man when he fought Ledoux, and he died of consumption five years later.

Left: Driscoll, called 'Peerless' because of his artistry and neatness, is one of Britain's greatest unsung sporting heroes. He was undisputed British featherweight champion for six years, and no challenger could get close to him, but he was consistently frustrated in his attempts to get world championship contests with American fighters. When he did, he wiped the floor with Abe Attell (by common agreement), but a State law turned his mastery of the champion into an insignificant exhibition bout.

Above: Freddie Welsh (1886–1927) was a great rival of Driscoll's, and their 1910 fight is one of the dirtiest on record, causing bitterness and resentment for years afterwards. Welsh won the world crown from Willie Ritchie in 1914 – an achievement Driscoll could never match.

Above: Abe Attell was, like Driscoll, a fighter more renowned for skill than power – which didn't prevent him from scoring more than forty-five knock-out victories in his career. Born in 1884, he held the world featherweight crown between April 30 1908 and February 22 1912.

Left: Forced out of retirement by financial problems, Driscoll (on the right) puts up a brave but hopeless struggle against Ledoux in his last fight.

SAM LANGFORD

One of the most talented boxers never to win a world championship was Sam Langford who, during his peak years, was denied opportunities to challenge for the ultimate crown because of the colour of his skin. Langford was born and brought up in Canada but moved south to the United States to seek his fortune and there turned professional in 1902.

Langford began his professional career as a featherweight and had a notable success in his second year when he beat Joe Gans who had at one time held the world lightweight title. Although he was small, standing no more than five feet seven and a half inches, and comparatively light, Langford was ambitious and craved the heavyweight title above all else. To his chagrin, however, he was consistently refused fights with the leading white heavyweight

BORN WEYMOUTH, NOVA SCOTIA, CANADA, FEBRUARY 12 1883 **TURNED PROFESSIONAL** 1902 **DIED** CAMBRIDGE, MASSACHUSETTS, JANUARY 12 1956

contenders. As a consequence he was forced to fight his fellow blacks and was obliged to take on the same people over and over again. He had an extraordinary catalogue of twenty-three battles against Harry Wills, fifteen against Sam McVey, fourteen against Joe Jeanette and eleven tough encounters against Jeff Clarke.

In 1906, he was pitched against the 'Galveston Giant', Jack Johnson, and gave the man who was to become the first ever black world heavyweight champion the fight of his life. Johnson won on a narrow points decision; he was so surprised at Langford's talent that he was afraid to box him again and steadfastly refused offers of a return contest, however hard Langford and his managers pushed.

Johnson became world champion in 1908 but proved to be so unpopular with the white American public that, if anything, he made it

Above: Langford knocks Bill Lang clear through the ropes.

Left: 'Iron' Bill Hague, the British champion, was no push-over, but Langford gave him a boxing lesson in 1909 before disposing of him in the fourth round.

more difficult than ever for black heavyweights to rise to the top. Nevertheless, the 'Boston Tar Baby', as Langford was dubbed, was at last allowed to fight white men, and he disposed of such 'white hopes' as Jim Barry, Jim Flynn, Sandy Ferguson and Tony Ross. In 1909, Langford crossed the Atlantic and took on the British champion, 'Iron' Hague. He put on an impressive display of skill and knocked the Englishman out in the fourth round.

To boost his career still further, Langford moved to Australia, where he lived for more than a year,

Right: Langford got to know Harry Wills pretty well during his career: they fought one another no less than twenty-three times. They had to fight each other because the leading white contenders and champions were persistently allowed to refuse fights with black boxers with the tacit approval of the authorities. Fighters such as Langford, Wills, McVey, and Jeanette were undoubtedly superior to most of the so-called 'Great White Hopes', but the prejudices of the times denied them the fame and riches of the world stage.

fighting ten contests and winning all but one of them. However with his years working against him, and with the world crown in the grasp of the reluctant Johnson, his hope of a title bout diminished.

The record books show that Langford only ever held one heavyweight title, the Mexican. He won that crown when he flattened Jim Savage in the opening round of a bout held in Mexico City in 1923. By that time, though, he was past forty and his best boxing years were behind him. He refused to retire, however, and continued to fight until he was forty-four. He would have continued further had his eyesight not been blighted by cataracts which rendered him partially blind.

Tragically, Langford's eyes continued to fail him and not long after his last fight he was completely unable to see. Thankfully, his many friends rallied round and saved him from a life of poverty, and before he died in early 1956 he at least had the satisfaction of knowing that he had been elected to *The Ring*'s Hall of Fame.

In his professional career Langford fought close to 400 contests, and, although he only weighed 145 pounds, most of his fights were against heavyweights. He owed his success to his massive shoulders and extraordinarily long reach.

GEORGES CARPENTIER

Georges Carpentier, dubbed the 'Pride of Paris', was the darling of France during his heyday and was fêted like a movie star by his adoring public. Yet, for all his debonair charm, he had humble beginnings, being the son of a miner. He started to box as a flyweight in his early teens and during his career he gradually progressed right up to heavyweight.

Carpentier won the French national lightweight title when he was just fifteen and he was still short of his eighteenth birthday when he clinched the European welterweight title. In 1913, he stepped up to heavyweight and got the better of the British champion, Bombardier Billy Wells, in a contest that lasted four rounds. After a repeat victory against Wells, he fought the American, Ed 'Gunboat' Smith, in London, for the 'white' heavyweight world championship (the genuine champion, Jack Johnson, was black, and at that time there was a scandalous attempt in the boxing world to seek a white boxer to beat him). Smith was disqualified in the sixth round but, as the contest was fought just before the outbreak of World War One, Carpentier was unable to capitalize on his victory. Instead, he joined the French Air Force and had a distinguished career during the war, winning the *Croix de Guerre* and the *Médaille Militaire*.

The war deprived Carpentier of his peak years but nevertheless, in 1920, he travelled to Jersey City to take on 'Battling' Levinsky for the world light-heavyweight championship. He got the better of the American in four rounds and the manner in which he fought convinced the promoter, Tex Rickard, that he was a worthy opponent for the world heavyweight champion, Jack Dempsey.

Conceding twenty-four pounds in weight, Carpentier faced Dempsey in a huge, purpose-built arena on Boyle's Thirty Acres, New Jersey, in 1921. More than 80,000 fans turned out to view the fight which became the first in history to gross more than $1 million at the gate. During the contest the brave Frenchman broke his thumb, which dramatically affected his punching power, and he was pulverized into defeat in the fourth round.

In May the following year Carpentier defended his light-heavyweight world title against Ted 'Kid' Lewis in London. He won in the first round but in controversial circumstances, the Englishman claiming that he was knocked out by an illegal blow. Four months after defeating Lewis, Carpentier fought the unknown Senegalese fighter, 'Battling' Siki in Paris. Carpentier and his manager, François Descamps, thought the fight would be an easy one but they were sorely mistaken. Carpentier had the better of the opening rounds but Siki, who was short of talent but extremely brave, badly damaged the handsome Frenchman's nose in the fourth round. Thereafter the challenger pummelled Carpentier and during the sixth round, Descamps threw in the towel. Whether out of loyalty to the champion or not, the referee ignored the towel and disqualified Siki for allegedly tripping Carpentier. The crowd was outraged and, amid booing, the decision was reversed in Siki's favour.

Carpentier was never the same after losing his world title to Siki. He beat the British heavyweight champion, Joe Beckett, for a second time in 1923, but during a tour of the United States in 1924 lost to Gene Tunney in the fifteenth round. In 1927 he quit boxing and retired to run a café in Paris.

Carpentier was a master of the ring, being a quick mover with a devastating right-hand punch that accounted for many of his opponents. He was a suave and charming man, and a hero in his beloved France.

BORN LENS, FRANCE, JANUARY 12 1894
TURNED PROFESSIONAL 1908 **WORLD LIGHT-HEAVYWEIGHT CHAMPION** 1920–1922 **WORLD CHAMPIONSHIP FIGHTS** (MIDDLEWEIGHT) LOST 1 (LIGHT-HEAVYWEIGHT) WON 2, LOST 1 (HEAVYWEIGHT) LOST 1 **DIED** PARIS, OCTOBER 28 1975

Left: The charming Frenchman with his equally dapper manager, François Descamps, arriving in New York to prepare for Dempsey.

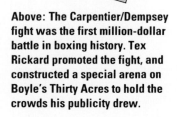

Top: The scene at the Thirty Acres Oval seconds before the Carpentier v Dempsey title fight commenced. The two boxers have returned to their corners after the preliminaries; the referee is Harry Ertle. Above: Carpentier damaged a thumb early in the fight, and this, combined with the amount of weight he was giving away, saw him going backwards virtually from the start. Here in the fourth, Dempsey has Carpentier reeling over the ropes. Right: Later in the fourth, and it is all over. Carpentier stayed down.

Above: The Carpentier/Dempsey fight was the first million-dollar battle in boxing history. Tex Rickard promoted the fight, and constructed a special arena on Boyle's Thirty Acres to hold the crowds his publicity drew.

TED 'KID' LEWIS

Gershon Mendeloff, who changed his name to Ted Lewis and was known as 'Kid', was born of Jewish parents in the heart of London's East End. He turned professional when he was just fourteen years old and went on to become one of the most successful and admired boxers ever to have been produced by England.

Lewis started as a featherweight, and in 1913 won the British title in a contest held at the illustrious National Sporting Club. A year later he went one better and picked up the European title, but was forced to give up both championships after he put on too much weight. Late in 1914 he travelled to Australia where he fought five twenty-round contests in nine weeks: then, fighting as a welterweight, he moved on to try his luck and skill in the United States.

Lewis became the undisputed world welterweight champion on beating the New Yorker, Jack Britton,

BORN LONDON, OCTOBER 24 1894 **TURNED PROFESSIONAL** 1909 **WORLD WELTERWEIGHT CHAMPION** 1915–1916, 1917–1919 **WORLD CHAMPIONSHIP FIGHTS** (WELTERWEIGHT) WON 5, LOST 3, NO-DECISION 2 (LIGHT-HEAVYWEIGHT) LOST 1 **DIED** LONDON, OCTOBER 20 1970

in August 1915. He again got the better of Britton the following month, but in a third clash, in 1916, he lost the decision in a twenty-round contest. The Londoner regained the title from his long-time adversary in 1917 and held on to it for two years. He successfully defended the championship four times, with two victories and two no-decision bouts, before being knocked out by Britton in nine rounds on March 17 1919. After this defeat Lewis returned to his roots in London.

Back on home territory Lewis was unbeatable. He knocked out Johnny Basham to win the British Empire and European welterweight titles in June 1920, and, full of confidence, he crossed the Atlantic once more in an attempt to wrest the welterweight world crown from none other than Jack Britton. Britton again proved to be too strong for the Englishman and won on points in front of his home crowd in New York.

Right: Lewis shakes hands with Jack Britton, but the civilities between these two great rivals were never more than cursory. Lewis was, to many critics, the finest British boxer of the twentieth century, and remains the only fighter from Britain to have won the genuine respect and approval of American fight fans and commentators. This reputation was founded on his twenty contests with the only welterweight of the time who could compare with him – Jack Britton. During Lewis' five-year stay in the States the title changed hands regularly between them: they once fought three times in less than three weeks.

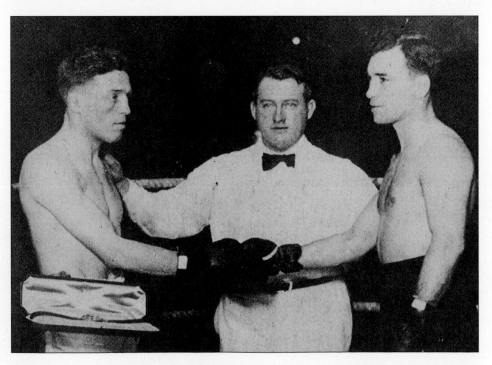

This was the last time these two great boxers met in the ring. In all they fought each other twenty times, including six championships bouts: these had the honours split, with both men winning three contests.

Returning once again to Europe, Lewis subdued Jack Bloomfield to win the British and European middleweight crowns, and in June 1922 he relieved the Australian, Frankie Burns, of the Empire middleweight title. In May 1922 Lewis fought the Frenchman, Georges Carpentier, for the world light-heavyweight championship in London and lost in controversial circumstances in the opening round. By his own account, Lewis was angered by Carpentier's holding, and turned to the referee to complain. While doing this, he dropped his guard and Carpentier landed a right-hand smack on his chin.

Lewis continued to fight after his brief encounter with Carpentier but he was never the force he had been. Roland Todd took the British and Empire middleweight titles from him in 1923 and Tommy Milligan beat him on points in 1924 to clinch his British and Empire welterweight crowns.

Lewis finally retired at the age of thirty-five and briefly flirted with a show-business career in a vaudeville act. He later became a boxing coach and an ever-popular figure in British boxing circles. Lewis won innumerable fans both in England and in the United States for his courageous, all-action style. He was rarely forced into retreat and his preferred tactic was to press forward with both fists flailing.

Above: Australia's Frankie Burns does his best to avoid a swinging right from a Lewis in typically aggressive form. Lewis knocked out Burns in the eleventh round at Holland Park in London on June 19 1922 to win the Empire middleweight championship.
Right: The 'Kid' in his prime.

JACK DEMPSEY

Born into an impoverished family, William Harrison Dempsey followed an elder brother's footsteps when he took up boxing. He adopted the name Jack after the famous 'Nonpareil' Jack Dempsey, the middleweight champion from the end of the nineteenth century. The new Jack Dempsey was born in the same year that the great old-timer passed away.

He honed his skills to perfection while working in local mining and lumber camps where life was tough and fights were frequent. His big break came when he was spotted by Jack 'Doc' Kearns, who became his manager, confidant and publicist. Under the guidance of Kearns he fought a series of carefully chosen fights that brought him into contention for the world championship.

Dempsey faced the champion, Jess Willard, on July 4 1919 and Kearns was so confident of his man that he bet Dempsey's entire purse of $27,500, at odds of ten to one, that he would win in one round. Dempsey very nearly became a rich man overnight. He knocked Willard down seven times in the opening round and was jumping out of the ring to collect his winnings when he was summoned back: the bell had sounded but in all the commotion nobody had heard it. Dempsey lost his purse but had the consolation of becoming world champion in the third round when the humiliated Willard retired.

Nicknamed the 'Manassa Mauler', the new champion knocked out Billy Miske and Bill Brennan the following year and then in 1921 the entrepreneur Tex Rickard promoted the first 'fight of the century', pitting Dempsey against the Frenchman, Georges Carpentier, who was the European champion. Rickard built a special arena for the contest at Jersey City and some 80,000 people flocked to see the contest, paying well over $1 million at the gate. The gallant Carpentier

BORN MANASSA, COLORADO, JUNE 24 1895 **TURNED PROFESSIONAL** 1914 **WORLD HEAVYWEIGHT CHAMPION** 1919–1926 **WORLD CHAMPIONSHIP FIGHTS** WON 6, LOST 2 **DIED** NEW YORK, MAY 31 1983

broke his thumb during the ferocious struggle in the ring and was knocked out in the fourth round.

Dempsey's next fight was not until 1923 when he easily outpointed Tommy Gibbons over fifteen rounds. Searching for suitable opposition for the champion, Rickard then produced the Argentinian, Luis Firpo, a giant of a man who had a formidable punch. Dempsey knocked Firpo to the canvas no less than seven times in the opening round but the courageous Argentinian retaliated by knocking the 'Manassa Mauler' through the ropes and into the ranks of pressmen. In the second round Firpo could not find any strength and was finished off by the champion.

The phenomenally successful Kearns–Dempsey partnership ended acrimoniously after the Firpo fight, the manager disapproving of the champion's marriage to the actress Estelle Taylor. Dempsey did not fight for three years and when he did he was in for a surprise. Gene Tunney took advantage of the champion's long spell away from the ring and convincingly beat him on points over ten rounds at Philadelphia in September 1926. The rematch almost exactly a year later ended in the same result but not before Dempsey had felled Tunney in the seventh round. This was the famous 'Long Count' when the referee did not start counting until Dempsey had retreated to a neutral corner. Tunney was in fact down for fourteen seconds, the extra four giving him enough time to recover and win the fight.

After his second fight with Tunney Dempsey retired to become a successful businessman. He will always be remembered for being a fighter in every sense of the word who had a clubbing punch in both fists. He was one of the greatest box-office draws of all time and five of his fights attracted more than $1 million at the gate – an extraordinary amount at the time.

Above: Looking here like a cross between a choirboy and an ad-man's dream, it is hard to believe that to most fight-fans Dempsey is emblematic of the twenties tough guy: the kid from the backstreets who made it to fame and fortune through a mixture of need and brute power. His life reads like a script for the archetypal boxing movie: flushed with his sudden status he is seduced away to Hollywood, where his new film-star wife edges out mentor 'Doc' Kearns; returning to the ring, he finds he does not have it any more, and lets clean-cut Gene Tunney walk off with his crown.

Top: Dempsey pulls another million-dollar crowd for the return against ex-Marine Tunney.

Above: One of Dempsey's finest hours. Matched as a relative unknown against champion Jess Willard, he put together a twenty-punch combination in the third that pummelled the older man to defeat. When he opened his Broadway restaurant, he had a whole wall painted with a mural of this scene.

Left: Dempsey persuades another great old-timer, Jack Sharkey, to play Willard's role in front of the famous painting.

GENE TUNNEY

Like many great champions, Gene Tunney came from a relatively poor family: he was born in Greenwich Village on Manhattan Island, New York. As a teenager he proved that he was highly intelligent and his parents had hopes of him taking up a literary career. However, the young Tunney dashed their aspirations and elected to become a professional boxer when he was eighteen.

Tunney sailed through his first fourteen fights undefeated but was then drafted into the United States Marine Corps. Far from wrecking his boxing hopes, the army positively boosted them, and he made a name for himself by winning the United States Expeditionary Force's light-heavyweight championship while stationed in France in 1919. It was at this time that Tunney first realised that he had the talent and power to be champion.

On returning to the United States after his army service, Tunney went back to his chosen profession full-time, and won twenty-two consecutive fights inside two years. At the beginning of 1922 he relieved the veteran 'Battling' Levinsky of the American light-heavyweight title but four months later lost it to Harry Greb. This was Tunney's only defeat in his professional career and it had a massive influence on his approach to boxing. He was obliged to spend a week in bed after the savage beating Greb gave him, but, instead of giving up, he spent the time hatching a tactical plan to beat his assailant. His plot worked to perfection and he got the better of Greb, the 'Pittsburgh Windmill', on four subsequent meetings.

With renewed confidence, Tunney began to take on heavyweights and achieved astonishing success. In 1924 he beat the great Frenchman, Georges Carpentier, in the fifteenth round of a bout at Yankee Stadium, and he gradually eliminated all the conten-

BORN NEW YORK CITY, MAY 25 1897
TURNED PROFESSIONAL 1915 **WORLD HEAVYWEIGHT CHAMPION** 1926–1928
WORLD CHAMPIONSHIP FIGHTS WON 3
DIED GREENWICH, CONNECTICUT, NOVEMBER 7 1978

ders for the world heavyweight crown. By 1926 Jack Dempsey had been world heavyweight champion for seven years: he agreed to a challenge from Tunney, and the two confronted each other in Philadelphia on September 23. Boxing cleverly, Tunney achieved his boyhood ambition and convincingly outpointed the 'Manassa Mauler', whom many had thought was unbeatable.

Tunney gave Dempsey a return match in Chicago the following year, and very nearly lost his title in the seventh round when Dempsey floored him. However, in one of the most notorious incidents in all of boxing history, Dempsey made the critical error of not immediately retreating to a neutral corner, and crucial seconds ticked away before the referee started the count. Tunney was in fact down for fourteen seconds and he recovered to win the ten-round fight on points. Talking about the 'Long Count' issue later, Tunney maintained that he could have got up in ten seconds and that it was his privilege to make the most of the count. In all truth, Dempsey only had himself to blame – he knew the rules well enough.

Tunney made only one more defence of his title before retiring. That was against the New Zealander, Tom Heeney, at Yankee Stadium in 1928. Heeney was stopped in eleven rounds and the fight proved to be something of a damp squib and never captured the imagination of the American public.

Tunney was one of the shrewdest of heavyweight boxers and he studied his opponents meticulously before he met them. On retiring, the undefeated champion was a wealthy man, having won nearly $1 million in his second fight with Dempsey alone. He married the heiress Polly Lauder and became a highly successful businessman, listing among his friends such figures as George Bernard Shaw.

Above: Still remembered by some fans as the greatest fight ever, the return between Tunney and Dempsey on September 22 1927 at Soldiers' Field, Chicago, had it all. With an eye for publicity, the promoter set the fight exactly a year and a day after Tunney's skill had won the title from Dempsey's aggression: so great was the excitement that the crowds filled the box-office coffers to a level that would not be matched for decades – $2,658,000 was taken, of which Tex Rickard personally pocketed over half a million. But above all, the fight was controversial: it was 'The Battle of the Long Count'. In the seventh, Dempsey floored Tunney, but failed to retire to a neutral corner to the satisfaction of referee Dave Barry. In the confusion, Tunney was down for, according to most sources, between fourteen and sixteen seconds. It is history that he recovered and went on to win a points result.

Left: Tunney at his peak. Unlike most champions, he coped well with the wealth and fame: he was a cultured man who mixed with writers and artists; he succeeded in business, and he saw one of his sons enter Congress.

Above: Dempsey and Tunney were still receiving recognition for their epic battles over thirty years later.

MICKEY WALKER

Known as the 'Toy Bulldog', as much for his tenacious fighting skills as for his facial features, Mickey Walker was Irish-American born, and was brought up in a tough district of New Jersey. He turned professional at the earliest opportunity and fought some forty-five bouts before earning the right to challenge the ageing Jack Britton for the world welterweight title. He eventually beat Britton on a points decision on November 1 1922 in New York.

Walker had successfully defended his welterweight title three times (one no-decision against Pete Latzo) when he took on Harry Greb for the middleweight crown in 1925. Greb won the New York fight on points and legend has it that Walker pursued Greb after the contest and the two of them continued to brawl in Times Square (this scrap lasted only a few seconds).

After one more successful defence of his welterweight title against Dave Shade, the 'Toy Bulldog' lost it to Pete Latzo in May 1926. The press had a field day on that occasion, as a rumour spread around that

BORN ELIZABETH, NEW JERSEY, JULY 13 1901 **TURNED PROFESSIONAL** 1919 **WORLD WELTERWEIGHT CHAMPION** 1922–26 **WORLD MIDDLEWEIGHT CHAMPION** 1926–1931 **TITLE BOUTS** (WELTERWEIGHT) WON 4, LOST 1, NO-DECISION 1 (MIDDLEWEIGHT) WON 4, LOST 1 (LIGHT-HEAVYWEIGHT) LOST 2 **DIED** FREEHOLD, NEW JERSEY, APRIL 28, 1981

Walker had entered the ring nursing a severe hangover. Headache or not, he managed to stay on his feet for ten rounds before losing on points.

Walker almost retired after being knocked out by Joe Dundee in a fight that followed the Latzo contest, but he was persuaded to keep going. He was not too upset at relinquishing his welterweight title as he had a tendency to put on weight and he set his sights on gaining the middleweight world championship. He achieved his ambition by outpointing 'Tiger' Flowers in Chicago on December 3 1926. He went on to defend his new title three times but, deciding to chase bigger fish, he gave it up in 1931 to concentrate fully on the heavier divisions.

Walker had two attempts at winning the light-heavyweight championship of the world, but lost on points on both occasions: first against Tommy Loughran in 1929, and then against Maxie Rosenbloom in 1933. Ironically, he outpointed Rosenbloom the following year in a non-title contest.

Forever ambitious, Walker still openly coveted the

Right: 'Tiger' Flowers took the middleweight title off Harry Greb on February 26 1926, and defended it in a return match on August 26 of the same year. He was the first black boxer to hold the crown at this weight. Flowers met Walker in Chicago on December 3 1926, and was relieved of the championship on a points decision after ten hard rounds. Walker remained champion until 1931.

Left: Not content with his great successes as a middleweight, Walker's ambitions constantly led him to challenge the giants of the ring, such as Jack Sharkey. His dream was the heavyweight championship: predictably, he never got close – he was giving away much too much in height, reach, and weight. His finest achievement outside the middleweight bracket was his draw against Sharkey, a rugged boxer who on June 21 1932 was to gain a points result over Max Schmeling to gain the heavyweight championship.

heavyweight title above all else. This was particularly foolhardy as he stood no more than five feet seven inches tall and weighed little more than one hundred and sixty-eight pounds at his heaviest. Still, he had some success against the big men and managed to hold the future world heavyweight champion, Jack Sharkey, to a draw. Against the rising Max Schmeling, however, he met his match and was pummelled into an eight-round defeat.

Walker was hugely popular with the American public and media during his heyday. Not only was he a ferocious and fearless fighter who was prepared to take on anybody, but he was also a flamboyant character who provided the press with a succession of juicy stories. He was an inveterate womanizer and he often liked to drink until dawn. He married seven times, including three remarriages, and his extravagant lifestyle was a considerable burden on his finances. However his manager was the wily Jack 'Doc' Kearns who amassed him a considerable fortune over their years together.

When he retired in 1935, the 'Toy Bulldog' took up the more passive art of painting, adopting a 'primitive' style. His canvases were widely acclaimed and he had several important exhibitions. More predictably, he also owned a popular bar sited, fittingly enough, next to Madison Square Garden in New York, the scene of many of his greatest triumphs.

Above: Walker challenged Tommy Loughran for the world light-heavyweight championship, but was out-gunned. Walker's obsession with boxing above his weight inevitably took its toll: it drained him of strength, and prevented him from fulfilling his full potential against boxers in his own class. At the same time it made him a hero with the public: they loved him for his courage and his attitude. Left: Mickey Walker, the boxer's boxer. He would fight anyone, anytime, and refused to believe that size counted for anything inside the ring.

MAX SCHMELING

Max Schmeling had a long and controversial professional career that spanned more than twenty years. He started out as a light-heavyweight and gained international recognition when he knocked out the Belgian, Fernand Delarge, in June 1927. This fourteen-round victory made him European champion and he successfully defended the title against Hein Domgoerger on November 6 1927.

In 1928 Schmeling moved up to heavyweight and began a campaign in the United States which had an impressive start, with five consecutive victories. The world title had by this time been vacated by the retiring Gene Tunney and in 1930 the two leading contenders, Schmeling and Jack Sharkey, were matched against each other to decide who should have the title. The fight took place in Yankee Stadium, and during the fourth round, Schmeling was dumped on to the canvas. While the German was being carried to his corner, his manager, Joe Jacobs, protested to the referee that the telling punch had been a foul, and a ringside judge agreed that it had landed below the belt. As a result Schmeling was declared the champion and went into the history books as the first heavyweight to win the ultimate crown on a foul.

In July 1931 Schmeling saw off the challenge of Young Stribling when the referee was obliged to call a halt in the fifteenth round. The following year, Sharkey was granted a return match with Schmeling and this time the contest went the full fifteen rounds. However, the outcome, a points victory to the American, did not seem entirely fair, even to the partisan American audience, and prompted Joe Jacobs to sob, 'We was robbed.'

Schmeling's first bout after losing his heavyweight title was against the gallant Mickey Walker, former welter- and middleweight world champion. In the eighth round of an all-action tussle in which fortunes fluctuated both ways, Schmeling felled the American and begged the referee to halt the fight. After several more knockdowns he was declared the winner.

The two fights for which Schmeling will always be remembered were against Joe Louis. The first took place in New York on June 19 1936. Louis was the over-riding favourite to win the non-title fight, but Schmeling was nothing if not clever, and he outwitted the 'Brown Bomber', ultimately sending him to the canvas in the twelfth round. The return contest two years later was rather different. Louis was by this time world champion and tensions ran high: the Nazi propaganda machine was at its peak, and the contest was seen as a battle between the black and white races as much as for the world crown. The fight was over within one round, Schmeling being decked by a devastatingly ferocious onslaught from the American.

Returning to Germany after his fight against Louis, Schmeling won the European heavyweight title against his fellow countryman, Adolf Heuser, in 1939. Soon after this one-round victory World War Two started, and Schmeling became a paratrooper in the German army. When hostilities ceased in 1945 he made a brief comeback but after a couple of wins he was beaten by Walter Neusel in 1948 and decided that it was time to retire from the ring.

It has been alleged that Schmeling had leanings towards the Nazi Party. It is certainly true that he met Hitler and he was once photographed giving the infamous Nazi salute before a fight in Germany. However, he always maintained, and most agree, that he was neither a racist nor a Nazi. When he quit boxing, he started several successful ventures and maintained close links with contacts in the United States, where he remained a respected and popular figure.

BORN BRANDENBURG, GERMANY, SEPTEMBER 28 1905 **TURNED PROFESSIONAL** 1924 **WORLD HEAVYWEIGHT CHAMPION** 1930–1932 **WORLD CHAMPIONSHIP FIGHTS** WON 2, LOST 2

Left: Schmeling had held the heavyweight crown for a brief period six years earlier, having beaten Jack Sharkey to take up the vacant title. But this, undoubtedly, was his finest hour. Joe Louis was still new on the scene, but was commonly regarded as a future champion who would be one of the all time greats. Schmeling was matched against him as a mature opponent who would provide experience, but no threat. Unfortunately, they forgot to give Schmeling the script, and he proceeded to take the youngster apart, felling him finally in the twelfth.

Right: The eighth round of a famous fight: Schmeling v Walker on September 26 1932. Still recalled by fans as one of the greatest slugging matches of all time, it was a typical instance of Walker never knowing when he was beaten. By the eighth, Schmeling's huge weight advantage had taken full toll, and, as Walker went down, he begged referee Denny to end the bout, which he eventually did.

Above: Two years after their first fight, Louis was champion, and not about to repeat his earlier error. Nobody imagined that so much damage could be done by one man to another in just over two minutes. Schmeling went down three times, and didn't get up on the third.

MAX BAER

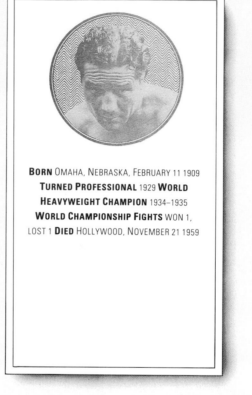

BORN OMAHA, NEBRASKA, FEBRUARY 11 1909
TURNED PROFESSIONAL 1929 **WORLD
HEAVYWEIGHT CHAMPION** 1934–1935
WORLD CHAMPIONSHIP FIGHTS WON 1,
LOST 1 **DIED** HOLLYWOOD, NOVEMBER 21 1959

Max Baer possessed one of the most devastating right hands that boxing has ever known, but he never truly capitalized on it, and his fickle temperament often let him down. He was the son of a tough Californian cattle butcher and legend has it that he only discovered his punching power when a man made an inappropriate comment as he walked his girlfriend home one evening. Baer was so incensed at the remark, and the insult to his girl, that he knocked the hapless individual clean through a shop door.

Turning professional at twenty, Baer had the hallmarks of a potential champion. He was a fearsome puncher, and he also had an impressive physique, though he lacked natural boxing skills. After a succession of impressive knockout wins he rose sufficiently high up the ladder to earn a fight with the former world champion, Max Schmeling.

The contest, held at Yankee Stadium in 1933, was close until Baer unleashed his right hand and stopped the German in the tenth round. This victory earned Baer a title bout against the Italian Primo Carnera. The Carnera versus Baer contest took place on June 14 1934 and turned into an almost comic spectacle. Carnera was an enormous man who lacked a heavy punch but was not short on skill. He weighed fifty pounds more than Baer, who found it easy to manoeuvre his way around the ponderous giant, landing blows at will. In all, the American floored the Italian eleven times in eleven rounds before the Italian decided he had taken enough punishment, and called a halt to the proceedings.

Baer's tragedy was that he could take nothing seriously and he even joked and played the comic during his fight against Carnera. He rarely bothered

Above: Primo Carnera looks like the clown here, but it was Baer's inability to take things seriously – in or out of the ring – that stopped him fulfilling his potential.

Left: A rare picture of Baer training. Baer was finally shocked into realising that boxing was a serious business when he lost the title on his first defence to the unrated Braddock – a fighter who was over-the-hill and who had been given no chance against Baer's firepower. For once in his life he went into training, aiming to pick off Joe Louis and start a comeback trail. Unfortunately Louis' talent was just coming into its prime: even an in-shape Baer stood no chance, and he went down in four.

to train and relied solely on his right-hand punch to win fights. His come-uppance came a year later when, on June 13 1935, he faced James J Braddock on Long Island, New York. Braddock, who had lost a light-heavyweight title contest against Tommy Loughran in 1929, was given virtually no chance against Baer's punch but he used his brain and steered clear of trouble, eventually outpointing the champion in one of the biggest upsets in heavyweight boxing history.

Shocked by his defeat at the hands of the ageing Braddock, Baer attempted to fight his way back to the top but this time he did not find it so easy to compete against some of the best heavyweights of the time. Joe Louis knocked him out in four rounds, a defeat that he found hard to stomach, and England's Tommy Farr outpointed him in London in 1937. In a return fight in New York a year later, Baer got the better of Farr but more trouble loomed for the former champion in the shape of Lou Nova. Baer fought Nova twice, once in 1939 and again in 1941. On both occasions he was stopped inside the distance and after the second fight he finally decided to retire.

Baer was one of the most popular of all American boxers for two reasons. Firstly, he thrilled audiences during his heyday by regularly knocking opponents flat on the canvas and, secondly, he was a natural clown who revelled in playing the fool. He had the talent and ability to become a truly great champion but discovered that being a high-profile playboy was more to his liking. He became a radio personality and made a film called *The Prize Fighter and the Lady* (1933), in which he starred with Jack Dempsey.

Right: Baer's defeat by Louis placed him firmly in the second division: as Louis was a one-man first division at the time, it was a situation he shared with virtually every other would-be contender. He is seen here with Tommy Farr (centre) the English champion with whom he fought two terrific battles, and with his brother Buddy (far right). Both Farr and Buddy Baer gave Louis tough fights (Buddy actually flooring the champ in the first of their two meetings), but the 'Brown Bomber' was unbeatable when they were at their best.

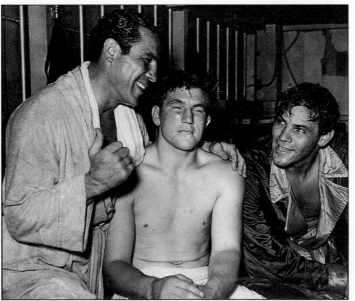

Above: If a film had been made about Baer's life in the thirties, the leading role would have been played by Errol Flynn. Baer had it all: speed, timing, strength, and a great punch for use inside the ring; and looks, physique and wit to apply outside it. All he lacked was dedication. The crowds adored him – any Baer fight, even after his defeats by Braddock and Louis, was an event and a spectacle. But in the end, he enjoyed life too much to make the sacrifices necessary to become a great fighter rather than a great personality.

HENRY ARMSTRONG

The eleventh child of a family of fifteen children, Henry Armstrong could boast that a potent mixture of Negro, Cherokee Indian and Irish blood flowed through his veins. He was born Henry Jackson and was brought up in a poor quarter of St Louis where, as a teenager, he boxed for trophies which he invariably sold to help keep his large family in food. At nineteen he left home and journeyed to Los Angeles, where he intended to make his fortune. Initially he earned his keep in California by boxing to orders: he got paid for winning, drawing or, most frequently, for deliberately losing fights that were promoted by heartless and unscrupulous businessmen for the benefit of crooked gamblers and mobsters.

Luckily for the young Jackson he was spotted by the famous entertainer Al Jolson, who prompted Eddie Mead, a prominent manager, to take the precociously talented boxer under his wing. Henry changed his surname to Armstrong to conceal his ignominious history as a 'paid' fighter and achieved immediate success.

1937 was a busy year for Armstrong. He had no less than twenty-seven fights, winning all but one of them inside the distance. During this unparalleled run of victories he defeated Mike Belloise, who, as the New York Athletic Association's featherweight champion, also claimed he was the world title holder. In October the same year Armstrong put paid to any arguments over who was the genuine world featherweight champion when he knocked out Petey Sarron in six rounds on October 29 in New York.

In May the following year Armstrong gained his second world title when he outpointed the great Barney Ross to become the welterweight king. Ever ambitious, he then sought the lightweight crown, and in the summer of 1938 he beat Lou Ambers on points

BORN COLUMBUS, MISSISSIPPI, DECEMBER 12 1912 **TURNED PROFESSIONAL** 1931 **WORLD FEATHERWEIGHT CHAMPION** 1937–1938 **WORLD LIGHTWEIGHT CHAMPION** 1938–1939 **WORLD WELTERWEIGHT CHAMPION** 1938–1940 **WORLD CHAMPIONSHIP FIGHTS** (FEATHERWEIGHT) WON 1 (WELTERWEIGHT) WON 20, LOST 2 (LIGHTWEIGHT) WON 1, LOST 1 (MIDDLEWEIGHT) DREW 1 **DIED** LOS ANGELES, OCTOBER 23 1988

in a bitterly-fought fifteen-round contest held at Madison Square Garden, New York.

Finding it difficult to make the weight he gave up his featherweight title, and on August 22 1939 he also lost his lightweight crown in another savage struggle with Lou Ambers. However, he successfully defended his welterweight title nineteen times, and in March 1940 he very nearly collected his fourth world championship when he drew with the reigning middleweight title holder, Ceferino Garcia.

In October 1940, Armstrong finally met his match in the shape of Fritzie Zivic, who outpointed him in fifteen rounds to take away his welterweight title. In a return match the following year, Zivic confirmed his superiority over the slowing Armstrong by pummelling him to a twelve-round knockout defeat in New York.

Armstrong announced his retirement after the second Zivic fight but he was back in the ring only eighteen months later. By this time, though, he was past his best, but even so he did not finally quit the ring until 1945.

Henry Armstrong is the only person in history to hold three world titles simultaneously, and in an era when there were fewer weight divisions than there are now, and consequently much greater competition, that says a lot for the man who was dubbed 'Homicide Hank'. He had an abnormally slow heartbeat which enabled him to go flat out for fifteen rounds without tiring, and he used to flail away with his fists non-stop.

Tragically, Armstrong went into a sorry decline in his retirement. Always one for the women and the good life, he frittered away the vast fortune he had earned in the ring and became addicted to drugs and alcohol. He was ordained a Baptist minister in 1951 and changed his ways, but when he died he was blind and living in abject poverty.

Above: On May 25 1939 British fight fans had one of their rare treats, when Armstrong came to London to give the British welterweight champion Ernie Roderick a shot at the world crown. Roderick put up a good fight, but Armstrong's non-stop windmill style saw him through to a points victory after fifteen rounds.

Right: Having taken the world featherweight championship away from Petey Sarron in October 1937, Armstrong went up a weight to challenge the superb Barney Ross for the welterweight crown on May 31 1938. Armstrong came through with a fifteen-round points victory at the Garden Bowl, Long Island City.

Top: Armstrong became the first boxer to hold three crowns at three different weights simultaneously when, at Madison Square Garden on the night of August 17 1938, he defeated the great Lou Ambers on points over fifteen rounds to take the lightweight championship.
Above: Armstrong fought hundreds of bouts but encountered only one boxer to whom he had to acknowledge true superiority. That was Fritzie Zivic, who defeated the champ twice at the end of his career.

JOE LOUIS

Christened Joseph Louis Barrow, the 'Brown Bomber', as he became known, was born into a poverty-stricken family in the deep South of the United States. His family moved to Detroit when he was ten and it was there that he learned to box while he should have been attending his violin lessons. After winning the Golden Gloves award for light-heavyweights in 1934 he turned professional, and proceeded to win twelve contests within a year. His reputation spread far and wide and in June 1935 he fought the former heavyweight champion, Primo Carnera, at Yankee Stadium before a crowd of 62,000 people. Carnera lasted just six rounds.

Three months after the Carnera fight, Louis tackled another former champion, Max Baer, who managed to last for just four rounds. It seemed as if nothing could stop the budding champion, until in 1936 Max Schmeling felled him, and he was counted out in the twelfth round of their contest.

Louis captured the world heavyweight crown in Chicago in 1937, when he knocked out James J

BORN LEXINGTON, ALABAMA, MAY 13 1914 **TURNED PROFESSIONAL** 1934 **WORLD HEAVYWEIGHT CHAMPION** 1937–1949 **TITLE BOUTS** WON 27, LOST 1 **DIED** LAS VEGAS, APRIL 12 1981

Braddock in eight rounds. Two months after winning the title he defended it against the Welshman, Tommy Farr. Louis won, but Farr became one of relatively few men ever to go the distance with the 'Brown Bomber'. After the Farr fight, Louis took on fighters at regular intervals in what came to be called his 'Bum of the Month' campaign. But his victories were against quality fighters as well, including solid professionals such as Arturo Godoy and Bob Pastor. A particularly satisfying victory for Louis was a return match against Max Schmeling, who was pulverized to an emphatic and humiliating defeat in two minutes four seconds.

In 1942 Louis joined the United States Army as a physical education instructor, but he returned to the ring in 1946. He defended his title four more times, including two bouts with 'Jersey' Joe Walcott, and then retired, undefeated, in 1949. However, pressure from the taxman forced Louis out of retirement a year later and he attempted to regain the championship from Ezzard Charles. By this time, the 'Brown

Right: Tommy Farr put up an extraordinary show against Louis when they met in New York City on August 30 1937. He was desperately unlucky to meet the new champion on his first defence – and the 'Brown Bomber' was in his prime. Even so, Farr was no 'Bum of the Month', and many critics, not only from the British Isles, considered that the fifteen-round points decision might have justifiably gone the other way under different circumstances.

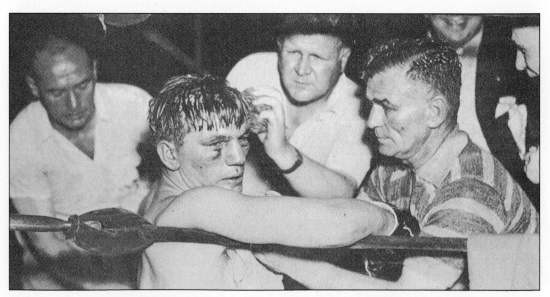

Left: Every decade or so there comes along a fighter who is so good, and so much better than the opposition, that the public comes to believe that he can never be beaten. In later years, Marciano was such a figure, and Ali and Tyson after him. But of all the greats in boxing's record books, it is difficult to think of a fighter who dominated his age to the extent that Louis ruled the twelve-year period from June 22 1937 to March 1 1949.

Below: Louis lost only three times: once, to Schmeling, on the way up; and then to Ezzard Charles and Marciano during an ill-conceived come-back. Schmeling must have regretted defeating the young 'Brown Bomber': when he later met a more mature Louis for the title, he took just about the worst beating in ring history, and is seen here going down in the first.

Bomber' was a shadow of his former self and he lost his twenty-seventh championship fight on points. Tragically, Louis' attempted comeback did not end there. He went on to have a fight against the rising Rocky Marciano in 1951: he was knocked through the ropes and the fight was stopped in the eighth round.

In his career Louis defended his title more times than any other heavyweight in history, and he succeeded in knocking out five former world champions. His style in the ring was deceptive. His footwork could look slow and ponderous, but the speed with which he delivered his power-laden punches was formidable, and few men could stand up to one of his onslaughts. He also took good care of his body and never appeared in the ring out of prime condition.

Despite winning some $5 million in his career as a boxer, Louis was perpetually in financial trouble, and when his boxing days were finally over he was obliged to earn his living as a casino host in Las Vegas. Whatever his later circumstances he will always remain a legendary figure in boxing, and he was a fine sportsman in every sense of the word.

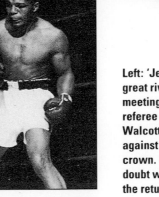

Left: 'Jersey' Joe Walcott was a great rival to Louis. In their first meeting on December 5 1947, the referee voted a victory to Walcott, but the two judges went against him to leave Louis the crown. Louis left no room for doubt with an eleven-round KO in the return match six months later.

ARCHIE MOORE

Archie Moore, whose original name was Archibald Lee Wright, had one of the most bizarre careers in boxing history. For a start, there is some confusion over his exact birth date: in his boxing days *he* maintained that he was born in 1916, while his *mother* said he was born in 1913. Whatever the case, he became champion extremely late, having boxed professionally for over fifteen years before winning his first crown, the world light-heavyweight title.

At the age of sixteen he was a welterweight, but he proceeded to gain in bulk as the years went by and he ultimately challenged for the world heavyweight title. One reason for his slow rise to the top was the fact that he had an extraordinary number of managers in his career, eight in all. Moore was acutely aware that managers frequently took advantage of black boxers at the time, so, possessing a fiery personality, he swapped managers as soon as he had any suspicion, however unfounded, that he was being exploited.

'Ageless Archie' had such a reputation as a knockout specialist during the late 1940s that champions were reluctant to fight him. Finally he teamed up with the extraordinary Jack 'Doc' Kearns, who eventually got him a fight against Joey Maxim for the world light-heavyweight title in 1952. The bout was held at St Louis and Moore won the fifteen-round contest on points. Over the next two years he had two return matches with Maxim and on each occasion he outpointed the challenger over the full fifteen rounds.

Moore defended his light-heavyweight title seven more times, winning on each occasion. However, there were some close calls. In 1956 he fought the West Indian Yolande Pompey in London. The fight turned into a yawn and in the ninth round the referee told the boxers that he was going to disqualify the contest unless they started to fight. Responding to the threat, Moore came out like a whirlwind in the tenth round and knocked out the hapless Pompey.

In 1958 he travelled to Montreal to face the Canadian, Yvon Durelle. The challenger had the champion on the floor three times in the opening round but Moore came back to win by a knockout in the eleventh.

During his career Moore made two challenges for the world heavyweight title. The first was against Rocky Marciano in New York in 1955. He floored Marciano in the second round, but eventually came off second best and was knocked out in nine rounds. A year later he challenged Floyd Patterson for the vacant heavyweight title, but came to grief in five rounds.

In 1960 the National Boxing Association stripped him of his light-heavyweight title for 'inactivity', but he was still considered the champion by other boxing authorities and made his final defence in 1961, outpointing Giulio Rinaldi.

After the Rinaldi conquest, Moore's world title was taken away from him by all the boxing authorities but he still continued to fight, mainly as a heavyweight. He took on the budding Cassius Clay in 1962, being knocked out in the fourth round, and the following year he finally decided to hang up his gloves for good.

In his career Moore succeeded in knocking out no less than 145 opponents. His technique was to soften up his man with an unrelenting stream of blows before moving in for the *coup de grâce*. He is remembered for his outrageous publicity gimmicks, as well as for his boxing skills. He secured his fight with Marciano only after writing to every sports editor in the United States and having posters made up showing Marciano as a wanted man and himself as a sheriff.

BORN BENOIT, MISSISSIPPI, DECEMBER 13 1916 **TURNED PROFESSIONAL** 1935 **WORLD LIGHT-HEAVYWEIGHT CHAMPION** 1952–1962 **WORLD CHAMPIONSHIP FIGHTS** (LIGHT-HEAVYWEIGHT) WON 9 (HEAVYWEIGHT) LOST 2

Above: Archie was a great light-heavyweight champion, but his two shots at moving up to challenge for the world heavyweight crown both ended in disaster. In the first, his historic clash with Marciano, Moore is seen on the canvas in the ninth, with referee Harry Kessler counting him out. This was Marciano's last defence before retiring undefeated. Moore immediately challenged Floyd Patterson for the vacant title, but was KO'd in five on November 30 1956. Below: Canadian challenger Yvon Durelle.

Above and left: Archie Moore was an all-time great, both as boxer and as ring character. He was over thirty-five years of age when he won his first world title by taking the light-heavyweight crown from Joey Maxim on points over fifteen rounds on December 17 1952. He held that title until it was finally stripped from him on the grounds of inactivity in February 1962.

FREDDIE MILLS

BORN PARKSTONE, DORSET, JUNE 26 1919
TURNED PROFESSIONAL 1936 WORLD
LIGHT-HEAVYWEIGHT CHAMPION 1946–
1950 WORLD CHAMPIONSHIP FIGHTS WON 1,
LOST 2 DIED LONDON, JULY 25 1965

Freddie Mills is famed for being one of the most recklessly brave fighters ever to have entered a ring. As a young teenager, he worked as a milkman, boxing as an amateur in his spare time. He took the hard route to boxing stardom by becoming a professional fighter in a fairground booth in which he took on all-comers, in all their various shapes and sizes. While still a booth fighter, he met the former British lightweight champion, Gypsy Daniels, who encouraged his endeavours and passed on much of his hard-earned experience.

Mills first rose to national prominence when he outpointed the able middleweight Jock McAvoy over ten rounds in August 1940. A return fight resulted in McAvoy being hurt and stopped in the opening round. This led to a contest against the British and Empire champion, Len Harvey, who also held the British Boxing Board of Control's version of the world championship. Harvey was

Left: The superb American light-heavyweight, Gus Lesnevich. During the 1940s, after Billy Conn had given up the crown in 1941 to challenge Louis as a heavyweight, the light-heavyweight class became highly confused, with no clear succession. Things were further complicated by the war, which effectively ruled out the British and European fighters. Most authorities recognized Lesnevich as the champion, a position he confirmed by defeating Mills in 1946. But Mills was out-of-shape because of years of inactivity during his war service, and triumphed two years later when he beat Lesnevich in London to take the world title.

knocked out of the ring in the second round and was unable to climb back to beat the count.

Service in the RAF during World War Two deprived Mills of some of his best years, and in 1946 his rustiness showed when he was stopped in ten rounds by the American holder of the world light-heavyweight championship, Gus Lesnevich. In the same year he rashly accepted an offer to fight the heavyweight, Joe Baksi, who was some twenty-five pounds heavier than himself. The inevitable happened, and Mills was stopped in six rounds.

Slipping back to the light-heavyweight division, Mills had a return fight against Lesnevich in 1948 and this time he came out on top, winning the fifteen-round contest in London on points. However, Mills was determined to emulate his boyhood hero, Jack Dempsey, and again challenged the heavyweights. He beat the South African champion, Johnny Ralph, in eight rounds, but his attempt to wrest the British and Empire heavyweight titles from Bruce Woodcock in 1949 was thwarted when he was stopped in the fourteenth round.

Mills had his last fight in 1950 when he faced the American, Joey Maxim, in London with his world light-heavyweight title at stake. The Englishman fought as bravely as ever but he was weary after his tussles with heavyweights and he was counted out in the tenth round. For Mills it meant more than just the loss of his world title, as several of his teeth went missing as well.

Deciding that he had had enough, Mills announced his retirement immediately after losing to Maxim and invested his considerable earnings in a restaurant. He also became a hugely popular radio and television personality, but, despite his cheerful demeanour, he was persistently troubled by personal and financial troubles. His life came to a horrific and

Left: Mills ranks alongside Henry Cooper as the most popular boxing hero of the British public. Sophistication and artistry were in small supply, but he had enough courage and fighting spirit for a man twice his size. His 1946 encounter with Lesnevich ranks as one of the bravest British boxing performances of all time. Mills had just been demobbed, having been ill in the Far East during the last part of the war. He found himself in the ring with a fight-hardened pro, who happened also to be one of the best light-heavyweights in history. For ten rounds the two men slugged it out in a frightening barrage, and it was only when Mills went down three times in the tenth that the referee saw sense and stopped the fight.

Left: Like Mickey Walker, Freddie Mills was a fearless fighter who constantly chose to mix it with the heavyweights, never knowing when he was beaten. He is seen here taking his second defeat from British heavyweight champion Bruce Woodcock in 1949.

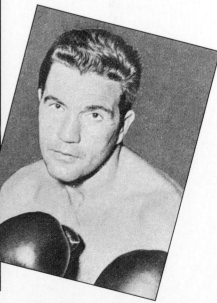

tragic end as a result of a gunshot wound. He was found dead in his car, and although the verdict was that he had committed suicide, his sad demise still remains something of a mystery. He will always be remembered for his quite remarkable courage.

Above: Joey Maxim took Mills' world title on January 24 1950, stopping the champ in a ten-round encounter. Maxim lost the crown to Archie Moore in 1952.

'SUGAR' RAY ROBINSON

'Sugar' Ray Robinson was christened Walker Smith and he did not adopt his 'stage' name until he turned professional. His mother and sisters moved from Detroit to a poor region of New York when he was a young lad, and he was obliged to keep the family by tap-dancing on the sidewalks. His great passion, however, was for boxing, and he worshipped the great heavyweight Joe Louis.

He had immense success as an amateur, winning eighty-five bouts, forty of them in the first round. He crowned his amateur career by winning Golden Gloves titles in the featherweight and lightweight divisions and elected to turn professional in 1940.

According to legend, he was substituted for a fighter by the name of Ray Robinson on his professional début and was so entranced by the other man's name that he decided to keep it. Later someone told his manager, George Gainford, that he had a sweet mover in his stable and Gainford is reputed to have answered, 'Yes, he's as sweet as sugar.' The name was complete and stuck with him.

'Sugar' Ray had unparalleled success in his first years as a professional, winning forty successive contests before losing to Jake LaMotta. In all Robinson fought LaMotta six times, and this was the only one of those six fights he lost. In 1946 he challenged Tommy Bell for the vacant welterweight world title and won on points. He went on to defend the title successfully five times before relinquishing it, reluctantly, on beating his old adversary LaMotta for the middleweight crown in 1951.

As the new middleweight champion Robinson toured Europe in 1951 complete with a veritable army of assistants and trainers, and accepted an offer from the promoter Jack Solomons to defend his title

BORN DETROIT, MICHIGAN, MAY 3 1921
TURNED PROFESSIONAL 1940 **WORLD WELTERWEIGHT CHAMPION** 1946–1951
WORLD MIDDLEWEIGHT CHAMPION 1951–1960 **WORLD CHAMPIONSHIP FIGHTS** (WELTERWEIGHT) WON 6 (MIDDLEWEIGHT) WON 8, LOST 6, DREW 1 (LIGHT-HEAVYWEIGHT) LOST 1 **DIED** LOS ANGELES, APRIL 12 1989

against Randolph Turpin. Over-confident and arrogant, Robinson under-estimated Turpin and lost the bout on a points decision. Turpin, however, did not have a grasp on the title for very long: sixty-four days later Robinson won it back at a contest held at the New York Polo Grounds before an audience of some 61,000 people.

The following year Robinson saw off the challenges of Carl 'Bobo' Olson and Rocky Graziano for the middleweight championship, and he then had the audacity to challenge Joey Maxim for the light-heavyweight title. Robinson drew ahead on points, but he failed to come out of his corner for the fourteenth round. It is true to say that he was beaten by the heat rather than his opponent; the atmosphere was so close that the referee had already collapsed in the tenth round and had been replaced.

Robinson announced his retirement soon after his fight with Maxim, but he returned to the ring in 1955 and regained the middleweight title after knocking out the usurper, Olson, in two rounds. He lost the title to Gene Fullmer in January 1957, but gained his revenge five months later by knocking Fullmer out in five rounds. Carmen Basilio took the title from him in 1957 but, never one to give up, he became a champion for the fifth time when he beat Basilio on points in a rematch in 1958. He finally lost the middleweight title for the last time when Paul Pender beat him in 1960. He challenged for the undisputed title one more time, and for the NBA version twice more, but finally gave up his ring career on December 10 1965 at a retirement party.

One of the most stylish and punishing boxers of all time, Robinson had an extravagant lifestyle that endeared him to the gossip columnists. Sadly he died of Alzheimer's disease in 1989.

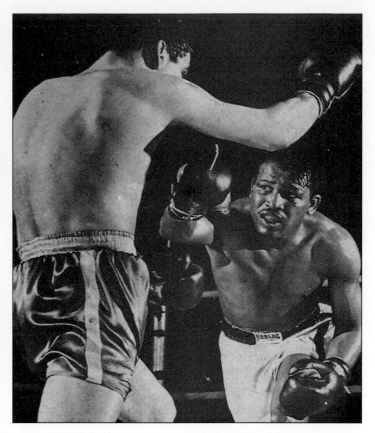

Above: A thirty-four-year-old Robinson comes out of retirement to despatch 'Bobo' Olson in two and take the middleweight title for the third time.

Left: One of the true legends of the ring, Robinson came out of retirement on countless occasions, and won the middleweight crown five times.

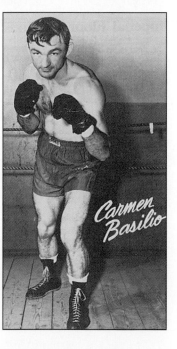

Above and left: One of Robinson's last great flurries was against Carmen Basilio, a fine fighter with an old-time slugger's heart. Basilio took Robinson's title on September 23 1957 on a split decision: Robinson came back eight months later to beat Basilio and take the crown for the fifth time.

EZZARD CHARLES

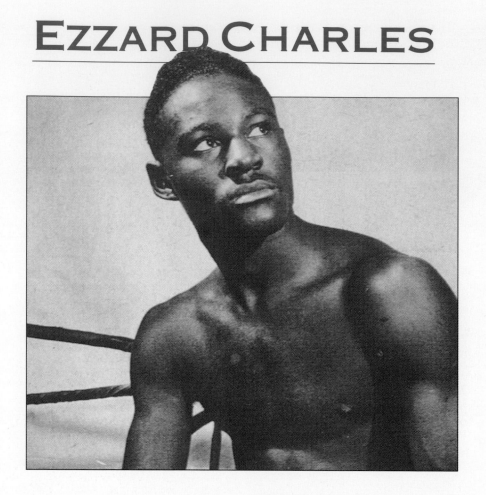

BORN LAWRENCEVILLE, GEORGIA, JULY 27 1921 **TURNED PROFESSIONAL** 1940 **WORLD HEAVYWEIGHT CHAMPION** 1949–1951 **WORLD CHAMPIONSHIP FIGHTS** WON 9, LOST 4 **DIED** CHICAGO, MAY 27 1975

Ezzard Charles has never really been forgiven by the American public for beating Joe Louis, and even Charles himself was sorry when he outpointed his hero. He was, however, a great boxer who deserves more recognition than he receives.

He rose to prominence as a teenager, winning all of his forty-two amateur contests including the middleweight Golden Gloves championship of 1939. Turning professional in 1940, he moved up to heavyweight in 1943 and had a run of success that earned him the nickname 'The Cincinnati Cobra'. In 1949, Joe Louis announced his retirement and the National Boxing Association pitted Charles and 'Jersey' Joe Walcott against each other to decide who should hold its world heavyweight title. The bout took place on June 22 1949 in Chicago, and Charles emerged the victor on points. To many people, however, Louis was still champion and consequently few people paid much attention to the new champion – despite the fact that he successfully defended his title three times, including once against Gus Lesnevich. In 1950, plagued by financial problems, Louis made a comeback and fought Charles for the world title in New York. Louis was by this time a shadow of the great boxer he had once been, and it was no surprise when Charles was proclaimed the points winner after fifteen rounds. Rather ridiculously, the public still refused to give Charles credit for his achievements.

In March 1951 Charles got the better of 'Jersey' Joe Walcott for the second time and in May he beat the talented Joey Maxim. In July the same year he had a third fight with his old adversary Walcott and this time he lost the title after

Below: Charles v Marciano in their still-remembered encounter of June 17 1954. At this time Marciano was a god of the ring; so supreme as to be considered invincible. He had won the world heavyweight title from Walcott on September 23 1952 on a knock-out, and every defence he made of his crown was also won inside the distance – except this first encounter with Charles. Despite his long and distinguished career, and his many championships and championship defences, it is thought by most critics that his performance in this points defeat by Marciano represented his finest hour.

Left and above: Charles' rivalry with 'Jersey' Joe Walcott was one of the greatest in ring history. They fought four times: Charles came out top in 1949, winning the vacant world crown, and in March 1951, in a title defence. Walcott took the title from him in July 1951, and successfully defended it against him in June 1952.

being knocked out in the seventh round. A fourth battle with Walcott a year later resulted in another defeat, and it seemed like the end of the road.

Two years later, however, he reappeared in the ring to challenge for the world title which was by this time held by Rocky Marciano. In their first fight, held in New York on June 17 1954, Charles used his wits and experience and boxed extremely cleverly. He was eventually well beaten on points, but he did at least earn the satisfaction of becoming the only challenger to take the 'Brockton Blockbuster' the distance. In a second battle with Marciano three months later, the thirty-three-year-old Charles put up another brave effort and badly hurt the champion's face, but it was

not enough and he was knocked out in the eighth.

After his two tussles with Marciano Charles lost much of his fire but he refused to quit. It was a mistake, as he lost the majority of his later fights and gained few admirers. He finally decided to retire in September 1959.

Sadly Charles retired an embittered man, sickened that his talent was never fully appreciated. During his career he fought and beat many of the best heavyweights around – it was sheer bad luck that he emerged at a time when Joe Louis was revered as a national hero and favourite. It was also unfortunate that he should encounter Rocky Marciano when his own best boxing days were behind him.

ROCKY GRAZIANO

Rocky Graziano's championship record does not appear very impressive on paper, but in each and every fight he gave his all, and his approach to boxing so captured the imagination of the American public that he became a legendary figure like Jack Dempsey and John L Sullivan before him.

He was born Rocco Barbella, the son of poor Italian immigrants who lived in a desolate tenement block in the shabby East Side of New York. As a child all he knew was crime. He frequently absconded from school and roamed the streets with gangs that stole anything that wasn't actually cemented to the sidewalk. He was perpetually in trouble with the law and saw the insides of remand homes and detention centres on a regular basis. He was called up to join the United States Army but could not bow to authority and ended up in military prison. He was eventually dishonourably discharged from the army and, had he not taken up boxing, would almost certainly have become an irredeemable hoodlum. As it was he learned to vent his deep-seated hatred in the ring and he became a success as an amateur, winning a middleweight Golden Gloves title.

He had earlier changed his name to Graziano to conceal his unenviable past, and he turned professional when twenty. For four years he fought his way up until he was given a chance to wrest the middleweight world title from Tony Zale. Graziano and Zale met for the first time on September 27 1946 in New York. The fight was savage and neither man gave any quarter. Both men were knocked down in the first round, but Zale was the quicker to recover: he retained the title on knocking out Graziano in the sixth round.

The following year Zale and Graziano had a rematch in Chicago which was contested equally viciously. Zale appeared to be heading for victory as he

BORN NEW YORK CITY, JANUARY 1 1922
TURNED PROFESSIONAL 1942 **WORLD MIDDLEWEIGHT CHAMPION** 1947–1948
WORLD CHAMPIONSHIP FIGHTS WON 1, LOST 3 **DIED** NEW YORK CITY, MAY 23 1990

mercilessly slugged away, but the challenger dredged up all his reserves of courage and energy in the sixth round and produced a stunning counter-attack that ended with Zale hanging on the ropes.

With the public baying for more, a third championship contest between Graziano and Zale was arranged. The bout took place on June 10 1948 in Newark, New Jersey and Zale emerged triumphant, knocking out Graziano in the third round to reclaim the crown.

Four years elapsed before Graziano again challenged for the middleweight world title, which was by this time in the possession of 'Sugar' Ray Robinson. The fight, which took place in Chicago in 1952, was embarrassingly one-sided. After knocking the champion down briefly in round one, Graziano proved no match for Robinson: the challenger was knocked out in three rounds.

Reluctant to retire, Graziano had one more fight after his defeat at Robinson's hands, but Chuck Davey outpointed him and this defeat finally convinced him that it was time to hang up the gloves.

Graziano could hardly be called a great technician or a clever boxer; when he fought, he fought for real and he was not concerned with the niceties of the game. He had phenomenal courage and determination and his three battles with Zale are among the bloodiest ever recorded. He enjoyed fighting men who had an explosive style similar to his own, but he was no match for anybody who was prepared to bide his time. However, his spirit and personality won him millions of admirers the world over.

Graziano's extraordinary career was retold in the book *Somebody Up There Likes Me*, which was later made into a film starring Paul Newman. He might have featured in the film himself, as he had considerable success in a second career as a screen actor.

Above and left: Graziano's name heads this page, but it might just as well be Zale's: the greatness of these two boxers comes not in their individual careers, but in their combined rivalry. Here Graziano (right of picture, on the scales) is seen at the weigh-in before his victory in the second fight of their epic series.

Above and right: Tony Zale defended his middleweight crown successfully against Graziano in 1946, but lost out to him in six rounds on July 16 1947 in Chicago. On June 10 1948, in one of the most keenly-anticipated fights ever, Zale KO'd Graziano in the third to prove to his own satisfaction that he was the better man.

JAKE LaMOTTA

BORN BRONX, NEW YORK, JULY 10 1922
TURNED PROFESSIONAL 1941 **WORLD MIDDLEWEIGHT CHAMPION** 1949–1951
WORLD CHAMPIONSHIP FIGHTS WON 3, LOST 1

Like his boyhood friend Rocky Graziano, Jake LaMotta was born and brought up in a run-down neighbourhood of New York and was destined to lead a life of crime until he was harnessed into a boxing career. Unlike Graziano, however, he never completely broke free from the criminal fraternity, and much of his career was blighted by powerful Mafia operators who manipulated his fights and his destiny.

A naturally aggressive man, LaMotta, whose original Christian name was Giacobe, saw boxing as an obvious way to earn a living. At the start of his career he shunned overtures made to him by mobsters and refused to be the hireling of a Mafia manager. However, organized crime virtually controlled boxing in New York at the time and the unfortunate LaMotta discovered that they could disrupt his career at will. For nine years he defied the gangsters and for nine years he fought without getting anywhere. During this period he had nearly one hundred bouts, many promoted by himself at his own venue (among his victims was a young 'Sugar' Ray Robinson). But the word was out from the mob, so promoters continued to look the other way until he finally succumbed to Mafia pressure and, for a considerable fee, was permitted to have a crack at the world middleweight title.

The champion at the time was an equally rugged fighter, Marcel Cerdan, and when they met in Detroit on June 16 1949 the Frenchman was the hot favourite. The fight was ferocious and in the third round Cerdan's arm was dislocated when LaMotta flung him to the canvas. The gallant champion fought on

Right: During his early career LaMotta refused to co-operate in the fight-fixing schemes of the criminal fraternity. As they virtually controlled boxing in New York, this left him with nowhere to go: no manager or promoter could afford to take an interest in him, so he had to set up his own contests against no-hope boxers in anonymous venues. In this 1943 slugfest he beat 'Sugar' Ray Robinson. At the time Robinson had won forty straight fights, and was contending for the championships. Such a victory should have set LaMotta up for the big-time, but his career continued to remain dormant for another six years.

Right: LaMotta could slug it out with the best, but had more problems against genuine ringcraft. He caught Robinson early in his career, and beat him; but the mature 'Sugar' Ray was a different matter. Robinson is seen here taking the crown by guilefully boxing 'The Bull' to defeat on Valentine's Day 1951.

Above left, and above right: LaMotta's big break came against the French slugger, Marcel Cerdan (above), at Briggs Stadium on June 16 1949. The European had taken the middleweight title from Tony Zale in 1948, and this was his first defence: he was heavily tipped to win. LaMotta came out like a bull, and mixed it from the start. The Frenchman damaged his arm in the third, when LaMotta threw him to the canvas: disabled, he soldiered on, but soaked up so much punishment that the fight was stopped in ten. LaMotta is seen (above left) celebrating his first title.

for six more rounds but failed to come out for the tenth – America had a new world champion.

LaMotta was contracted for a return fight against Cerdan but the Frenchman was killed in a plane crash. His new challenger was the Italian Tiberio Mitri, whom he outpointed over fifteen rounds in 1950. Another Frenchman, Laurent Dauthille, was coasting to a points victory in LaMotta's third defence when, with seconds to go in the last round, the champion flattened his opponent to retain the title.

'Sugar' Ray Robinson put an end to LaMotta's reign as middleweight champion of the world in February 1951 when, utilizing his immaculate technique, he stopped him in the thirteenth round. The former champion attempted a comeback, but after two defeats he lost his chance of having another title fight and he finally decided to retire in 1954.

After hanging up his gloves, LaMotta started a second career as a stand-up comedian with a modicum of success, but he led a turbulent and troubled life and was not exactly a quiet, contented man. He lived his life outside the ring rather like he did when in it: fiercely and to the limit. While he was fighting professionally, he earned the nickname 'The Bronx Bull', which was an apt description of his style: he crouched low and charged with both fists flailing.

The film of LaMotta's extraordinary life, *Raging Bull* (1980), starred Robert de Niro, and did much to bring the boxer back into the public eye. One of the tragedies of LaMotta's career was that he was never allowed to box world-class opposition while in his prime: by the time he was able to compete he was very nearly past his peak and had soaked up an astonishing amount of punishment.

ROCKY MARCIANO

Rocky Marciano fought forty-nine professional fights as a heavyweight without losing one – a record that many have tried to emulate without success. He was born Rocco Marchegiano, the eldest of six children whose parents were poor Italian immigrants. At school he excelled in several sports, including baseball, but it was boxing that captured his heart. He served in the United States Army at the end of World War Two and, while based in England, made an impression in military boxing competitions. On returning to the United States, he wrote to Madison Square Garden for a trial in the gymnasium and was granted an invitation to perform in front of the famous matchmaker, Al Weill. With no money to his name Marciano hitchhiked from Brockton to New York and was disappointed when Weill and others who watched him were unimpressed. He was considered too small to have any potential as a heavyweight and in addition they reckoned he lacked style.

Marciano returned to his roots, but he continued to box as an amateur while earning a living as a factory worker. He decided to turn professional in 1947 and had a remarkable run of success, winning thirty-five contests in a total of just 146 rounds. This earned him a fight with the much-respected Rex Layne in 1951, and after he won in six rounds, Al Weill started to sing a different tune and took him into his management stable.

Weill matched Marciano against the former world title holder Joe Louis, who gave the youngster something of a boxing lesson but was finally swatted to defeat in the eighth round. The victory over Louis earned Marciano a crack at the world title which belonged to 'Jersey' Joe Walcott. The two met in Philadelphia on September 23 1952 and Walcott knocked the upstart on to the seat of his pants in the opening round. Marciano recovered quickly, however, and remorselessly battered the champion into a thirteen-round defeat.

During May the following year Walcott was given a rematch, but his spark had gone and Marciano dispatched him in the opening round. Over the next two and a half years Marciano defended his title five more times. The only man to take him the distance was Ezzard Charles in 1954. His last fight, on September 21 1955, was against Archie Moore who had the satisfaction of putting the champion on the canvas. Marciano once more displayed his phenomenal powers of recovery, and stopped Moore in the ninth round.

After this fight Marciano was determined to spend more time with his family, so he decided, on April 27 1956, to quit boxing while he was at the top. Despite many lucrative offers he steadfastly refused to return to the ring: he was satisfied with the $4 million he had already amassed. Unlike many champions who wasted their wealth, he was financially acute, and had saved and used his money wisely.

Outside the ring Marciano was a mild-mannered, gentle man, but inside he was devastatingly brutal. He was short, just five feet ten and a half inches tall, and he had remarkably small fists for a heavyweight, but what he did have in abundance was physical strength. He could take heavy blows as well as deliver them and what he lacked in technical skills, he made up for with brute force and power. His other great asset was his fitness; he always trained rigorously before a fight and took nothing for granted.

Marciano's final 'fight' was a farcical contest against Muhammad Ali in which the two men acted out a script created by a computer. The machine reckoned that Marciano was the better man and he came out on top with a knockout in the tenth round.

BORN BROCKTON, MASSACHUSETTS, SEPTEMBER 1 1923 **TURNED PROFESSIONAL** 1947 **WORLD HEAVYWEIGHT CHAMPION** 1952–1956 **WORLD CHAMPIONSHIP FIGHTS** WON 7 **DIED** IOWA, AUGUST 31 1969

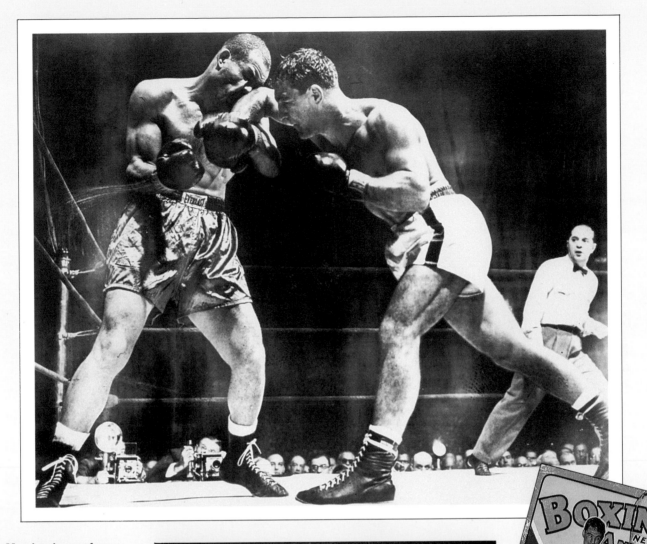

Above: Marciano's most famous punch was unique to him: a swinging right that gave the 'Brockton Blockbuster' two chances to score. If the glove failed to club the side of his opponent's face, the luckless victim would be swatted with forearm and elbow. Given a choice, most boxers would prefer Marciano to land a clean blow with the leather.

Right: Marciano won the heavyweight title from 'Jersey' Joe Walcott in thirteen rounds in Philadelphia on September 23 1952. If most boxers attempted to land a blow from this stance – at right angles to the opponent, and hitting with the left against the grain – it would be too weak to cause problems. With Marciano, it proved to be the first punch in a combination that finished Walcott in the thirteenth.

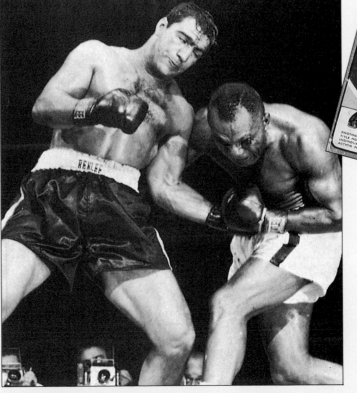

Above: Marciano was beloved by the media and the public. He was a sensible man, who handled his fame with grace. Outside the ring he was kind, gentle, and well-mannered.

RANDOLPH TURPIN

One of three famous boxing brothers, Randolph Turpin is regarded by many as having been the most able fighter to have emerged from the English boxing scene since World War Two.

It was while he was serving as a cook in the Royal Navy that Turpin's amateur career began to take off. He won the Amateur Boxing Association (ABA) welterweight title in 1945 when still just seventeen, and the following year he was crowned ABA middleweight champion. Shortly after winning his second ABA title he turned professional and in October 1950 he became British middleweight champion on beating Albert Finch in five rounds. This was sweet news to the Turpin family, as brother Dick had lost the middleweight crown to Finch six months earlier.

Early the following year Turpin took the European middleweight crown in dramatic fashion when he flattened the Dutchman, Luc van Dam, in forty-eight seconds. This remarkable victory put him in line for a world title challenge against the mighty 'Sugar' Ray Robinson. His chance came in July 1951 and he very literally grasped it with both fists, outpointing the American in a memorable bout held at Earls Court in London. A clause in the fight contract stipulated that a return match should be held within sixty-four days, and so it was that Turpin travelled to New York to meet Robinson for a second time two months later. If Robinson had been slap-dash in his preparation for their first clash, he most certainly was not for their second. Turpin appeared to be on the way to a successful defence when, in the tenth round, Robinson surged in and floored the Englishman with a heavy right. Shortly afterwards the referee called a halt and Robinson, complete with a bloody eye, was declared the world middleweight champion once again.

Turpin was never again quite the same boxer after

BORN LEAMINGTON, ENGLAND, JUNE 7 1928
TURNED PROFESSIONAL 1946 **WORLD MIDDLEWEIGHT CHAMPION** 1951 **WORLD CHAMPIONSHIP FIGHTS** WON 1, LOST 2
DIED LEAMINGTON, MAY 17 1966

losing his world title, although, at the age of twenty-three, he still had a lot of gusto left in him. In June 1952 he claimed the British and Commonwealth light-heavyweight titles when he humbled Don Cockell, and in the same year he also won the Commonwealth middleweight title from the South African, George Angelo. In June the following year he successfully defended his European middleweight title against a challenge from the Frenchman, Charles Humez. Robinson had temporarily retired at this stage and, outside the United States, Turpin was hailed as the world champion; in America Carl 'Bobo' Olson was hailed as the supremo.

Turpin and Olson duly met to sort out the rivalry on October 21 1953 in New York. Unfortunately the Englishman was dogged by personal problems at the time, and put up a poor showing by his standards, losing the fifteen-round contest on points. More disappointment was to follow. In May 1954 he was knocked cold in sixty-five seconds by the Italian Tiberio Mitri and consequently lost his European middleweight title.

After these two surprise defeats, Turpin's career tailed off. He successfully fought both Alex Buxton and Arthur Howard for the British light-heavyweight title, but after a surprising two-round defeat by Yolande Pompey in 1958, he retired.

Turpin had earned a sizeable fortune in the ring but when he retired he had little of it left. He dabbled in boxing and wrestling promotion for a time but was a tragically unhappy man. Unable to take the burden of financial and domestic pressures he shot himself at home just a few weeks short of his thirty-eighth birthday. That was a sad day for English and world boxing: it lost not only a great personality but one of the most aggressive and hardest-hitting boxers of the post-war era.

Left and below: The great 'Sugar' Ray Robinson was Turpin's opponent for the two most important fights of his career. In July 1951 Robinson came to London for what was intended to be an easy and lucrative first defence of the middleweight title he had just taken from LaMotta. The odds were twenty-to-one against a British victory, but Robinson was out-of-shape, and Turpin took him on points. On September 12 of the same year (left), a finely-tuned Robinson corrected his mistake by stopping Turpin in ten.

Above: Turpin was a tragic figure. Like many boxers from impoverished backgrounds, he found it hard to cope with the pressures of fame and riches, and this probably contributed to his eventual suicide.

Right: Like many tough middleweights, Turpin loved to take on the big boys. Here he decks Don Cockell to take the British light-heavyweight title on June 10 1952.

INGEMAR JOHANSSON

BORN GOTHENBURG, SWEDEN, OCTOBER 16 1932 **TURNED PROFESSIONAL** 1952 **WORLD HEAVYWEIGHT CHAMPION** 1959–1960 **WORLD CHAMPIONSHIP BOUTS** WON 1, LOST 2

In 1959 Ingemar Johansson became the first European since Primo Carnera to hold the world heavyweight title, and he simultaneously placed Swedish boxing on the map. His amateur career was blighted by a curious decision in the 1952 Olympic Games in Helsinki. He reached the final in the heavyweight division but was disqualified for 'not giving of his best' against the intimidating American, H Edward Sanders; it was not until 1982 that he was finally awarded his silver medal.

After the Olympics Johansson turned professional, and, under the guidance of his canny manager Eddie Ahlquist, made steady progress. He won the European heavyweight title in 1956 by knocking out the Italian, Franco Cavicchi, in thirteen rounds and made an impression on British fight fans a year later when he disposed of Henry Cooper in five rounds. His most impressive win, however, was against the American, Eddie Machen, who was considered to be the number one contender for the world heavyweight title. Johansson dispatched Machen in one round in 1958 on his home turf of Gothenburg and consequently elevated himself into a world championship fight.

Johansson faced the world champion, Floyd Patterson, on June 26 1959 in the rowdy atmosphere of Yankee Stadium, New York. Prior to the fight Johansson and his manager played up the Swede's playboy image and were careful to conceal his devastating right-hand punch from members of the press at the challenger's training sessions. When the day of the fight arrived Patterson was the hot favourite to win, but Johansson unleashed his 'secret weapon' and floored the champion no less than seven times. The contest was stopped in the third round and Europe had its first heavyweight champion for more than twenty-five years.

In the return fight a year later Patterson was fully aware of the potential of Johansson's right hand, and he became the first heavyweight in history to regain his title with an emphatic knockout victory in five rounds. A third match against Patterson in March 1961 proved that the American was the superior boxer – Johansson was counted out in the sixth round of their clash at Miami Beach, Florida.

Right: In an important contest for both fighters, Johansson puts an end to Britain's Henry Cooper in 1957 in the Swedish sunshine. For Johansson, who had won the European heavyweight championship the previous year, it was a valuable stage in rehabilitating his reputation after the 1952 Olympic Games *débâcle*, and the win pushed him further up the ladder towards a world title bout. For Cooper, it meant another few years in the backwoods before a title shot against Ali.

Below: Johansson called his right hand 'The Hammer of Thor', and it was a well-kept secret from American boxers and fight-fans until he unleashed it against Patterson on June 26 1959 in an amazing odds-against victory.

Right and below: Johansson may have looked and behaved like a playboy, but he differed from similar figures like Max Baer in one important respect – he took his fights very seriously. No amount of training and preparation, however, could protect him from Patterson's ire in their June 20 1960 rematch.

On June 17 1962 Johansson regained the European title (which he had been obliged to relinquish when he became world champion) by knocking out England's Dick Richardson in eight rounds. However, he was later stripped of the European title for failing to defend it and in 1963 he decided to embark on another quest for the world title which was at this time held by Sonny Liston. On April 21 he fought England's Brian London in Stockholm in what he reckoned to be a stepping-stone fight for a world championship challenge. He beat London on points but only just: he was floored by a flurry of punches in the last round and would have been counted out had he not been saved by the final bell. Deciding that his match with London was too close for comfort, he acknowledged that it was time to retire.

Johansson's three fights with Patterson had made him wealthy and when he finally hung up his gloves he invested wisely and became a successful business-man. A lover of the good life, he used to frequent clubs and bars even while in training; he also, however, took his fights seriously, even when he pretended that he was doing otherwise. He relied heavily on a right-hand punch, which he kept unobtrusively in reserve until he found an opening in his opponent's defence; most recipients of 'Thor's Hammer' (also known as 'Ingo's Bingo') never knew what hit them and ended up with their backs on the canvas.

HENRY COOPER

Henry Cooper, 'Our 'Enery' to his loyal fans, without doubt remains the most popular British heavyweight since World War Two. He and his identical twin brother, George, who also became a professional boxer, were brought up in Bellingham in south-east London. Henry became a plasterer while at the same time sustaining a successful amateur career as a boxer. In 1952 he won the Amateur Boxing Association (ABA) light-heavyweight title and also represented Great Britain at the Helsinki Olympic Games. He won a second ABA title in 1953 and the following year elected to make a career as a professional.

Cooper experienced mixed fortunes in his early years as a professional. He fought his way up the ladder, but was beaten in nine rounds by Joe Bygraves in 1957 in an attempt to win the Commonwealth heavyweight title. Further defeats by Sweden's Ingemar Johansson and Joe Erskine deprived him of both the European and British crowns.

In 1958 Cooper staged a comeback, and had two impressive victories against Dick Richardson and the American, Zora Folley. These wins marked a turning point in his career and on January 12 1959 he humbled Brian London to gain the British and Empire heavyweight titles. During the next ten years Cooper saw off eight challengers for the British title and thus became the first man in history to win three Lonsdale Belts outright.

Perhaps Cooper's greatest moment came on June 18 1963 when he fought the precocious Cassius Clay (later to become Muhammad Ali) at Wembley Stadium in a non-title fight. In the fourth round he floored Clay with his fabled left hook and the American would almost certainly have been counted out if he had not been saved by the bell. As it was, Clay's trainer, Angelo Dundee, indulged in some time-wasting tactics during the break and when a refreshed Clay succeeded in worsening a cut over the Englishman's left eye during the fifth round the fight was stopped by the referee.

In February 1964 Cooper achieved a points victory over his old adversary Brian London to win the European heavyweight title, and two years later he challenged Muhammad Ali for the world heavyweight crown. At their meeting at Highbury Stadium in London Cooper again put in a courageous effort but the fight had to be stopped in the sixth round because of the blood that was streaming down his face from an open wound above his left eye.

After winning two more European title fights, against Karl Mildenberger in 1968 and Piero Tomasoni in 1969, Cooper was matched against Jimmy Ellis for the WBA world heavyweight crown. However, the British Boxing Board of Control did not recognize the WBA and refused to grant the contest official status, so a disappointed Cooper gave up his British and Empire title in protest.

Overcoming the disappointment of not being allowed to challenge Ellis, Cooper staged a comeback in 1970 and proved his worth by outpointing Jack Bodell to regain the British title. This was followed by another European championship win over Spain's José Urtain. In March 1971, however, Joe Bugner took the British, Commonwealth and European titles from Cooper in a hotly disputed points victory.

Cooper quit boxing after his contest with Bugner and went on to become a highly successful businessman, boxing commentator and star of television commercials. In the ring he was extremely brave and tenacious, which greatly endeared him to a British public starved of boxing success. He is now as much a national institution as a sporting hero.

BORN WESTMINSTER, MAY 3 1934 **TURNED PROFESSIONAL** 1954 **WORLD CHAMPIONSHIP FIGHTS** LOST 1

Top: This was Great Britain's most notable challenge for the heavyweight crown in the second half of the twentieth century. The whole nation was emotionally involved in Henry's big shot at the title, but Ali stopped him, again with a cut, in the sixth round on May 23 1966 at the Arsenal soccer ground, Highbury Stadium.

Above: Cooper's left eye was badly damaged by young Cassius Clay in the fifth round of their 1963 non-title fight. Henry was a victim of cuts throughout his career: even pictures of his finest victories seldom show him without blood flowing freely on his face. This vulnerability was the principal reason he did not fulfil all of his ambitions.

Left: Britain's most popular boxing figure.

MUHAMMAD ALI

Muhammad Ali once boasted that he was the most famous man in the world, and certainly while he was at his peak his face and voice were immediately recognizable to many millions around the globe. It is beyond doubt that he is the most famous boxer ever, and he has done more to promote the sport than anybody in its history.

He was born Cassius Marcellus Clay, the son of a signwriter whose forebears had been slaves. He started boxing at the age of eleven and had a highly successful amateur career, culminating in a light-heavyweight Golden Gloves award followed by an Olympic gold medal in Rome in 1960.

Returning triumphant from the Olympics he turned professional and after one fight came under the guidance of the trainer Angelo Dundee. He had a flair for creating publicity and one of his gimmicks was to predict the round in which he would defeat opponents. His prophecies proved remarkably

BORN LOUISVILLE, KENTUCKY, JANUARY 17 1942 **TURNED PROFESSIONAL** 1960 **WORLD HEAVYWEIGHT CHAMPION** 1964–1967, 1974–1978, 1978–1979 **WORLD CHAMPIONSHIP FIGHTS** WON 22, LOST 3

accurate and he was consequently labelled 'The Mouth'.

Few pundits gave the twenty-two-year-old Clay much of a chance against the hard-hitting heavyweight world champion Sonny Liston when the two met in Miami in 1964. But Clay ran rings around the champion, who relinquished his title when he refused to come out of his corner at the start of the seventh round. Later in the same year Clay embraced the Black Muslim faith and gave up what he called his 'slave name' to call himself Muhammad Ali.

In his rematch with Liston in 1965, Ali produced a lightning-quick right hand that floored the former champion who was counted out in the first round. Thereafter nobody doubted that the brash young champion could punch as well as he talked. He succeeded in defending the heavyweight title eight more times, including once against England's Henry Cooper, before he was deprived of his crown in 1967 for refusing on religious and moral

Right: A twelve-year-old Cassius Clay has no doubts about where his future will lead him.

Far right: Who could dispute that Ali was king? Not only was he invincible in his prime, but he was also the greatest showman the sport has ever seen. To some, his persistent publicity gimmicks and mouthings became grating: nevertheless, Ali must be credited with pulling boxing out of the doldrums and giving it popular credibility in an increasingly suspicious modern climate.

Left: It is difficult to tell who was more outraged by Liston's pathetic performance in their 1965 rematch – Ali, or the crowd.

Below: Ali at his best against Floyd Patterson.

Above: Ali at his absolute peak – shortly after his Olympic gold medal victory in Rome in 1960, and on his way towards the heavyweight crown only four years later.

grounds to join the United States Army.

Returning to the ring in 1970, Ali lost a title bid against Joe Frazier on points, and then in 1973 he had his jaw broken by Ken Norton. He still claimed he was the 'Greatest', however, and he regained the world title by unexpectedly knocking out George Foreman at a contest held in Zaïre, in 1974.

After successfully defending the title ten more times, including rematches against Frazier and Norton, Ali suffered the third defeat of his career when he lost on points to the relatively unknown Leon Spinks in 1978. Seven months later, though, he became the first man in history to win the heavyweight title three times when he outpointed Spinks in New Orleans.

Ali then retired, but could not resist coming back after a two-year lay-off to take on Larry Holmes for the championship in 1980. Nearly thirty-eight, he was by this time a shadow of his former self and he was stopped for the first time in his career when he retired after ten rounds. One more foolish fight against Trevor Berbick ended in defeat and finished the great champion's career on a sad note.

'Float like a butterfly, sting like a bee' was one of Ali's favourite sayings, and in many respects that is exactly what he did during his early years as a professional. He used to dance round the ring doing his famous Ali Shuffle, pouncing in to strike whenever his opponent lost concentration or became distracted by his outrageous exhibitionism. In later years, when he was heavier, he used different tactics. In his memorable fight against Foreman he had his legion of fans in despair as he absorbed punishment while resting on the ropes. This was all part of his 'rope-a-dope' ploy, and when Foreman had exhausted himself he unleashed his knockout punch.

Suffering from a disease which makes his every movement appear slow and awkward, Ali is now a sorry figure, but still holds the love and respect of fight fans everywhere in the world.

JOE FRAZIER

The seventh son of a large, poor family, Joe Frazier had little to look forward to as a boy. After a spell of working on his father's humble farm he followed the example of his elder brothers and migrated to the metropolis of Philadelphia where he worked as a butcher in an abattoir.

He showed great promise as an amateur boxer and lost only two fights, both to Buster Mathis. It was Mathis who got the better of him in the showdown to decide who would represent the United States as a heavyweight in the 1964 Olympic Games but, as luck would have it, Mathis broke a bone in his hand and it was Frazier who was picked. He did not let his country down and returned from Tokyo with a gold medal, a prize which convinced him that he should turn professional in 1965.

He had an impressive run of success, winning nineteen consecutive fights and beating the likes of Oscar Bonavena and George Chuvalo. In 1968 he was pitted against his old adversary, Mathis, in a fight brokered by the New York Athletic Commission for the world championship. At this time Muhammad Ali had been stripped of his world heavyweight title for not joining the United States Army and rival organizations set up separate competitions to decide who would be 'world champion'. Frazier avenged his two defeats against Mathis by stopping him in eleven rounds. He successfully defended his new title four times, leading to a showdown with the WBA heavyweight champion, Jimmy Ellis, at Madison Square Garden on February 16 1970.

Frazier gave Ellis a ferocious hiding which only lasted four rounds and he was finally acknowledged as the undisputed champion of the world – although faithful followers of Muhammad Ali still claimed that their hero was the best heavyweight around. When

BORN BEAUFORT, SOUTH CAROLINA, JANUARY 12 1944 **TURNED PROFESSIONAL** 1965 **WORLD HEAVYWEIGHT CHAMPION** 1968–1973; (UNDISPUTED, 1970–1973) **WORLD CHAMPIONSHIP FIGHTS** WON 10, LOST 2

Ali returned to boxing the whole world willed him to fight Frazier and in due course a $1 million fight was arranged. In one of the most exciting heavyweight contests in history Frazier outpointed the former champion in New York on March 8 1971.

Two easy fights followed the Ali battle and then, in 1973, Frazier was matched with George Foreman, who was given little chance of victory by the *aficionados* but who pulled off a remarkable victory by stopping the champion in two rounds.

Frazier continued to box after his humiliating defeat by Foreman and gradually won back some of his confidence. He beat the European champion Joe Bugner in a bruising battle before agreeing to a return match against Ali. The second Frazier versus Ali match, on January 28 1974, was another great fight but this time Ali finished victorious on points.

A year later Muhammad Ali was champion of the world once more and Frazier challenged him to a third fight. This was the celebrated 'Thriller in Manila' and it lived up to all expectations. Both men fought courageously but, sapped of energy, Frazier did not come out of his corner for the final round.

Never one to give up easily, Frazier attempted to take his revenge on Foreman in 1976 but lost again in five rounds. He continued to fight until 1981 when he quit after drawing against 'Jumbo' Cummings.

An all-action fighter, Frazier was a hustler who liked to press forward. He was not a particularly big heavyweight but his non-stop approach earned him the nickname 'Smokin' Joe'. When he retired, he tried his luck as a pop singer but it was a career that never really got off the ground. He was more successful at managing his promising son, Marvis, but his hopes were dashed when the young Frazier came unstuck against both Larry Holmes and Mike Tyson.

Above and right: Frazier's great moments came against Ali. This first encounter was on March 8 1971, when Frazier was champ, and Ali was making his comeback. Ali looked supremely confident – even toying with Frazier at times – but he couldn't finish him off, and Frazier kept the crown on a unanimous decision after a superb contest.

Left: Frazier, in his powerful pomp, unleashes a stunning combination on Jerry Quarry.

Right: 'Smoking' Joe' was a likeable and popular figure outside the ring. He tried his luck as an entertainer, and stayed involved with boxing by managing his son Marvis.

GEORGE FOREMAN

BORN MARSHALL, TEXAS, JANUARY 22 1948
TURNED PROFESSIONAL 1969 **WORLD
HEAVYWEIGHT CHAMPION** 1973–1974; 1994
WORLD CHAMPIONSHIP FIGHTS WON 4,
LOST 3

Born into poverty, George Foreman had a turbulent childhood and might well have taken to a life of crime had he not discovered that organized boxing was a good alternative to a hoodlum's existence on the streets.

He first rose to prominence as an amateur, winning the Olympic heavyweight gold medal in 1968. A year later he turned professional and went through a procession of thirty-seven consecutive victories before confronting the world heavyweight champion Joe Frazier in 1973. At the time Frazier was looking for warm-up fodder for his rematch with Muhammad Ali, and few people reckoned that the hard-hitting Foreman would be serious competition for the champion. It was, indeed, a one-sided contest but very much in Foreman's favour. Frazier was punched all around the ring and went down no less than six times before the referee called a merciful halt in the second round.

The new champion knocked out his first challenger, Joe Roman, in one round and in March 1974 he took on Ken Norton, the man who had gained a fearsome reputation the previous year when he broke Muhammad Ali's jaw. Norton proved no match for Foreman and was dispatched in two rounds.

Foreman's next challenger was the former champion, the great Muhammad Ali. The fight took place in Kinshasa, Zaïre, in 1974, and was dubbed the 'Rumble in the Jungle' by Ali, who, despite all his cockiness, was rated the underdog. For seven rounds Ali allowed Foreman to pummel him as he hung on to the ropes. Then in the eighth, with his man exhausted, Ali caught Foreman on the chin and the champion folded and was counted out.

Shaken by the defeat, Foreman reverted to his former lifestyle and much of the fortune he had earned in the ring was frittered away. In order to try and regain some of his former wealth he came out of retirement, and had convincing victories over Ron

Right: Foreman endeared himself to the American public by unveiling and waving a tiny Stars and Stripes on the winner's podium at the 1968 Olympics. Five years (and thirty-seven victories) later, he was world heavyweight champion, taking the title from Joe Frazier on January 22 1973 on a KO after one minute thirty-five seconds of the second round.

Left: Foreman was one of the hardest punchers who ever lived. He showed this on his phenomenal comeback trail – here against Terry Anderson. In his forties he was not very mobile, but opponents found that his power was undiminished.

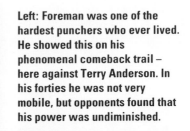

Above: A larger-than-life character, Foreman is the greatest popularizer of the sport since the young Ali. He has shown the human side of the fight-game, proving that boxers can be quick-witted and funny, and, through his great charitable works, that they can put something back into society in a responsible manner.

Lyle and Joe Frazier. Then he suffered a shock defeat by Jimmy Young in 1977 and announced to the world that he was giving up boxing to become a preacher.

For ten years, Foreman was out of the reckoning but the call of the ring was too strong and he decided to put on his gloves again and try once more to become world champion. Sceptics were surprised by what they saw. Although the former champion was slow around the ring he still possessed a hugely powerful punch, and his defeat of Gerry Cooney in January 1990 put him in line for a title challenge.

He fought Evander Holyfield in 1991 and Tom-my Morrison in 1993 both for versions of the world championship. Although losing, George performed well and when both Holyfield and Morrison were later deposed, he was again poised to challenge for the title. At the age of 46, he became the oldest man ever to win boxing's major prize by knocking out Michael Moorer in the tenth round. He patiently waited for an opening and when he saw it, threw a right hand that dropped Moorer on his back and put himself back on the championship throne that he'd occupied twenty years earlier. It was one of boxing's outstanding achievements.

LARRY HOLMES

The life story of Larry Holmes is a classic rags to riches tale. He was one of eleven brothers and sisters, and when he was a youngster he was forced to work as a shoeshine boy to earn much-needed cash for the family. When he was not on the streets seeking customers with tarnished shoes, however, he was in the gym learning to box. He nearly represented the United States at the 1972 Olympic Games but was disqualified in the final of the Olympic Trials for holding Duane Bobick. Not prepared to lose any more time as an amateur, he turned professional in 1973 and launched a career that was to make him a millionaire several times over.

He became recognized as a genuine heavyweight title challenger after twenty-six consecutive victories, twenty of them inside the distance. His chance came in 1978 when he was pitted against the man who had been awarded the WBC version of the heavyweight title, the ageing Ken Norton. They fought a close contest in Las Vegas and Holmes was adjudged the winner on points after fifteen rounds. He successfully defended his title seven times before meeting his boyhood hero Muhammad Ali in 1980. In his youth he had acted as a sparring partner for Ali but by now 'The Greatest' was well past his best and Holmes forced the former champion to retire in the tenth round. 'I love that man and didn't want to see him getting hurt,' Holmes said after his victory.

Perhaps Holmes' most satisfying bout was against the 'Great White Hope', Gerry Cooney, who was convincingly beaten in thirteen rounds but who nevertheless proved to be a courageous challenger. After humbling Marvis Frazier, son of the former heavyweight champion Joe Frazier, in 1983, Holmes relinquished the WBC title and became recognized as heavyweight champion of the newly-formed IBF.

BORN CUTHBERT, GEORGIA, NOVEMBER 3 1949 **TURNED PROFESSIONAL** 1973 **WORLD HEAVYWEIGHT CHAMPION** 1978–1985 **WORLD CHAMPIONSHIP FIGHTS** WON 20, LOST 4

His first defence of the IBF crown was against James 'Bonecrusher' Smith in 1984, and he went on to beat two more challengers before meeting the light-heavyweight Michael Spinks in September 1985. Spinks won the contest on a points verdict that was bitterly disputed by Holmes: it was his first ever professional defeat. In the return match in 1986 Spinks again won on points and Holmes was so unhappy with the result that he announced his retirement from boxing.

Two years later, however, Holmes was offered $2 million to fight Mike Tyson for the undisputed heavyweight championship of the world. It was too much for the thirty-eight-year-old former champion to resist and the two men met at Atlantic City in June 1988. Holmes was painfully and brutally dispatched in four rounds by a man in his prime, who was some seventeen years his junior.

Holmes seldom gets the recognition he deserves as a boxer because he followed in the wake of the irrepressible Muhammad Ali, to whom he is often compared. The two had very different personalities and styles, so any such comparison does not do Holmes justice. He had a formidable left jab and a long reach that he used to good effect. He was not generally considered to be a knockout specialist and yet he stopped thirty-four opponents within the distance.

When well into his forties, Holmes, dismissive of the quality of current heavyweight boxing, announced another comeback. He ran up six wins then lost to Evander Holyfield in a title challenge in 1992. The following two years saw him unbeaten and his success put him in line for a title fight with Oliver McCall early in 1995. At that time he'd won 60 times in 64 outings and had lost to only the very best confirming his status as a legend of the ring.

Top, left, and right: Larry Holmes claimed the heavyweight crown between 1978 and 1985, but, despite his terrific record of twenty successful defences (including one against Gerry Cooney, left), he never made his mark with the public, and was not a particularly popular fighter. He retired after losing to Michael Spinks, but was lured back in 1988 to take an unsuccessful crack at Tyson (top).

ROBERTO DURAN

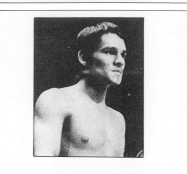

BORN GUARARE, PANAMA, JUNE 16 1951
TURNED PROFESSIONAL 1967 **WORLD LIGHTWEIGHT CHAMPION** 1972–1978
WORLD WELTERWEIGHT CHAMPION 1980
WORLD JUNIOR-MIDDLEWEIGHT CHAMPION 1983 **WORLD MIDDLEWEIGHT CHAMPION** 1989 **WORLD CHAMPIONSHIP FIGHTS** (LIGHTWEIGHT) WON 13 (WELTERWEIGHT) WON 1, LOST 1 (JUNIOR-MIDDLEWEIGHT) WON 1, LOST 2 (MIDDLEWEIGHT) WON 1, LOST 1 (SUPER-MIDDLEWEIGHT) LOST 1

Few people ever witness the kind of poverty that Roberto Duran had to endure as a boy. He grew up in his native Panama when he was almost literally required to fight for his survival. With absolutely nothing to lose, he turned professional in 1967 at the age of just sixteen and rapidly built up a reputation that was truly awesome: amazingly, he polished off seven of his first ten victims inside the opening round.

At the beginning of the 1970s, he went to the United States to seek his fortune and was called the 'Hands of Stone', an apt nickname for such a ferocious puncher. On June 26 1972 he was pitted against the WBA world lightweight champion Ken Buchanan in New York. The able Scot was no match for Duran who won when the referee stopped the fight in the thirteenth round.

The new WBA world champion successfully defended his title twelve times against all-comers and only one man, Edwin Viruet, stayed the distance with him. In his final fight as a lightweight, in 1978, against Esteban De Jesus he became undisputed champion of the world. He then gave up that title in a bid to win the welterweight crown which was then being worn by the great 'Sugar' Ray Leonard.

In a remarkable fight in Montreal in 1980 Duran denied Leonard the space to box in his natural style and dragged the champion into a brawl. It was a tactic that paid handsomely and the Panamanian won an unexpected points decision. In the return match in November the same year Leonard was a wiser man and in the eighth round, in an extraordinary moment, Duran turned his back, saying 'no mas, no mas' ('no more, no more').

Duran's decision to quit against Leonard did little

Right: Pound-for-pound, Duran is placed amongst the great fighters of the twentieth century. Other than the still-mysterious episode against Leonard, in 1980, when he turned his back and refused to fight on, he has the reputation for being a boxer of courage, resilience, determination, and power. He is an old-fashioned street-style fighter, comparable to the likes of LaMotta and Graziano: it is tempting to think that he would have been more at home in the darker boxing world of the 1930s and 1940s, rather than the modern era of Las Vegas, cable TV, and the highly-staged and promoted spectacles in which he has featured so prominently.

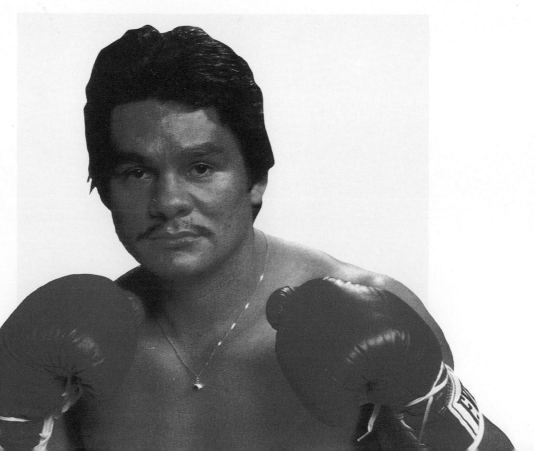

Below: In his thirty-seventh year, Duran still had the power and stamina to beat Iran Barkley and take his middleweight title.

Right: Duran boxed on until he was nearly forty: a natural fighter, it is easy to assume that he clung to the ring because boxing was all he knew.

for the WBC junior-middleweight crown. Hearns proved to be much the stronger man and Duran was knocked out inside two rounds. After this fight Duran quit for a time, but made an extraordinary comeback in February 1989 to take the WBC middleweight title from Iran Barkley in a closely fought contest that resulted in a split decision. This victory sparked off the imagination of promoters who pushed for a final showdown between Duran and Leonard for the super-middleweight title. The fight was an unmitigated flop and Leonard won on points.

Duran was still boxing, infrequently, at the age of 43. In his 103rd contest he took the former IBF lightweight champion Vinny Pazienza to an exciting 12-round points loss, but he no longer had his former speed and accuracy, and Pazienza won the rematch.

for the WBC junior-middleweight crown. Hearns proved to be much the stronger man and Duran was knocked out inside two rounds. After this fight Duran quit for a time, but made an extraordinary comeback in February 1989 to take the WBC middleweight title from Iran Barkley in a closely fought contest that resulted in a split decision. This victory sparked off the imagination of promoters who pushed for a final showdown between Duran and Leonard for the super-middleweight title. The fight was an unmitigated flop and Leonard won on points.

Tough but temperamental, Duran was a warrior boxer who could end a fight very quickly with either fist. He was at his best when fighting as a lightweight but proved his worth in other divisions and has four world championships to prove it.

MARVIN HAGLER

Marvin Hagler, or 'Marvelous Marvin' as the American press dubbed him, was something of a late developer. He turned professional in 1973 and suffered two defeats (later both were avenged) which led observers to believe that he was vulnerable when put under intense pressure. He had been a professional for a full seven years before he had worked his way into a position to challenge for the world middleweight crown. Given the awesome reputation he earned later in his career, it is also surprising that he did not win his first world title bout. It was against the unremarkable Italian, Vino Antuofermo, in Las Vegas in 1979, and although many ringside spectators reckoned that Hagler had done enough to win, the aspiring champion was left disappointed with a draw, and no title. He was soon to put this right.

It was the Englishman Alan Minter who relieved Antuofermo of the world championship in March

BORN NEWARK, NEW JERSEY, MAY 23 1952
TURNED PROFESSIONAL 1973 **WORLD MIDDLEWEIGHT CHAMPION** 1980–1986
WORLD CHAMPIONSHIP FIGHTS WON 13, LOST 1, DREW 1

1980, and in September that year Hagler flew to London for a second attempt at the title. This time he was successful: he severely punished the Englishman, who was so badly lacerated that the referee had to intervene and stop the fight in the third round. Unfortunately Hagler left London with mixed feelings. Although he was ecstatic at having won the championship he was less than happy with the British public's response. Some members of the partisan audience reacted with a vengeance when they saw their man go down. They hurled missiles and racial abuse at the American, who had to have a police escort from the ring to the dressing room. It was a sorry day for British boxing and severely damaged its reputation.

Whether it was in response to the British public's shameful behaviour or not, Hagler was a changed man after his fight with Minter. He disposed of three opponents in rapid order in 1981, and in the spring

Right: These two great ring gladiators, Hagler and Duran, slugged it out in a superbly entertaining and exciting bout in Las Vegas in 1983 for the middleweight crown. At this time the championship was fragmented, with different authorities recognizing different contenders and champions. But as far as the public was concerned, Hagler was the title-holder, and he remained so after defeating Duran on a points verdict.

Left: Duran lands a powerful punch on Hagler in their 1983 contest. During the 1980s, bored by the lack of a truly charismatic figure to head the heavyweight class, the public turned its attention to the middleweight and welterweight divisions. There they found Hagler, Duran, Hearns and Leonard, who between them created a golden age: it is hard to think of another era when four such great boxers fought in the same divisions at the same time.

Right: Hagler lines up with the all time greats: he took the world middleweight title from Alan Minter in 1980 and held it for six years against an array of high-quality challengers. His ferocious hairstyle and pre-fight scowl disguise an amusing and easy-going personality.

of 1982 he dispatched William 'Caveman' Lee in just over one minute of the first round. The referee had to save England's Tony Sibson from taking a terrible beating at the start of 1983, and in November the same year Hagler beat the great Panamanian fighter, Roberto Duran, on points in Las Vegas.

One thing Hagler never did was shirk a fight. In 1985, he took on Thomas Hearns in a much-publicized and extremely lucrative fight in Las Vegas. Early on, with a badly cut eye, Hagler was in danger of being stopped, so he went for broke and smashed the 'Hit Man' to the canvas in the third round.

Hagler's next contest was a tough match against the unbeaten John Mugabi, but it all ended for the Ugandan in the eleventh round when he was knocked

out. Then in April 1987 came the fight that the world wanted to see: Hagler versus 'Sugar' Ray Leonard in Las Vegas. Huge sums of money had to be placed on the table to draw both men into the ring and it turned out to be the richest fight in boxing history with Hagler getting $17 million and Leonard $11 million. It was a close and thrilling bout with Leonard winning controversially on a split decision. Hagler was sure that he had won, and so deep were his feelings that he never boxed again.

Hagler will always be remembered as a great champion. He was a southpaw with a punishing jab and a devastating right hook and, as if that was not enough, he shaved his head and cultivated a steely stare that put fear into all but the very bravest.

'SUGAR' RAY LEONARD

BORN WILMINGTON, NORTH CAROLINA, MAY 17 1956 **TURNED PROFESSIONAL** 1977 **WORLD WELTERWEIGHT CHAMPION** 1979–1982 **WORLD LIGHT-MIDDLEWEIGHT CHAMPION** 1981–1982 **WORLD MIDDLEWEIGHT CHAMPION** 1988–1990 **WORLD SUPER-MIDDLEWEIGHT CHAMPION** 1988–1990 **WORLD LIGHT-HEAVYWEIGHT CHAMPION** 1988–1990 **WORLD CHAMPIONSHIP FIGHTS** (WELTERWEIGHT) WON 6, LOST 1 (LIGHT-MIDDLEWEIGHT) WON 1 (MIDDLEWEIGHT) WON 1 (SUPER-MIDDLEWEIGHT) WON 1, DREW 1 (LIGHT-HEAVYWEIGHT) WON 1

Leonard was named after the great jazz singer Ray Charles by his parents, but he always preferred boxing to a career in music and he began to show off his talents at the tender age of fourteen. He had a meteoric career as an amateur and won the light-welterweight gold medal at the 1976 Olympic Games. After the Montreal games he intended to forego boxing, but was tempted into becoming a professional in order to help pay the family bills and keep them fed.

He started his professional career with twenty-seven consecutive victories and won the WBC world welterweight title at his first attempt in 1979 by stopping Wilfred Benitez in the fifteenth round. He defended the title successfully against Britain's Dave 'Boy' Green in 1980 but then lost the title three months later in an epic battle with Roberto Duran. Recovering well from this setback, he fought Duran again in November 1980 and recaptured the title when, in a notorious and still controversial incident, the Panamanian gave up in the eighth round saying 'no mas, no mas' ('no more, no more').

In June 1981 Leonard stepped up to light-middleweight and took the WBA world title from Ayub Kalule, knocking the Ugandan out in nine rounds. Determined to become undisputed world welterweight champion, Leonard then challenged Thomas 'Hit Man' Hearns, the WBA champion. The epic fight lasted for fourteen rounds before the referee called a halt, declaring Leonard the victor.

After humiliating Bruce Finch in three rounds at the beginning of 1982, Leonard was forced to have an eye operation for a detached retina and announced his retirement later in the year. He made a comeback in 1983, but his nine-round win over Kevin Howard was not entirely convincing, and he immediately decided to announce his retirement once more.

Leonard stayed out of the ring for over three years but was tempted back to fight 'Marvelous' Marvin Hagler for the WBC world middleweight title. The fight was held in the car park of Caesar's Palace, Las Vegas, in April 1987 and is reputed to have grossed more than $100 million. With no warm-up fight beforehand, and with only one contest in the previous five years, Leonard boxed his way to a sensational points victory over Hagler.

After winning the richest contest in boxing history Leonard gave up the middleweight crown, but hinted that he might still continue to fight. Sure enough, in November 1988 he fought Donny Lalonde and won in nine rounds. This victory enabled him to claim the WBC light-heavyweight and super-middleweight titles. In 1989, aged thirty-three, he had two more fights: one against Thomas Hearns, with whom he drew, and a second in which he beat, for the second time, the only man who had defeated him, Roberto Duran.

'Sugar' Ray Leonard ranks as one of the shrewdest tacticians boxing has produced and his mastery is beyond doubt. When he overwhelmed Donny Lalonde in 1988 he became the first person to win world championship titles at five different weights. He has proved equally successful outside the ring.

Right: Leonard was an amazing boxer: as much businessman and entrepreneur as fighter, he, above all, was clever enough to benefit from the new era, when boxing contests evolved into a form of world-wide TV spectacle rather than a simple test of strength and skill between two ordinary mortals. At the same time he was a boxer of rare artistry, and an extraordinary mixture of cool intelligence and reckless courage.

Above: 'Sugar' Ray Leonard raises his fist in triumph after a victory over Hagler which confirmed him as probably the richest and most successful boxer of all time. The fight took place on April 6 1987: it was over twelve rounds, in a purpose-built arena in Caesar's Palace parking lot. The decision was split, but went narrowly in Leonard's favour. This was an amazing performance by a man who had been retired for three years and had not even had a warm-up fight to prepare.

Right: Another great money-spinner against Tommy Hearns. What stopped these Leonard/Hearns/Hagler/Duran fights from being perceived as merely cynical paydays (like some of the ludicrous contemporary heavyweight mis-matches) was the quality of the fighting. These men were legitimate pugilists who would have stood their ground in any era, and their battles are an honourable part of boxing's history.

BARRY McGUIGAN

The son of a singer who had once represented Ireland in the Eurovision Song Contest, McGuigan (who was christened Finbar Patrick) was brought up in Clones, a small town that lies on the border between the Republic of Ireland and Northern Ireland. He showed great promise as a teenager, winning the Commonwealth Games bantamweight gold medal in 1978 at the age of seventeen. However, he disappointed at the 1980 Olympics, where he was eliminated in the second round.

Turning professional as a featherweight a year after the Olympics, under the guidance of Belfast's Barney Eastwood, McGuigan had a setback in his third fight when he was outpointed by Peter Eubanks. Tragedy was to follow in June 1982 when Young Ali, a Nigerian opponent he knocked out in six rounds, died from brain injuries after their fight. But McGuigan was made of stern stuff and he continued

BORN MONAGHAN, IRELAND, FEBRUARY 28 1961 **TURNED PROFESSIONAL** 1981 **WORLD FEATHERWEIGHT CHAMPION** 1985–1986 **WORLD CHAMPIONSHIP FIGHTS** WON 3, LOST 1

to box, relieving Vernon Penprase of the British featherweight title in April 1983. Later in the same year he knocked out Valerio Nati in six rounds to claim the vacant European featherweight title.

After eighteen consecutive wins McGuigan was ready to challenge the veteran holder of the WBA world featherweight title, Eusebio Pedroza, who had remained undefeated since 1978 and had successfully defended his crown nineteen times. Pedroza was reluctant to come to Britain to fight but eventually a price and venue were agreed upon. McGuigan fought Pedroza at the Queen's Park Rangers soccer ground in Shepherd's Bush, London, on June 8 1985 in front of a 25,000 crowd, most of whom were Irish. It turned out to be a remarkable fight with McGuigan flooring the champion in the seventh round and going on to win on points after fifteen rounds.

Right: Although a national hero in Ireland, and one of the few boxers from the British Isles to gain international esteem in the last three decades, there is nevertheless a feeling that, with a little luck, McGuigan could have gone further and achieved more. His career was interrupted by injury and by managerial disputes, and a record of four world championship fights does not truly reflect McGuigan's excellence and courage. That having been said, his career record of thirty-two wins from thirty-five outings ranks alongside the very best.

Left and above: Two images from the greatest fight of McGuigan's life – the night he took the title from the great Pedroza. On the left, he has the champion on the run and is moving in to complete a numbing combination. Above, his fans and family chair him in triumph from the ring.

After successfully defending his title twice, McGuigan was lured to Las Vegas where he fought a little-known substitute by the name of Steve Cruz in 1986. After getting the better of the early rounds, the Irishman was troubled by the sweltering heat and succumbed to a points defeat by the young Texan.

For a year or more McGuigan fought a tedious and acrimonious battle with his manager, Eastwood, during which time he was kept out of the ring. He was determined to have another try for the world title, however, and won three comeback contests while under new management. Luck was not with McGuigan, though, and in his fight against Jim McDonnell in 1989 his eye was badly cut and the referee stopped the fight in the fourth round. Deciding that enough was enough, McGuigan retired.

McGuigan developed into an extremely forceful boxer who sapped the strength of his opponents with heavy body blows. He also had a stout heart and a determination that rattled the most experienced of fighters, including Pedroza. His engaging personality has made him a successful television commentator.

The 'Clones Cyclone', as McGuigan was dubbed, hails from a troubled part of Ireland and his popularity was such that both Republicans and Loyalists would flock to see him at Belfast's King's Hall in crowds that were a promoter's dream. He became an Irish hero, and when he beat Pedroza in Shepherd's Bush the folk song 'Danny Boy' was sung by tearful but jubilant Irishmen in pubs and clubs all over the world. His professional record of thirty-two victories, twenty-eight of them inside the distance, out of a total of thirty-five fights shows that in McGuigan all Ireland had a figure of which they could be proud.

FRANK BRUNO

For almost a decade Frank Bruno has carried the hopes of all Englishmen who crave a British world heavyweight champion. Yet Bruno has never won a British title: his fame has largely been gained from bouts against European and American opposition.

Born in Hammersmith in the west of London, Bruno had a successful amateur career which culminated with victory in the Amateur Boxing Association heavyweight finals in 1980. Two years later he turned professional and notched up a remarkable string of victories, winning twenty-one bouts inside the distance. He rapidly rose up the ranking lists and many thought that he had the makings of a world champion. The one blot on his impressive record sheet was his fight against James 'Bonecrusher' Smith. Bruno was way ahead on points against the American but in a slack moment during the tenth round he was felled by a scything blow and failed to beat the count.

Recovering from his ignominious defeat at the hands of the 'Bonecrusher', Bruno came back to take on Anders Eklund for the European heavyweight title in 1985. He had a convincing four-round victory over the giant Swede and his hopes of a world title fight were further boosted after a one-round win over the highly rated South African, Gerrie Coetzee.

In July 1986 Bruno's wishes came true and he fought Tim Witherspoon, the WBA world champion. For Bruno, however, history repeated itself. He was winning the contest on points in front of a vast, partisan audience at Wembley when, in the eleventh round, the champion launched an attack that had him in such severe trouble that the referee had to step in quickly to stop the fight.

Determined to continue fighting after his setback against Witherspoon, Bruno had four conclusive

BORN LONDON, NOVEMBER 1 1961 **TURNED PROFESSIONAL** 1982 **WORLD CHAMPIONSHIP FIGHTS** LOST 3

victories in 1987. The most important of these was against Joe Bugner, the former British and Commonwealth champion who had embarked on the comeback trail. Bruno and Bugner fought in London and the contest was considered to be an eliminator for a world title challenge. Bugner, who had never been a popular figure in England and who had emigrated to Australia, was soundly beaten in eight rounds. After his win against Bugner, Bruno was again thrust to the forefront of world boxing but he had to bide his time for over a year before being granted a fight against Mike Tyson.

Bruno and Tyson met on February 25 1989, in Las Vegas. The press and media did not rate the Englishman's chances of success very highly and in the end their predictions were accurate. Tyson was, however, momentarily stunned in the first round by a blow from Bruno, and the challenger put in a courageous effort before the contest was stopped in the fifth.

Bruno was inactive for two years then launched a comeback. After a series of wins under the management of Micky Duff, he challenged Lennox Lewis for Lewis's WBC heavyweight crown in October 1993. One big left from Lewis, in round 7, cancelled out the excellent showing of Bruno in the previous rounds. Despite losing, Bruno emerged with his prestige enhanced. He scored a couple more wins and, following Lewis's surprise defeat by Oliver McCall, was again in the chief contender's slot. If his challenge to McCall comes off, the winner – which could well be Bruno – will figure in the plans of Mike Tyson.

Bruno has a superb physique for a boxer, being both tall and strong. He is, however, regarded by some critics as ponderous and slow around the ring, and, as age catches up with him, it remains to be seen how he faces up to young opponents. Humorous, polite, and occasionally witty, Bruno is hugely popular.

Above: The fight between Bruno and Bugner had tremendous emotional significance in the UK. The British public had been devastated when Bugner had beaten their all-time favourite, Henry Cooper: the new favourite, Bruno, avenged his predecessor in fine style, and to tremendous acclaim.

Top: A scene from Bruno's career high-point – a match with the champion Tyson. Truth be told, nobody expected Bruno to win, and when he shook the champ there was tremendous, but short-lived, excitement. Tyson mopped up in five. **Right:** Bruno has always looked the part: he has a fine physique and great strength.

99

JULIO CESAR CHAVEZ

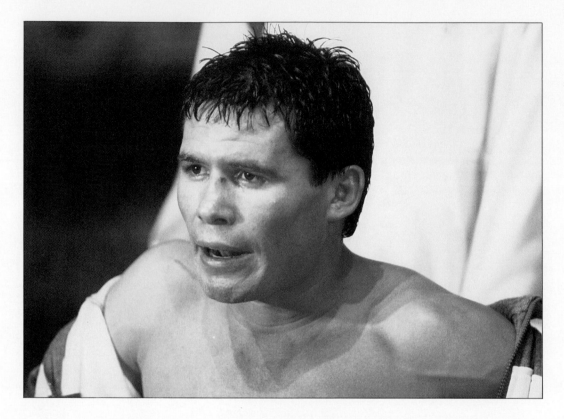

Many people claim that Julio Chavez is the greatest boxer, pound for pound, of the twentieth century. His record of one defeat in more than ninety professional fights supports that opinion and without doubt he ranks alongside the very best who ever boxed.

He was born and brought up in Mexico where many boys look to boxing as a way of making a living. His three elder brothers all turned professional and Julio Cesar, or 'JC' as he is often called, followed suit in 1980 when he was only seventeen. He had a tough start with twenty-two fights in his first two years, but he won all of them with knockouts.

He won his first world title, the WBC junior-lightweight championship, in September 1984 when he stopped Mario Martinez in the eighth round. He defended the title no less than nine times over

BORN CIUDAD OBREGON, MEXICO, JULY 12 1962 **TURNED PROFESSIONAL** 1980 **WORLD JUNIOR-LIGHTWEIGHT CHAMPION** 1984–1987 **WORLD LIGHTWEIGHT CHAMPION** 1987–1988 **WORLD JUNIOR-WELTERWEIGHT CHAMPION** 1989–1994 **WORLD CHAMPIONSHIP FIGHTS** (JUNIOR-LIGHTWEIGHT) WON 10 (LIGHTWEIGHT) WON 3 (JUNIOR-WELTERWEIGHT) WON 14 LOST 1 (WELTERWEIGHT) DREW 1

the next three years, winning all but four of the contests inside the distance. Among his victims were Roger Mayweather who went out in two rounds, and Rocky Lockridge who managed to survive for the full twelve rounds but lost on points.

Late in 1987 Chavez gave up his junior-lightweight crown and stepped up to lightweight, relieving Edwin Rosario of the WBA world title in November. Almost a year later he was able to add the WBC lightweight prize to his trophy cabinet when he got the better of José Luis Ramirez in Las Vegas.

In the spring of 1989 Chavez moved further up the weight ladder to fight his old adversary Roger Mayweather for the WBC junior-welterweight world championship. The referee had to stop the fight in the tenth round, declaring Chavez the winner. After picking off two contenders for his

Below: Chavez is so good, that if he is run close in a bout it makes the headlines. Probably his hardest fight was against Meldrick Taylor in 1989: JC, behind on points in the last round, saved the day by a crushing attack which finished the bout with only two seconds left on the clock.

Right: Chavez prepares to despatch Ramirez. Although it is impossible, and invidious, to make comparisons between weights and decades, if the title Fighter of the Century was on offer, Chavez would be one of the most serious contenders.

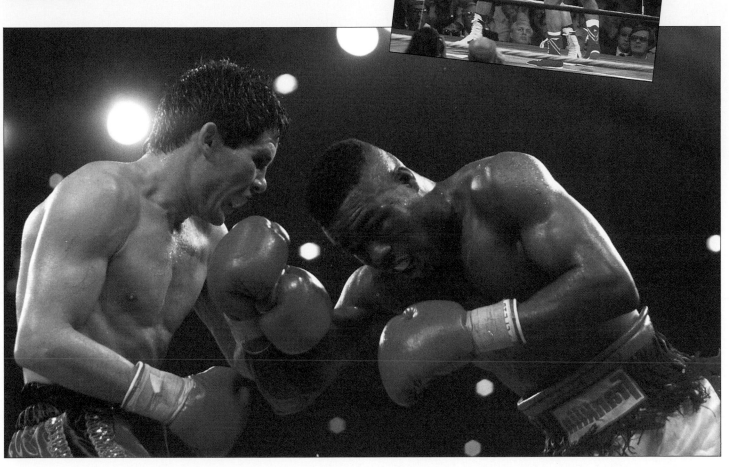

new title late in 1989, a contest was arranged between Chavez and Meldrick Taylor who was in possession of the IBF junior-welterweight crown. In a bitterly-fought brawl in Las Vegas Chavez looked in danger of losing, but in the final round he produced a whirlwind of punches and the referee stopped the fight. It was a close call for Chavez: there were just two seconds to go on the clock!

Taylor had to wait five years for a return but his best days were then behind him and he was comprehensively beaten in eight rounds. Chavez had ambitions at welterweight level and forced WBC champion Pernell Whittaker to a draw in 1994 after successfully defending his junior welterweight title against Terrence Ali.

Chavez's long winning streak was broken in his 90th fight when slick boxing Frankie Randall floored and outpointed him. Randall was boxing well in the return match when a cut, caused by a head clash, made it impossible for the Mexican to continue. Chavez was awarded a 'technical' points win and thereby regained his title.

Tony Lopez, a former champion, was ground down in ten rounds and the manner of Chavez's victory dispelled any suspicions that he was on the slide.

It is likely that he'll retire after his hundredth fight provided he has achieved his ambition to beat Pernell Whittaker for the welterweight championship. Their drawn fight in 1993 means that Whittaker is the only component that Chavez has failed to beat.

MIKE TYSON

Mike Tyson was born and brought up in one of the grimmer ghettos of New York City, and as a young teenager he discovered that the easiest way to get money was to mug people. He learned to box in a reform school for delinquents where he was spotted by Cus D'Amato, who had managed the former world heavyweight champion, Floyd Patterson. D'Amato recognized the reckless fourteen-year-old's potential and became his legal guardian, friend, father-figure and mentor.

Under the expert tutelage of D'Amato, Tyson flourished: he had mixed success as an amateur, but won the Golden Gloves heavyweight championship in 1984. He turned professional in 1985 and rapidly earned a formidable reputation as a knockout specialist, disposing of fifteen opponents in a total of just twenty-two rounds. In his second year as a professional he had thirteen straight wins before being pitted against the WBC world heavyweight champion, Trevor Berbick. Tyson despatched Berbick in two rounds and, at twenty years and 145 days, he became the youngest man ever to claim a world heavyweight title. In March 1987 he took on the mighty James 'Bonecrusher' Smith for the WBA heavyweight crown. Smith retained some credibility by going the distance, but he lost his title on points.

Over the next two to three years Tyson put away eight challengers, including the former champion Larry Holmes in four rounds, and Frank Bruno in five in February 1989. One of his most remarkable fights was against the unbeaten Michael Spinks who lasted a paltry ninety-one seconds in a contest held in Atlantic City in 1988. A quicker victory was to follow, however: on July 21 1989 he knocked out the IBF champion Carl Williams in just eighty-three seconds, which confirmed his status as undisputed heavyweight champion of the world.

BORN BROOKLYN, NEW YORK, JUNE 30 1966
TURNED PROFESSIONAL 1985 **WORLD**
HEAVYWEIGHT CHAMPION 1986–1990
WORLD CHAMPIONSHIP FIGHTS WON 10,
LOST 1

Many thought Tyson to be unbeatable, but Frank Bruno had shown that the champion could at least be hurt; the Englishman had temporarily stunned Tyson with a clip to the head during the first round of their 1989 contest. Then in 1990 occurred one of the greatest upsets in boxing history. Tyson faced James 'Buster' Douglas in Tokyo and virtually nobody gave the challenger a chance. In the eighth round it all seemed to be over when Douglas went down for what turned out to be a 'long count', but he got up and continued to box. By this time Tyson was tiring and Douglas finished the fight in the tenth round. Some controversy raged over the long count, mainly whipped up by Tyson's new handler, Don King, in an attempt to get the verdict quashed, but Douglas was heralded as the new champion.

Douglas' reign as champion was short-lived, and he lost to Evander Holyfield later in the year. Tyson immediately sought a showdown with Holyfield, but their proposed fight in November 1991 had to be postponed due to an injury sustained by 'Iron Mike'.

Tyson is not a clever fighter but then he claims he does not have to be subtle to win. He is fearless and has the most wicked punch known to modern boxing, a combination which has brought him extraordinary success. Until he was stopped by 'Buster' Douglas, his aura of invincibility had been cultivated to such an extent that many of his opponents had effectively lost before they crossed the ropes into the ring.

A much-publicized divorce, a street brawl, a split with manager Bill Cayton and a rape conviction sullied his public image. He was incarcerated for 3 years in February 1992 and in his absence, the heavyweight championship became fragmented. It comes as no surprise that the public expects his release from jail to herald his return to the ring. The talk is of purses worth millions.

Above: Leaving aside events away from the ring, Tyson must be viewed as a truly exceptional champion – a colossus who dominated his age, albeit during a truncated reign. If his power and aggression could have been properly harnessed and controlled, he might well have been the greatest ever.

Right: There was little artistry in Tyson's ring technique, but his brute power and sheer savagery were enough to see off all-comers. Of past greats, the most obvious comparison is with Marciano, and a fight between the two would have been spectacular indeed.

RIDDICK BOWE

By impressively deposing Evander Holyfield in a classic, all-action encounter, Riddick Bowe emerged as a formidable heavy-weight champion. Some critics had expressed prior doubts as to his 'heart' and durability – citing his struggle to outpoint former WBA champion, Tony Tubbs – but the way in which he beat Holyfield soon made them change their tune.

Bowe went into the fight with thirty-one victories and an unbeaten professional record that included the scalps of Everett Martin, Bert Cooper and former WBC champion, Pinklon Thomas. His first defence emphasised his power when Michael Dokes failed to last one round. Yet Dokes was a former WBA champion!

The WBC tried to enforce an agreement that Bowe should defend against Lennox Lewis, rather than against Dokes, so Riddick promptly relinquished the WBC title. After dropping the WBC belt in a

BORN BROOKLYN, NEW YORK, AUGUST 10 1967 **TURNED PROFESSIONAL** 1989 **WBA AND IBF CHAMPION** 1992–93 **WBO HEAVYWEIGHT CHAMPION** 1995 **WORLD CHAMPIONSHIP FIGHTS** WON 4, LOST 2

rubbish bin, he invited Lennox to remove it if he so desired. Lewis is the last man to have beaten Bowe. That was at the 1988 Olympic finals when family misfortunes were, perhaps, playing on Riddick's mind and impeding his concentration.

Bowe put on weight and eventually lost his title to Holyfield in their second meeting in 1993. Once again it was a magnificent battle and Bowe was great in defeat.

He put that loss behind him and kept winning. When he was offered a fight with WBO champion Herbie Hide in March 1995, he promptly accepted and emerged as the new champion, with Hide succumbing in six rounds after being floored nine times.

Eddie Futch, a veteran trainer who has handled some great fighters, has this to say of Bowe: 'He has the potential to become the best heavyweight I ever had.' And Futch is seldom wrong.

Right: Bowe in unstoppable form against Bruce Seddon in Atlantic City. The New Yorker knocked the 'Atlantic City Express', once ranked world ~~num~~

ROY JONES JNR.

BORN PENSACOLA, FLORIDA, JANUARY 16 1969 **TURNED PROFESSIONAL** 1989 **IBF MIDDLEWEIGHT CHAMPION** 1993 **IBF SUPER-MIDDLEWEIGHT CHAMPION** 1994 **WORLD CHAMPIONSHIP FIGHTS** (MIDDLEWEIGHT) WON 2 (SUPER-MIDDLEWEIGHT) WON 2

Roy Jones emerged as one of the superstars of the 90s when he took the IBF Super Middleweight Championship from an outstanding title holder in James Toney. There were those who favoured Jones to win but the odds were short whoever you chose. It was a classic pairing, full of imponderables, between two men who went into the Las Vegas ring with unblemished professional records. It looked like being a close, hard-fought battle with Toney a slight favourite in the opinion of the cognoscenti. In the event, Jones won clearly and the manner of his victory sent the press reporters searching for superlatives to describe the skills of the new champion.

Jones had turned twenty before he boxed for pay. He entered the pro ranks with a wealth of amateur experience behind him. He was a silver medal winner in the 1988 Olympics with the Val Barker trophy awarded to him as a bonus.

He'd been a professional for four years before he was taken to a points win. Jorge Castro lasted the 10 round course in Jones's home town of Pensacola and by then Jones seemed a cert bet for world title honours.

He'd knocked out Ricky Stockhouse, Reggie Miller and – ominously – former world welterweight champion Jorge Vaca. Vaca lasted less than a round, as had Art Servano and Glenn Wolfe.

Jones got his first world title shot at the middleweight limit in 1993 and clearly outpointed Bernard Hopkins for the vacant crown. Hopkins was made to look very ordinary and Jones extended himself only enough to clinch the decision. He'd shown the same casual approach before. "Professional boxing is all business and I do only what I need to. Only if the money is adequate will I extend myself", was his response.

There were some who thought he'd be casual against Toney. Even when he defended his middleweight title – the one he wrested from Hopkins – against experienced Thomas Tate, he was accused of lacking zest and enthusiasm. A strange and incorrect analysis that – Tate went out in two rounds and once again Jones had made it look easy.

The doubters were converted after the Toney win. Jones emerged as the best pound-for-pound fighter in the world and, as if to prove it, he beat his first challenger, Antoine Byrd, in three minutes.

Right: Roy Jones moment of triumph, as he salutes his new IBF Super Middleweight World Championship victory over James Toney on November 18 1994. Jones's superior ringcraft and lightening quick hands and feet saw him home against an opponent who was sluggish on the night.

BRITISH STARS

TERRY DOWNES
MIDDLEWEIGHT

Left: Terry Downes was born in London on May 9 1936. After a successful amateur and army boxing career he turned professional in 1957. He became British middleweight champion on defeating Phil Edwards on September 30 1958, and world middleweight champion on beating Paul Pender on July 11 1961. He fought forty-three professional bouts, winning thirty-four; twenty-seven of his victories were knockouts.

Downes was born in 1936 in London's Paddington district. After military service – some of which was spent in the United States in the Marine Corps – he turned professional, and took the British middleweight title from Phil Edwards in his twentieth bout. After some domestic ups and downs, he earned a world title eliminator against the highly experienced Joey Giardello: to everyone's, except Downes' surprise, he gave Giardello a boxing lesson, tempering, for once, his rushing windmill style to

mix in a few artistic jabs.

On January 14 1961, Downes got his shot at the new champion, Paul Pender, who had taken the crown from Sugar Ray Robinson the previous year. Probably over-awed, he wasted the opportunity by attempting to go forward too relentlessly, and received such a badly gashed nose that the fight was stopped in the seventh round. Sensing an easy and lucrative rematch, Pender agreed to come to London for the return.

On July 11 1961 Downes achieved his dream of a

world title by stopping Pender after nine rounds. The fight ended oddly and suddenly: Pender was ahead on points, and did well in the ninth round, but he stayed on his stool for the tenth. The air of controversy robbed Downes of some of the glory he deserved.

Downes lost a return with Pender in Boston on April 7 1962 by a unanimous decision. He boxed on, but, other than a rather sad win against his boyhood hero Sugar Ray Robinson, had only one more fight of international

significance, in 1964. This was against Willie Pastrano, who had become the world light-heavyweight champion in June 1963. In their encounter, which was for the world light-heavyweight title Downes ran him desperately close, but lost on a stoppage.

Downes was much loved both in the ring and after his retirement. A natural character, with no airs or graces, he stayed in the boxing world and used some of the great wealth he had shrewdly accumulated for the good of the sport and for many charities.

JOHN CONTEH
LIGHT-HEAVYWEIGHT

Conteh's story is similar to Barry McGuigan's: he achieved a lot by ordinary standards; won a world title, and became a hero to his people – yet somehow he never fulfilled his potential, and a question is left hanging about what might have been.

His career was launched in 1970 when he won a Commonwealth Games middleweight gold medal agcd ninctccn. Hc bcat thc fine German, Rudiger Schmidtke, in 1973 to take the European light-heavyweight crown, and a match was arranged with the other great British favourite of the time, Chris Finnegan, to settle the British and Commonwealth titles. Conteh won the first match and a controversial return, proving himself the best in Britain. The manner of his victories, and his all-round win-at-all-costs approach, ensured that, although he was undoubtedly the most admired and respected boxer of his generation, some elements of the 'sporting' British public (who tend to favour a good loser over an out-and-out winner) never took him to their hearts. An exception was the fans in his hometown of Liverpool, who adored him.

Conteh had earned a shot at the world title, and was lined up to fight the Argentinian, Jorge Ahu-

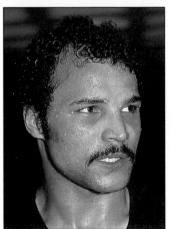

Above: John Conteh. Top: Conteh in action against Parlov in Belgrade.

mada, for the light-heavyweight title vacated by Bob Foster. The battle took place at Wembley Pool, London, on October 1 1974, and Conteh was not about to lose. He contested every second of a brutal fifteen rounds, emerging the points victor.

Conteh defended his title three times in the next three years, against Lonnie Bennett, Yaqui Lopez, and Len Hutchins, but neither the quality of the opposition, nor the frequency of

his outings impressed the boxing authorities, who stripped him of the title. In truth, things had gone wrong for Conteh at this stage: he got entangled in disputes with his managers, and he was sidetracked by the lifestyle his fame and filmstar looks had brought him. He had chances to come back, and was the victim of an awful decision against Parlov in Belgrade, but his career was ended when his licence was revoked on medical grounds.

CHARLIE MAGRI
FLYWEIGHT

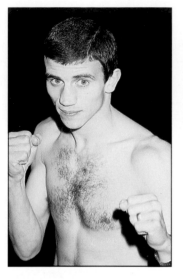

Above: Charlie Magri.

Right: Magri has Eleoncio Mercedes trapped against the ropes during his famous victory of March 15 1983. Magri stopped his man in the seventh round to fulfil his dream of the world title.

Magri was born in Tunisia in 1956, and having moved to London was carefully nurtured by manager Terry Lawless. He made it through to the 1980s undefeated, and with a reputation as an exceptional prospect for the world title. He was a brilliant and artistic boxer; a great points scorer with exceptional speed and technique.

Having come onto the scene like a shooting star, winning the British flyweight championship in only his third professional fight, Magri's progress was slowed down by Lawless, who only nudged him towards the world stage several years later, when he matched him against the ageing Italian, Franco Udella, in a fight that brought Magri the European title.

It came as a great shock to the boxing world to find out in the early 1980s that Magri – tipped to be the greatest British fighter of the century – had a weakness which was likely to upset their hopes. Magri still violently denies that he has a 'glass jaw', but it began to look distressingly like it when one opponent after another began to knock him over with well-timed clips. Whatever the nature of the problem, in most cases, and against all but the finest opposition, his skill and resilience allowed him to overcome the handicap, and he held on to his career until he achieved his dream of a world title fight. It was held at Wembley Arena on March 15 1983, and the opponent was the tough Dominican Republican, Eleoncio Mercedes, who had won the crown from Freddie Castillo the previous November. Britain held its breath, but Magri avoided disaster and had his day in the sun, stopping his man in the seventh round. His reign was brief: the title was taken from him on his first defence by Frank Cedeno. Magri continued to fight, having one more unsuccessful shot at the world title, and winning the European crown, but realizing he would not get back to the top, he retired early.

Magri was a boxer's boxer: he loved his sport and was a great credit to it. A delightful man outside the ring, he was enormously popular with British fight-fans, who still recall his superb ringcraft and his great artistry.

LLOYD HONEYGHAN
WELTERWEIGHT

Honeyghan was born in Jamaica in 1960, and was raised in Great Britain. He turned pro in 1980, and did his fair share of journeyman fighting before making a sudden breakthrough onto the championship scene in 1983. From a relatively lowly ranking, he got a shot at a title-fight eliminator as a late substitute, and when reigning champ Kirkland Laing gave up his crown, he found himself fighting Cliff Gilpin for the British championship. Decked in two, he came back off the canvas to win a bruising encounter on points.

Honeyghan had to wait another three years for his challenge for the world title. As with Charlie Magri, another fighter brought along with extreme caution, Honeyghan was managed by the great Terry Lawless. There were out-of-ring disputes, and it was only after Honeyghan's switch to the Mickey Duff stable that a match was arranged against the world champion, Don Curry.

This was the kind of fight that makes boxing legend. At the time, Curry was, frankly, invincible. He had won the vacant WBA crown by defeating Jun-Sok Hwang on February 13 1983 and defended it in the interim against such excellent fighters as Roger Stafford, Marlon Starling, Elio Diaz, Nino la Rocca, Colin Jones, Milton

McCrory, and Eduardo Rodriguez (unifying the division in the process). Only Starling took him beyond the seventh round. Against Curry, critics allowed Honeyghan the proverbial two chances: hardly any, and none. Still relatively inexperienced at international level, he was matched against a boxer who, pound for pound, was seen as one of the world's best.

Honeyghan, a fighter who could never be accused of under-rating his own talents, didn't fancy the loser's role for which he had been cast by the press. With Duff and trainer Bobby Neill he put together an all-or-nothing tactical package designed to put Curry in the unfamiliar position of going backwards from the start. Honeyghan kept up the pressure, and to the boxing world's amazement, he won when the referee decided that at the end of the sixth Curry was too damaged to continue.

From then on it was

Left: Lloyd Honeyghan – always immaculate, both inside and outside the ring.

showtime: Honeyghan was seldom out of the headlines for either his in-ring mastery or his out-of-ring glitz and controversy. He fought many excellent defences, but as well as taking the record for the fastest world championship finish in history – forty seconds against Gene Hatcher – was also involved in money arguments and disputed decisions. He also made the news when he relinquished the crown for a period after his principled decision not to defend his title in South Africa as a stand against apartheid.

When Honeyghan's career is reviewed in full, it will be seen as a great story. A boxer who was good for the sport, he thrilled the crowds and fascinated a broader public with his pizzazz and flamboyant lifestyle. A real battler in the ring, his win over Curry against all the odds ranks amongst the very finest twentieth-century British boxing achievements.

JOE BUGNER
HEAVYWEIGHT

Bugner was born in Hungary in 1950, and was raised in Great Britain, where he took up citizenship. His personality, like his career, was an enigma from start to finish. Here was a boxer who had been given everything, and whose obvious potential should have made him a natural hero to a nation that could never remember having had a world heavyweight champion: yet he never gelled with the British fight fans, and in retrospect it was this lack of support and sympathy that contributed as much as anything to Bugner's alienation and his failure to fulfil his dreams.

The real watershed in his career occurred not in the world title challenges that came later, but in a parochial match for the British championship at Wembley Pool on March 16 1971 in front of an audience of 10,000 baying enthusiasts. The opponent was Henry Cooper, and all but a handful of the crowd had paid good money to see their hero whip the twenty-one-year-old upstart: but Bugner beat Cooper on a highly controversial points decision, and if he had knocked out the Queen of England it would have left him more popular with the fans.

Bugner went on to achieve more in the ring than any other British

heavyweight for fifty years, yet he would always be known as the man who beat Cooper. He fought Ali twice: the first effort a tremendous battle over the full twelve rounds in a non-title bout, and the second a losing world-title match over fifteen rounds. He then had his greatest night of all in a narrow but hugely courageous defeat against Joe Frazier, but as far as the ungrateful Brit-

ish public was concerned, he could do no right. Eventually the bemused Bugner had had enough of the unjustified criticism and ridicule: he retired early, and headed off to take up Australian citizenship. His last ring appearance was in a well-paid 1987 comeback against Frank Bruno: the thirty-seven-year-old Bugner was well past his best, and was denied a victory he would have loved.

Top and above, left: Joe Bugner, the man the British fans refused to love. He had a tremendous physique, and all the attributes and requirements of a great heavyweight, but never managed to put it all together to the satisfaction of the crowds.

Above: In action, Bugner sinks a hefty right into the body of Danny Sutton.

TERRY MARSH
JUNIOR-WELTERWEIGHT

Marsh was one of the brightest individuals ever to put on professional gloves – a fact that has stood him in good stead in the last few years, as speaking engagements and commentating have had to take the place of fighting for a living. For in 1987, with Marsh freshly-crowned as world light-welterweight champion, it was suddenly revealed to the public (though Marsh is reckoned to have known for some time) that he had epilepsy – an ailment which immediately disqualified him from his ring career.

Always a pragmatist about ring glory – perhaps because he secretly knew that one day it would be denied him – Marsh was never fully seduced by either fame or the champion's lifestyle. Throughout his career he maintained a full-time job as a fireman, and he delighted in taking this as seriously as his boxing.

Born in 1958, he came up through schoolboy boxing and the amateur ranks to win most of the non-professional honours available except for Olympic selection. Turning professional, he was twenty-six when he won the British light-welterweight crown from Clinton McKenzie, and the following year, 1985, he went one further by beating Alessandro Scapecchi to win the Euro-

Above: Terry Marsh is chaired from the ring in triumph on March 4 1987, after taking the world junior-middleweight title from Joe Manley. But less than six months later his career was over, when his epilepsy became public knowledge.

pean championship. His shot at the world title came on March 4 1987, when he took on the formidable American, Joe Manley. Marsh was on his own home turf in Basildon, Essex, and after a brutal battle the referee stopped the fight in the tenth when Manley went down for the second time.

After just one defence, against Japan's Akio Kameda in London on July 1

1987, the news of Marsh's epilepsy leaked to the press, and his career in the ring was over. There was an enormous wave of public sympathy – especially when he also lost his job as a firefighter – and he remains today a charming and highly popular, if slightly eccentric, figure, who is still heavily involved with his sport and media coverage by the press and television.

AUSTRALIAN STARS

Australia has produced many fine boxers over the past one hundred years, but never, until recently, any fighters who have dominated a weight division at the highest level or who have made a real and lasting impact on the world boxing scene. In the past decade two bright stars – Fenech and Harding – did emerge on to the world stage, and their success may point the way to the future.

As well as the men specially featured below, any round-up of Australian greats would be incomplete without mentioning two other Australian world title winners, Lionel Rose and Jimmy Carruthers, and Peter Jackson, a fine Puerto Rico-born black boxer at the turn of the century who was denied a world title only by the colour bar. Other local heroes who never quite made it to world fame include Les Darcy, Jack Carroll, Ambrose Palmer, Fred Henneberry (who had a long and bitter rivalry with another exceptional Australian middleweight, Ron Richards), Billy Grime, Vic Patrick, and Dave Sands.

Left: Ron Richards, who took on the renowned Fred Henneberry ten times.

FRANK SLAVIN
HEAVYWEIGHT

Slavin was born of Irish parents in Maitland, New South Wales, on January 26 1862. Like Bob Fitzsimmons, he worked for a blacksmith in his youth, and developed an impressive and muscular frame: he later went on to find adventure as a gold prospector. He was twenty-three when he fought his first bout, winning a purse of fifty pounds by knocking out Martin Powers.

When the Irishman Jack Burke arrived in Australia in 1889, Slavin was a seasoned professional, and he beat his man in eight rounds. Sensing riches on the world scene, he sailed for England, where he drew with the renowned Jem Smith in a championship contest held at Bruges, Belgium. The championship of England was at stake, and Slavin was having the best of the contest when the fight was deliberately broken up by a gang of toughs who were wearing knuckledusters, who wanted to protect their bets on Smith. Slavin was later awarded the fight, the purse, and the championship title.

He then sailed on to America, where he started his visit with a famous fight against Jake Kilrain, which Slavin won in nine rounds.

While in the United States he sparred with Charlie Mitchell and Jim Daly.

The most significant challenge in the later part of his career came on May 30 1892, against the legendary Peter Jackson, at the National Sporting Club, London, for the title of champion of England and Australia. Slavin was knocked out in the tenth.

In a long and distinguished career, Frank Slavin fought most of the greats of his era, including Smith, Jackson, Jake Kilrain, Joe McAuliffe, Jim Hall and Jack Burke. During a period when the 'world' title was never officially reconciled, he could with some justification lay claim to being the best boxer of his age. He fought on with decreasing frequency until 1907, and died in Canada, in 1929.

'YOUNG GRIFFO'
FEATHERWEIGHT

Right: 'Young Griffo' – Albert Griffiths – (left) takes up a publicity pose against Walter Campbell.

Left: The redoubtable Frank Slavin.

Albert Griffiths was born at Miller's Point, Sydney, in 1871. He started work as a newspaper boy, until a series of successes in street fights tempted him to try his hand as a professional boxer. In modern terms, Griffiths was a featherweight, but in that period of the fight game's history such subtle distinctions were seldom respected, so 'Young Griffo' made his name by taking on all-comers of many shapes and sizes. His most famous early encounters came in a series of five bouts against a black boxer from Mel-bourne called Pluto: they drew each contest, the longest being over seventy rounds.

Griffiths' first big success came when, weighing only 112 pounds himself, he won a contest for 140 pound boxers: having won national recognition, he proceeded to best all the competition available in his homeland (including Billy Murphy, the darling of the local crowds, on two occa-sions) before setting sail for America to try for world fame and bigger prizes.

In the United States he immediately showed his class by getting the better of draws with three truly excel-lent fighters: Solly Smith, Johnny Van Herst and George Lavigne. He came to be recognized as a ring marvel, and boxing his-torians compare Griffiths to one of the all-time greats in the featherweight div-ision, Abe Attell.

He was never a title hol-der, but must be regarded as one of the finest boxers never to wear a crown. He is a legend in the land of his birth, still recognized as one of the earliest and greatest of Australia's sporting heroes.

JOHNNY FAMECHON
FEATHERWEIGHT

In the middle years of the twentieth century one of the most noted Australian ring characters was Johnny Famechon. He was born into a great French boxing family (his uncle, Ray, fought for the world championship under the French national colours), but moved to Australia as a child, and began his boxing career in Melbourne in 1961. During the early 1960s he fought only in Melbourne, working his way up through the ranks, until he finally took the Australian featherweight title in his twenty-second professional bout, by beating Ollie Taylor on September 24 1965. Ranging a little further afield – to New South Wales, Queensland, and even Christchurch – he continued to fight regularly and to defend his title, but he always preferred to box in Melbourne whenever possible. It was there, in front of an adoring home crowd, that he advanced his career on November 24 1967 by taking the British Empire crown from Johnny O'Brien. It was not until the following year, 1968, that Famechon fought outside of Australasia for the first time: his fifty-first fight as a professional was held in Paris, against Réné Roque.

Famechon got his shot at the WBC world featherweight title on January 21 1969 in London, and he took the crown by defeating José Legra on points after the full fifteen rounds. He defended the title successfully on two occasions, both fights against 'Fighting' Harada, before being bested by the great Vincente Saldivar on May 9 1970 in Rome. At the age of thirty-five he decided to hang up the gloves, drawing a line under a distinguished career in which he suffered only five defeats in sixty-eight contests.

JEFF FENECH
BANTAMWEIGHT/FEATHERWEIGHT

Fenech was born in Sydney in 1964. Turning professional in 1984, he shot into the limelight by taking a world championship – the IBF bantamweight title – in only his seventh bout, when he defeated Shitoshi Shingaki on April 26 1985.

He defended his new crown three times, including a rematch with Shitoshi, before relinquishing it after a victory on July 18 1986 against Steve McCrory in order to move up to light-featherweight. Less than a year later he was WBC champion in that division after a fourth-round win over Samart Payakarun of Thailand. Again, he defended only twice before giving up the title to move up and fight the featherweights.

On March 7 1988 Fenech met Victor Callejas in Sydney for the WBC featherweight championship, and beat him when the referee stopped the contest in the tenth round. In an extraordinary period of only four years, he had remained unbeaten and taken world titles at three different weights.

Perhaps the most amazing thing about Fenech was that this early success came when he was still a raw fighter with an unrefined technique and an obvious lack of experience: he learnt his trade on the job, and got better every time he entered the ring. One of the highlights of his career was his emphatic victory over Marcus Villasana, which turned into a superb exhibition of ring mastery. Another was a hard-fought fight against Azumah Nelson, in which Nelson was lucky to escape with a draw; although an eventual defeat by the same boxer in March 1992 represented a major set-back. Nevertheless Fenech, by virtue of holding three titles and of gaining world recognition for Australian boxing, lays claim to being the greatest of all the products of the Australian fight game: he is revered as a national hero.

Top left: Johnny Famechon (left) misses with a left in a non-title encounter with a young Miguel Herrera.

Right: Jeff Fenech, arguably Australia's finest boxer ever.

JEFF HARDING
LIGHT-HEAVYWEIGHT

Left: Jeff Harding, looking formidably aggressive even between rounds.

Although Fenech may have put together the more impressive track record, there is no doubt that 'Hit Man' Harding produced the greatest ever night for Australian boxing when, in June 1989, he came from nowhere (as a late substitute for Donny Lalonde) to beat the established world light-heavyweight champion, Dennis Andries, and take the title.

Came from nowhere, that is, according to the American and British critics: the home commentators had seen enough of Harding's toughness, fitness, and firepower during the first seven years of his career to know that an upset was on the cards. Andries, too, was taken by surprise, and later admitted that he had failed to do his homework on the relative unknown. The result was that, after his normal strong start, showing his experience and highlighting the Australian's weaknesses, Andries gradually found himself going further and further backwards, until, to the astonishment and delight of the New Jersey crowd (who knew they were witnessing the start of something special), Harding stopped him for good after one minute twenty-five seconds of the twelfth round.

The highs and lows of Harding's career have all come against Andries. His first professional defeat came in their rematch, when the challenger, better prepared now he realised what he was up against, came through strongly to recover his title. Then Harding, proving to be one of the most determined and bloody-minded boxers in history, bested Andries in their third encounter to recapture the crown.

His grittiest performance was to follow when, after a period of inactivity, he took on that crafty veteran Mike McCallum in July 1994. The experienced Jamaican took Jeff's title but Jeff is young, durable and a fast learner. 1995 could well see him at the forefront again.

★

INTRODUCTION

THE
GREAT FIGHTS

Above: Referee Paul Cavalier goes to the assistance of Tony Zale as the marvellous French-Moroccan fighter Marcel Cerdan looks back to make sure his man is finished. On September 21 1948 in Jersey City, in one of the toughest fights ever witnessed, Zale soaked up more punishment than the crowd could believe, but just wouldn't go down. This picture shows the scene at the end of the eleventh round: Cavalier stopped the fight between rounds, and Cerdan became world middleweight champion on a technical knockout.

Left: A great fight, and one of the greatest moments in British boxing history, as an unfancied Lloyd Honeyghan shocks the fans by taking the world welterweight title from Don 'The Cobra' Curry on September 27 1986.

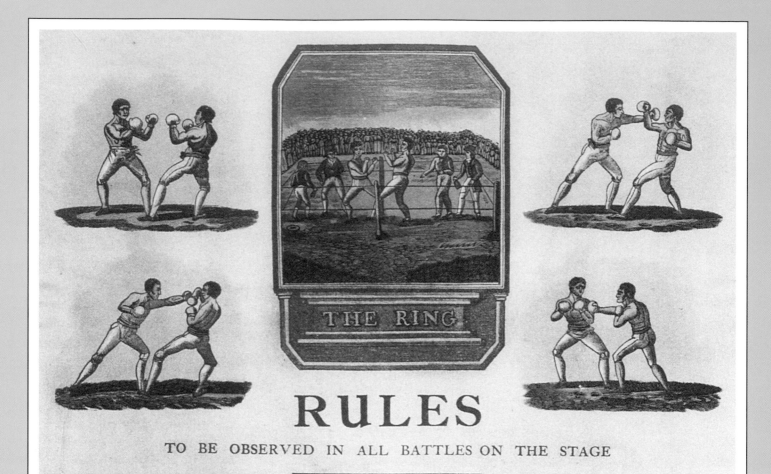

RULES

TO BE OBSERVED IN ALL BATTLES ON THE STAGE

I. THAT a fquare of a Yard be chalked in the middle of the Stage; and on every frefh fet-to after a fall, or being parted from the rails, each Second is to bring his Man to the fide of the fquare, and place him oppofite to the other, and till they are fairly fet-to at the Lines, it fhall not be lawful for one to ftrike at the other.

II. That, in order to prevent any Difputes, the time a Man lies after a fall, if the Second does not bring his Man to the fide of the fquare, within the fpace of half a minute, he fhall be deemed a beaten Man.

III. That in every main Battle, no perfon whatever fhall be upon the Stage, except the Principals and their Seconds; the fame rule to be obferved in bye-battles, except that in the latter, Mr. Broughton is allowed to be upon the Stage to keep decorum, and to affift Gentlemen in getting to their places, provided always he does not interfere in the Battle; and whoever pretends to infringe thefe Rules to be turned immediately out of the houfe. Every body is to quit the Stage as foon as the Champions are ftripped, before the fet-to.

IV. That no Champion be deemed beaten, unlefs he fails coming up to the line in the limited time, or that his own Second declares him beaten. No Second is to be allowed to afk his man's Adversary any queftions, or advife him to give out.

V. That in bye-battles, the winning man to have two-thirds of the Money given, which fhall be publicly divided upon the Stage, notwithftanding any private agreements to the contrary.

VI. That to prevent Difputes, in every main Battle the Principals fhall, on coming on the Stage, choofe from among the gentlemen prefent two Umpires, who fhall abfolutely decide all Difputes that may arife about the Battle; and if the two Umpires cannot agree, the faid Umpires to choofe a third, who is to determine it.

VII. That no perfon is to hit his Adverfary when he is down, or feize him by the ham, the breeches, or any part below the waift : a man on his knees to be reckoned down.

As agreed by feveral Gentlemen at Broughton's Amphitheatre,
Tottenham Court Road, Auguft 16, 1743.

DANIEL MENDOZA & RICHARD HUMPHREYS

THE EVOLUTION OF BOXING RULES

When Englishman James Figg opened his London amphitheatre in 1719, effectively heralding the rejuvenation of the sport after more than a thousand years of dormancy, the rules of boxing were rudimentary to say the least. It was not unheard of for a man to have his eyes gouged out or to be 'purred' (kicked while down): and in those days fighters wore spiked boots!

At this time all fights were bare-fisted – nothing was allowed or used to protect the hands. Most fights took place in cordoned-off booths, but in 1723 King George I ordered a square 'ring' to be erected in Hyde Park where anybody could go and spar or fight if they so wished.

In 1741, George Stevenson died of injuries that he had sustained in the ring. The man who beat him, Jack Broughton, was so devastated that he drafted a

Above: Mendoza (left) and 'Gentleman' Richard Humphries fought each other four times, each winning two contests. At their second meeting, in January 1788, they fought for 150 guineas on a twenty-four-foot stage and Humphries got the better of his opponent in twenty-nine minutes. Mendoza became champion in 1792 on beating Bill Ward but lost the crown to 'Gentleman' John Jackson, in 1795.

Opposite: The first rules of Prize Ring boxing were introduced by Jack Broughton in 1743. Although there is no mention of gloves in the text, the illustrations at the top show fighters wearing 'mufflers' and Broughton encouraged their use at his amphitheatre so that his pupils would be saved 'from the inconveniency of black eyes, broken jaws, and bloody noses'.

Right, and below: These two prints illustrate the second Tom Cribb v Tom Molineaux encounter. Cribb had beaten Molineaux in 1810 in thirty-nine rounds and their return match the following year attracted a crowd of some 25,000 to the arena at Thistleton Gap, Leicester. Cribb trained seriously for the fight, reducing his weight from 224 pounds to 188 pounds, and his endeavours paid off: he broke his opponent's jaw in the ninth round and Molineaux failed to get up in the eleventh.

set of rules that effectively governed boxing for nearly a hundred years. Broughton's Rules were hardly extensive, but they were at least a start. He recommended that boxers be brought to a square in the centre of the ring before sparring again after a knockdown; that when a man was knocked down he should be given up to thirty seconds to recover; and that a man should be disqualified if he wrestled below the belt or hit his opponent when he was down.

In his bid to make boxing safer, Broughton also encouraged the use of 'mufflers' – an early form of boxing-glove. He recommended their use, not for competition fights, but for amateurs and for professionals while training.

Broughton's Rules still left plenty of room for manoeuvre. There was no limit to the number of

rounds a bout should consist of, and individual rounds only ended when a man was knocked to the ground. This explains why some fights lasted for several hours, or were known to continue for more than a hundred rounds. Nor did the great man's ideas outlaw some outrageous tactics. 'Gentleman' John Jackson is said to have beaten Daniel Mendoza in 1795 by using a very ungentlemanly ploy: he held Mendoza's head by the hair while he pounded punches into his face.

Broughton was also instrumental in introducing original skills and basic tactics into boxing. He taught his pupils to block and to retreat when they were being pummelled; until these apparently obvious ideas were introduced, men simply stood up to each other and slugged it out. Both Mendoza and 'Gentleman' Jack advanced these skills: Mendoza was one of the first to appreciate the importance of footwork, and Johnson realized the importance of jabbing.

At the turn of the eighteenth century boxing was in a sorry state with fighters and their backers all but openly taking and offering bribes. In an attempt to

Above: Tom Spring and the Irish champion, Jack Langan, fought for the championship at Worcester racecourse in January 1824. During the second round, one of the stands, holding some 2,000 people, collapsed and the fight was temporarily stopped. When the contest was resumed, it lasted for another seventy-three rounds before Langan was knocked senseless. In their return fight, Spring won again in seventy-seven rounds.

The illustrations on this page originally appeared in *Famous Fights*, and show scenes from the infamous second fight between Thompson and Caunt. Even allowing for the renowned imagination of the *Famous Fights* artists, it is obvious that this was no ordinary encounter. William 'Bendigo' Thompson fought Ben Caunt three times, and each battle was won or lost on a foul. There was no love lost between them, and they were in any case two of the dirtiest boxers in an age in which boxing was not known for its obedience to rules. 'Bendigo' eventually lost this encounter in the seventy-fifth round on a disqualification, when he went to ground without being hit. It was quite normal in this period for as much violence to take place outside the ring as inside it, as can be seen below.

stamp out such behaviour, the Pugilistic Club was formed at 'Gentleman' Jack's home in London in 1814. For a time this club was influential in sponsoring and organizing contests, and it called upon ring officials to wear special uniforms so that they could at least be noticed.

When 'Brighton Bill' died after his battle with Owen Swift in 1838, the Pugilists' Protective Association issued a new set of rules, the so-called London Prize Ring Rules, which were intended to make boxing safer still. However even these did not limit

On this page are shown scenes from the match arranged after Tom Sayers, a rising star, was challenged to a fight by Harry Paulson in 1856. What followed was one of the bloodiest of battles, lasting no less than 109 rounds. Both men had been knocked to the floor many times, and both were drenched in blood, when Sayers finally delivered the finishing punch after three hours and eight minutes.

the number of rounds in a bout and a round still lasted until a man was knocked down. The Prize Ring Rules were subsequently revised in 1853 and 1866, largely to catch out such tricksters as 'Bendigo' Thompson and 'Deaf 'Un' Burke who would use any ruse or deceit to win a contest, including head-butting and attempting to throttle an opponent. The Prize Ring Rules also replaced Broughton's square in the middle of the ring with a 'scratch' line at which the two contestants had to face up to each other (hence the term 'up to scratch').

By this time boxing was actively outlawed in England and many fights were broken up by that early version of the modern police force, the Bow Street Runners. Consequently most contests took place in the remote countryside beyond the reach of the law: boxing's word-of-mouth network still ensured considerable audiences. To this day boxing has never been officially legalized in England: it is permitted through a loophole in legislation because it can be described and considered as an 'exhibition of skill'.

In 1866 the Marquess of Queensberry, together

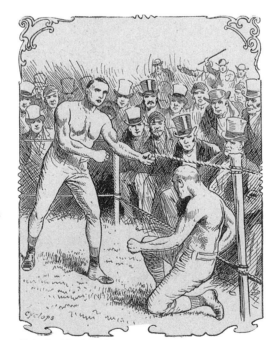

The illustrations on this page show the highlights from the Sayers v Paddock championship match in 1858. Paddock had disputed Sayers' right to the belt (which was then the champion's trophy), and a match was arranged for June 16 to settle the affair. Paddock had been dangerously ill with a fever, but was still heavily backed because of his size: he weighed in at over 170 pounds, while Sayers was under 150. Sayers started strongly, and things looked bad for Paddock after twenty minutes. Then Paddock's main backer and best friend, Alec Keene, with whom he had quarrelled, stepped into the ring to make up their differences (top), and this, together with Keene's tactical advice, gave Paddock the motivation to come back powerfully. But it was not to be for the challenger: drained of energy by his recent fever, he faded after a tremendous effort, and Sayers bested him after a brutal one hour and twenty minutes.

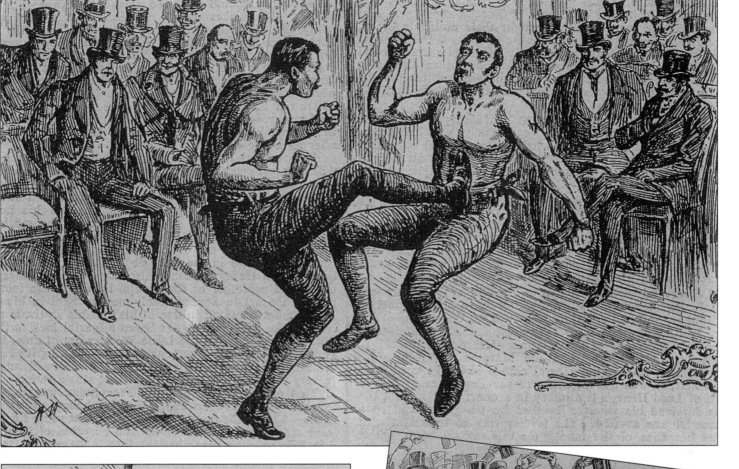

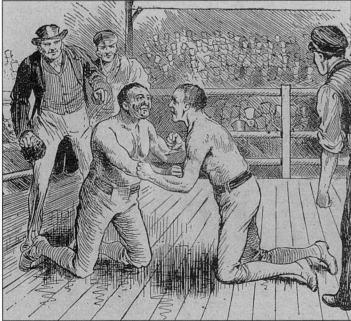

The group of artists' impressions on this page graphically illustrates, even allowing a due degree of scepticism about the lurid quality of the fight pictures of the time, the state of boxing in the early and mid-nineteenth century. Gouging, scratching, kicking, wrestling and butting were quite normal, and the fighters were expected by their backers, who had wagered huge sums, to fight on virtually to the death before quitting.

with Lord Lonsdale and Arthur Chambers, issued new rules which completely revolutionized boxing. The so-called Queensberry Rules had twelve clauses, the most important being: *a*) a ring should be twenty-four feet square, *b*) that wrestling should be illegal, *c*) that rounds should last for three minutes and that there should be a one-minute break between rounds, and *d*) that gloves should be worn. The rules were subsequently revised to limit the number of rounds to twenty, and the minimum weight for gloves was regulated to six ounces. A scoring system was also

One of the last and most famous bare-knuckle contests was fought out between the American hero, John L Sullivan (with moustache), and England's Charlie Mitchell on March 10 1888, highlights of which are illustrated, left. The venue for the encounter was Chantilly, in France, and the world title was at stake. After thirty-nine rounds and three hours and ten minutes of combat, the contest was declared a draw because of the muddy conditions. After the fight both men were arrested and were obliged to nurse their heavy heads in police cells. On the right is shown the magnificent physique of Charlie Mitchell, champion of England. He boxed on after his defeat by Sullivan, with great success, and eventually challenged James J Corbett for the championship of the world on January 25 1894 at the Duval Athletic Club, Jacksonville, Florida. A phenomenal purse of $20,000 was put up, but Mitchell was soundly and brutally dispatched in the third round.

introduced, with each combatant being awarded points according to his performance.

Queensberry's rules did not catch on immediately and bare-knuckle fighting continued to take place until the turn of the century: the last heavyweight bare-knuckle title fight took place in 1889 between John L Sullivan and Jake Kilrain. Gradually, however, the sense in Queensberry's rules prevailed, and even the likes of Sullivan accepted them (ironically Sullivan lost his first fight under the Queensberry Rules, against James J Corbett).

The concept of weight categories was first mooted in the 1850s and there were originally three divisions: heavyweight (over 156 pounds), middleweight (up to 156 pounds) and lightweight (up to 133 pounds). As boxing grew increasingly popular under the Queens-

berry Rules, more divisions were gradually introduced: there were nine divisions in 1910 and there are no less than seventeen today.

Several important organizations such as the Amateur Boxing Association (in 1880), the Pelican Club (in 1890), and the National Sporting Club (in 1909) adopted and revised the Queensberry Rules in England, and the powerful International Boxing Union (IBU) was created in Paris in 1910. In the United States, the New York State Athletic Commission was established in 1920 and did much to publicize the 'new' sport, which really boomed in the period between the two world wars.

In Britain the welfare of professional boxers was overseen by the British Boxing Board of Control (BBBofC), and around the world a number of new

Above: The last bare-knuckle fight for the world championship was held between John L Sullivan and Jake Kilrain. The fight took place at Richburg, Mississippi on July 8 1889, with Sullivan emerging victorious after seventy-five rounds. The fight marked the end of one era and the dawn of another in more ways than one. This is thought to be the earliest photograph of a boxing match and shows the two men in a clinch during the seventh round.

Jake Kilrain

Far left, and left: These two images of Jake Kilrain at the time of the Sullivan fight emotively illustrate the ending of the early years and the beginning of the modern age. At the same time that the rules were recodified, and gloves became standard for all fights, the charming and imaginative woodcut images of the great fights and famous boxers were finally superseded by the new art of photography.

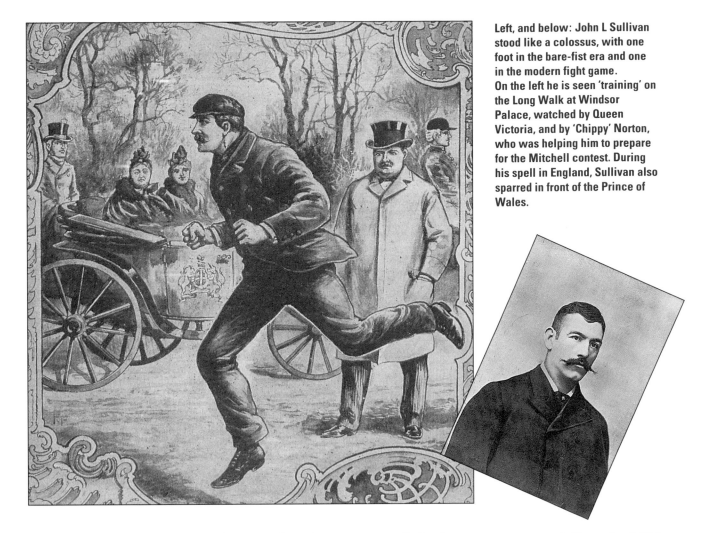

Left, and below: John L Sullivan stood like a colossus, with one foot in the bare-fist era and one in the modern fight game.
On the left he is seen 'training' on the Long Walk at Windsor Palace, watched by Queen Victoria, and by 'Chippy' Norton, who was helping him to prepare for the Mitchell contest. During his spell in England, Sullivan also sparred in front of the Prince of Wales.

regulatory bodies began to spring up. Unfortunately they more often than not squabbled with one another about their areas of responsibility and a large degree of chaos, which has never been resolved, ensued. In the United States, the National Boxing Association (NBA) was formed in 1921 in opposition to the New York Athletic Association, which had effectively monopolized championship boxing up until then. By the 1930s there were State champions, New York champions, NBA champions and IBU champions, each of whom frequently claimed that they held the world title. It was only when the various claimants fought each other that a genuine and undisputed world champion emerged.

The IBU became the European Boxing Union (EBU) in 1946 and the NBA changed its name to the World Boxing Association (WBA) in 1962. Despairing at the arrogance of the WBA, the BBBofC, several American state organizations, the EBU and various other governing bodies combined to create the World Boxing Council (WBC) in 1963. Numerous attempts were made to unify the WBA with the WBC,

but to no avail. In fact worse was to follow. In 1983 the International Boxing Federation (IBF) was formed, and in 1988 the World Boxing Organization (WBO) was created. Consequently it is now possible to have four world champions in each of the seventeen weight divisions. Many believe that this fragmentation has done much to devalue titles and diffuse interest in boxing in the last two decades.

Today boxing rules for professionals vary only marginally between the various different organizations (and all are based on the Queensberry Rules). For example, a professional bout can last for eight rounds or twelve; a round can be two minutes long or three; the referee can be the sole arbiter, or a panel of three independent judges can be used.

Amateur boxing has taken its own route, and by and large the rules for the amateur game are much more stringent than those used for professional contests. Rounds can last two or three minutes but there are usually only three rounds in a bout. It is normal now for amateurs to wear head-guards in their fights, in addition to their traditional vests.

LANDMARKS IN BOXING HISTORY

James Figg v Ned Sutton, 1720
Figg defeats Sutton to become the first recognized champion of England.

'Gentleman' John Jackson v Daniel Mendoza; April 15 1795; Hornchurch, Essex.
Jackson beats Mendoza in ten and a half minutes for a purse of 100 guineas, heralding a new age of 'scientific' boxing.

Tom Cribb v Tom Molineaux; December 10 1810; Copthall Common.
The first title fight in which a black person was involved. The two fought for 200 guineas a side plus 100 guineas prize money. Cribb won in fifty-five minutes (thirty-nine rounds).

Tom Cribb v Tom Molineaux; September 28 1811; Thistleton Gap, Leicester.
An estimated crowd of 25,000 turned out to watch this rematch for a prize of 600 guineas.

Cribb won again in twenty minutes (eleven rounds).

Jacob Hyer v Tom Beasley; 1816; New York.
The first American fight that was open to the public. Hyer won and claimed the American championship.

Tom Spring v Jack Langan; January 7 1824;
The first title fight for which a grandstand was built; an estimated 30,000 watched. Spring won in two hours twenty minutes (seventy-five rounds).

James 'Deaf 'Un' Burke v Simon Byrne; May 30 1833; No-Man's-Land, Hertfordshire.
The longest title fight on record, lasting three hours six minutes (ninety-nine rounds). Burke won, and Byrne later died of his horrific injuries.

Tom Sayers (Eng) v John C Heenan (USA); April 17 1860; Farnborough Common.
The first international world championship fight.

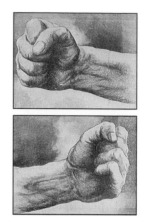

The contest, for £200 a side, ended in chaos and was declared a draw after two hours six minutes (thirty-seven rounds).

Jack 'Nonpareil' Dempsey (Ire) v George Fulljames (Can); July 30 1884; Staten Island, New York.
Dempsey becomes the first world champion (middleweight) fighting to Queensberry Rules. He knocked out Fulljames in the twenty-second round.

John L Sullivan (USA) v Jake Kilrain (USA); July 8 1889; Richburg, Mississippi.
The last heavyweight title

fight to be fought with bare knuckles. Sullivan won the $10,000 a side contest in seventy-five gruelling rounds.

John L Sullivan (USA) v James J Corbett (USA); September 7 1892; New Orleans.
Corbett becomes the first heavyweight world champion under the Queensberry Rules. He knocked out Sullivan in the twenty-first round to gain $45,000.

Jack Dempsey (USA) v Georges Carpentier (Fr); July 2 1921; New Jersey.
The first fight to gross more than $1 million at the gate ($1,789,238). Dempsey knocked out Carpentier in four rounds to retain the world heavyweight title.

'Marvelous' Marvin Hagler (USA) v 'Sugar' Ray Leonard (USA); April 6 1987; Las Vegas.
The richest fight in boxing history. Gross takings for the fight are thought to have exceeded $100 million; Hagler pocketed $17 million of the $28 million purse and Leonard $11 million. Leonard won the middleweight contest on a split decision.

Opposite page: First column; Mendoza smashes a left into the chin of 'Gentleman' John Jackson, but Jackson came back to win very quickly. Second column; John C Heenan tried to avoid capture after the break-up of his fight with Sayers, but was eventually taken into custody. Third column, top; *Famous Fights* illustrated the boxers' fists in their coverage of the 1860 fight – Sayers' above, and Heenan's below. Third column, middle; Jack Dempsey, 'The Nonpareil', in shape for his 1884 battle against George Fulljames.

Left: Weight divisions were not devised until the middle of the nineteenth century. This print shows Thomas Johnson (left) fighting Isaac Perrins in 1789.

WEIGHT DIVISIONS

Heavyweight	unlimited	**Featherweight** (WBC super-bantamweight)	up to 126 pounds
Cruiserweight	up to 190 pounds	**Junior-featherweight** (WBC super-bantamweight)	up to 122 pounds
Light-heavyweight	up to 175 pounds	**Bantamweight**	up to 118 pounds
Super-middleweight	up to 168 pounds	**Junior-bantamweight** (WBC super-flyweight)	up to 115 pounds
Middleweight	up to 160 pounds		
Junior-middleweight (WBC super-welterweight)	up to 154 pounds	**Flyweight**	up to 112 pounds
Welterweight	up to 147 pounds	**Junior-flyweight** (WBC light-flyweight)	up to 108 pounds
Junior-welterweight (WBC super-lightweight)	up to 140 pounds	**Straw-weight** (IBF and WBA Mini-flyweight)	up to 105 pounds
Lightweight	up to 135 pounds		
Junior-lightweight (WBC super-featherweight)	up to 130 pounds		

GREAT FIGHTS OF THE GLOVED ERA

Above: Ted 'Kid' Lewis gets in a handy left against Johnny Basham at the Royal Albert Hall, London, on November 19 1920, in their second fight. The European title was at stake, and was retained by Lewis when he knocked out the courageous Basham in the nineteenth round.

Left: Bruno and Tyson exchange blows in their 1989 heavyweight title bout. Although this was 'just another championship fight' in world terms, it was an emotional contest for British fans, and Bruno did more than expected before Tyson came through with the heavy guns to stop him in the fifth round.

PETER MAHER V BOB FITZSIMMONS

February 21 1896
near Langtry, Texas

Above: Peter Maher was born in County Galway, Ireland, in 1868. He fought his way to the championship nomination with famous victories over Gus Lambert, 'Bubbles' Davis, Jim Daly, Jack Fallon, 'Sailor' Brown and George Godfrey. He had previously lost to Fitzsimmons in New Orleans on March 2 1892.

Below: The unusual shape of Bob Fitzsimmons.

Peter Maher, an Irish heavyweight, was chosen by James J Corbett to be his successor as world champion in 1895. The English-born Fitzsimmons challenged Maher to a fight which was to have taken place at Langtry in Texas. However the Rangers arrived on the scene (Prize Fighting was illegal in Texas at the time), and the contest was moved over the Rio Grande into Mexico. The bout was filmed, but the fight was over so quickly, with Fitzsimmons winning in one round, that Kinetoscope refused to pay.

Above: Fitzsimmons (right) about to finish off Maher with his famous left hook in the opening round. In the background can be seen enthusiastic Mexicans who turned up to view the fight which was unexpectedly fought on their territory.

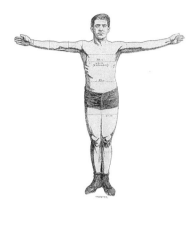

James J Corbett v Bob Fitzsimmons

March 17 1897

Carson City, Nevada

Obliged to come out of retirement to defend his world title against Fitzsimmons, Corbett was the hot favourite to win the challenge. The champion had the best of the opening rounds but during the thirteenth, Fitzsimmons' wife yelled 'Hit 'im in the slats, Bob.' Fitzsimmons did just that and floored Corbett in the fourteenth with a punishing blow to the solar plexus. Unable to get up, Corbett finally relinquished his world title.

Top left, Corbett, and top right, Fitzsimmons, as weighed and measured by *Famous Fights* prior to their epic encounter. Far right: The fight was a subject of speculation for months, and the boxing magazines were full of anticipation and profiles.

Right: Corbett (right) leaves his midriff vulnerable; it was a body-blow slipping through just such a defensive weakness that ended his reign as champion.

Bob Fitzsimmons v James J Jeffries

June 9 1899

Coney Island, New York

Fitzsimmons lost his world heavyweight title to Jeffries in his first defence, being knocked out in eleven rounds. A return match in 1902 ended in similar fashion.

Right: Jeffries shakes hands with the balding Fitzsimmons before the contest.

Left: Cameramen were now in regular attendance at title fights, and this was one of the last fights to be covered by press artists. From here on, the truth of photography would replace the romanticism of the pen and brush.

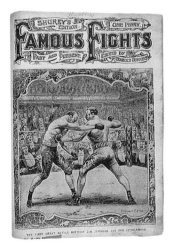

JOE GANS V 'BATTLING' NELSON

September 3 1906
Goldfield, Nevada

In an epic contest that lasted forty-two rounds, Gans successfully defended his world lightweight title against the Dane, Nelson, who was disqualified. In two subsequent bouts, however, Nelson emerged victorious.

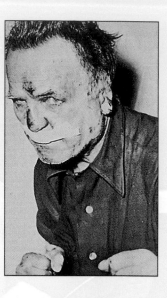

Top left: Joe Gans is thought by many to be the greatest lightweight who ever lived. He was born on November 25 1874 in Philadelphia, and died of consumption on August 10 1910.
Top right: A later portrait of 'Battling' Nelson.

Left: The two boxers shake hands before their second fight in 1908. Nelson won on a knockout.

Below: Despite having consumption, the stylish Gans outboxed 'The Durable Dane'.

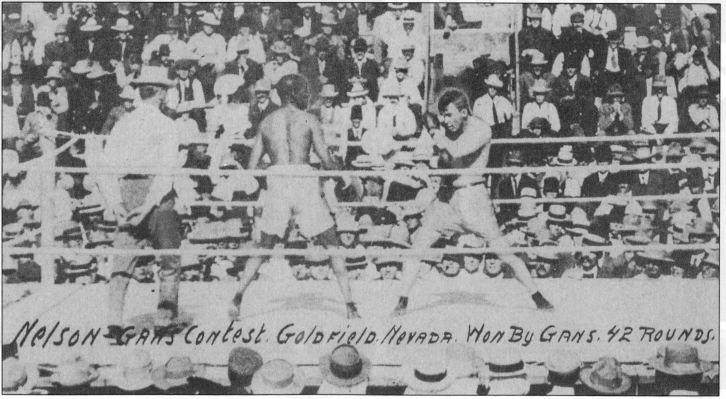

Nelson-Gans Contest. Goldfield. Nevada. Won By Gans. 42 Rounds.

TOMMY BURNS V
JACK JOHNSON

December 26 1908
Sydney, Australia

Johnson was forced to follow Burns all the way to Australia to secure a title fight. He verbally riled the Canadian heavyweight remorselessly throughout the contest and became world champion when the bout was stopped in the fourteenth round.

Top left: The immortal Jack Johnson.

Above: The arrogant Johnson toyed with Burns during the fight, and the clinches gave him the opportunity to taunt the champion with abuse.

Left: The two boxers being introduced to the crowd with Burns standing on the left.

JACK JOHNSON V
STANLEY KETCHEL

October 16 1909
Colma, California

Johnson's first defence of his world heavyweight title was against the 'Great White Hope', Ketchel. An agreement was reached beforehand whereby the contest would end in a draw, thus ensuring a lucrative rematch. However, when Ketchel floored him early in the twelfth round, Johnson immediately retaliated in lethal fashion and knocked the challenger out cold.

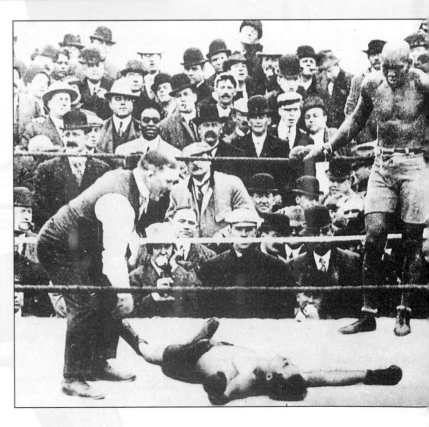

Right: Ketchel takes the count as the infuriated champion looks on.

Left: The extraordinary Stanley Ketchel. He was shot one year after this fight, on October 15 1910, by a jealous rival in love, Walter A Dipley, when aged only twenty-five.

JACK JOHNSON V JAMES J JEFFRIES

July 4 1910
Reno, Nevada

Jeffries, a former heavyweight champion, was hauled out of retirement to take on Johnson. Many racists in the United States could not come to terms with the idea of a black heavyweight title holder, and were desperate for a white champion to put Johnson 'in his place'. But Jeffries was no longer the boxer he once was, and the hopes of the bigots were dashed when the fight was stopped in the fifteenth round.

Left: Foolish money and racist hopes made Jeffries the bookmaker's favourite before the fight, but from the start it was obviously a lost cause. Above: The referee holds back the champion, who is keen to go in for the kill. Right: A familiar pose for Johnson, who towers gloating above his fallen opponent, having taunted him throughout.

JACK JOHNSON V JESS WILLARD

April 5 1915
Havana, Cuba

Johnson finally met his match in Jess Willard, a huge cowboy from Kansas. Johnson controlled most of the fight but, aged thirty-seven and out of condition, he began to wilt under the intense sunlight and was knocked out in the twenty-sixth round.

Right: Johnson (left) was overweight when he fought Willard, and the younger, fitter man was more able to cope with the stifling heat.

Left: Jess Willard was born on December 29 1883 in Pottawatomie County. He held the world title for four years before losing to Dempsey.

Right: Between grim portraits of Dempsey (left) and Willard, Dempsey can be seen launching a ferocious assault on the champion.

Left: These are the last few moments of Willard's tenure of the heavyweight championship. Dempsey (left) unleashes a flurry of blows that pin Willard in a corner. Willard retired on his stool between rounds three and four, saying that he could not go on. The former champion later learned that his jaw had been broken in two places, that he had six broken ribs and that he had lost six of his teeth.

Right: Dempsey in training. Perhaps sensing that this might be his last fight, Willard demanded, and got, a $100,000 fee from Tex Rickard. Dempsey received $27,500, but his big paydays were still to come. Dempsey wagered his whole purse that he would knock out Willard in the first: he very nearly won his bet.

JESS WILLARD V
JACK DEMPSEY

July 4 1919
Toledo, Ohio

Willard was out of shape when he met the trim Jack Dempsey and the challenger was the hot favourite to win. The experts were proved right and Willard retired in the third round after taking a terrible beating.

Jack Dempsey v Georges Carpentier

July 2 1921
Jersey City, New Jersey

In a fight promoted by the great Tex Rickard, and which grossed more than a million dollars at the gate, Dempsey, the world heavyweight champion, was pitted against the popular French war hero, Carpentier, who was the light-heavyweight title holder. The gallant Frenchman broke his thumb in the second round and was counted out in the fourth.

Above: Badly hurt, Carpentier attempts to haul himself back into the ring after being knocked through the ropes. But the end is near for the Frenchman.

Top left: Even in a posed shot, Dempsey looks threatening. After his victory over Willard, he successfully defended twice, firstly against his friend and sparring partner Billy Miske, on September 6 1920, and then against Bill Brennan, on December 14 1920. He then became embroiled in a scandal over draft evasion in the First World War, for which he was indicted by a Federal Grand Jury. Enterprising as ever, Rickard made this a promotional feature of the Carpentier fight, casting the French war hero against the American draft dodger to drum up rivalry and excitement.

Top right: The Frenchman manages to look debonair even without his three-piece suit and button-hole orchid.

GEORGES CARPENTIER V 'BATTLING' SIKI

September 24 1922
Paris, France

Carpentier lost his light-heavyweight title to the little-known Senegalese in one of the major upsets in boxing history. The Frenchman was knocked out in the sixth round.

Below: Carpentier has to be lifted to his feet after being levelled by a stunning punch from Siki in the sixth round.

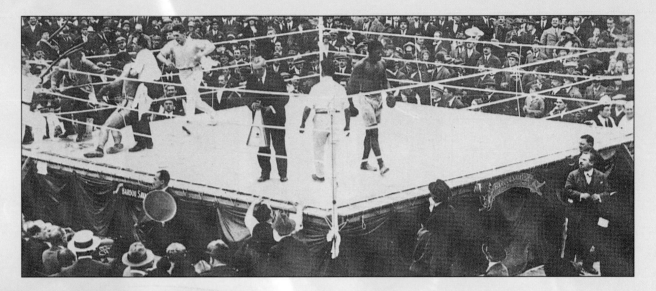

'BATTLING' SIKI V MIKE MCTIGUE

March 17 1923
Dublin

Siki lost his light-heavyweight title to McTigue in his first defence. Performing on his home turf in Dublin, and backed by a chanting Irish crowd on St Patrick's Day, McTigue won on points after twenty rounds.

Far left: McTigue (left) grapples with Siki who was an able and courageous slugger but not a particularly skilful or talented boxer.

Left: Mike McTigue welcomes 'Battling' Siki to Ireland, the land where he was born on November 26 1882 in County Clare. After his victory, McTigue held the world light-heavyweight title until May 31 1925, when he was beaten in Yankee Stadium by Paul Berlenbach.

Right: A famous portrait of Dempsey (left), and a handsome picture of the brooding Argentinian. In between, things do not look quite so attractive, as the South American lays flat out on the canvas and Dempsey lounges in a neutral corner.

JACK DEMPSEY V LUIS ANGEL FIRPO

September 14 1923
New York

In one of the most exciting heavyweight contests of all time, Dempsey put his title on the line against Firpo, an Argentinian giant. The contest only lasted two rounds but in that time Firpo was knocked down nine times and Dempsey twice. The champion also had to endure the indignity of being knocked clean through the ropes before rallying to deliver the *coup de grâce*.

Above: Seen from the other side of the ring, things look no better for Firpo. In this most amazing contest, both fighters were knocked down, but in truth Dempsey looks little bothered by affairs, and it was Firpo who soaked up the real punishment. Nevertheless, he lives on in legend as the man who knocked Dempsey out of the ring. Left: Firpo lived a long and contented life. He died a millionaire in August 1960.

GENE TUNNEY V JACK DEMPSEY

September 22 1927
Chicago

Gene Tunney won the world heavyweight title from Jack Dempsey by outpointing the champion in 1926. The return match a year later has become one of the most famous in boxing history and has been dubbed the 'Battle of the Long Count'. Tunney was floored by Dempsey in the seventh round but the challenger failed to retreat to a neutral corner and the seconds that elapsed before the referee started the count were enough to enable Tunney to recover. He retained his title by winning the ten-round bout on points.

Above: The seventh round. Dempsey clips Tunney with a right hook and the champion slumps to the canvas.

Right: The referee (extreme left) instructs Dempsey to retreat to a neutral corner so that he can commence the count over the floored Tunney, but the challenger lingers a while to eye his foe.

Left: With Dempsey (left) in a corner, the referee starts the count but by this time Tunney is on his way up. The champion was said to be down for fourteen seconds – but it is the referee's count that matters.

Far left: Clean-cut ex-Marine Gene Tunney was every mother's dream: he retired as undefeated champion in 1928, and became a highly successful businessman.

JACK SHARKEY V
MAX SCHMELING

June 12 1930
New York

Above: Max Schmeling. The retirement of Tunney ended what many still think of as the golden age of gloved boxing. No obvious champion immediately emerged, so there was a succession of eliminators involving many little-known and little-regarded boxers: this process did not catch the imagination of the fight fans. The long-awaited contest between Schmeling and Sharkey to settle the heavyweight crown after nearly two years came as a relief. In the end, the fight was both a disappointment and a sensation: it was a let-down because it lasted only four rounds, and ended in confusion; and a sensation because it was resolved on a foul – the fight being awarded to a groggy Schmeling when his manager, Joe Jacobs, and the famous reporter Arthur Brisbane drew the unsighted referee's attention to Sharkey's killer low blow. Sharkey had already gained a reputation for hitting low against British champion Phil Scott on February 28 of the same year in the final eliminator: Scott always claimed that Sharkey's low punching cost him a shot at the title.

Sharkey and Schmeling were matched against each other for the vacant world heavyweight title. When Sharkey punched the German below the belt towards the end of the fourth round, the German's manager claimed a foul and the referee agreed, so the title was won, but in a most unsatisfactory fashion. As fate would have it, Schmeling lost the title to Sharkey two years later on a controversial points decision.

Above: Schmeling takes a count with Sharkey watching from a neutral corner. The German won the title on a disputed foul after the intervention of his manager, Joe Jacobs.

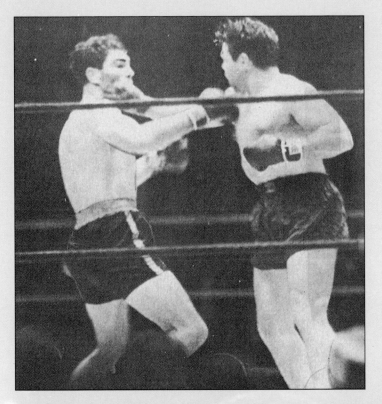

MAX SCHMELING V MICKEY WALKER

September 26 1932
New York

Chasing heavyweight glory, the former middleweight world champion Mickey Walker took on Schmeling, who had lost his world title to Jack Sharkey three months earlier. It was a bad mistake: the 'Toy Bulldog' took a heavy hammering and failed to come out for the ninth round.

Left: Walker (left) clips Schmeling on the chin in the third round but the 'Toy Bulldog' was himself on the receiving end for most of the fight.

Below: Walker tumbles to the canvas in the eighth round and Schmeling suggests that it might be time for the referee to stop the contest. Walker failed to come out for the ninth.

PRIMO CARNERA V
MAX BAER

June 14 1934
Long Island

Top left and top right: A full view of Max Baer's fighting form, and a typically cheery portrait. Baer missed being among the very greatest only because he could not focus on the seriousness of what he was doing. He had all the talents required, but loved the good life too much. This win against Carnera was a superb highlight in a dashing and crowd-pleasing career. Above: Here he is dwarfed by Carnera at the weigh-in, standing on the scales to match up their heights. Note the Italian's dapper two-tone shoes and elegant sock suspenders – he was a fashion giant as well.

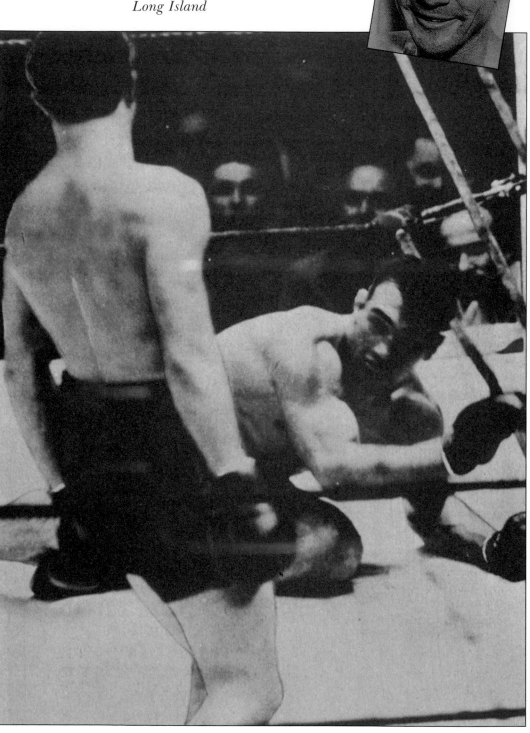

Baer took the heavyweight world title from Carnera in a battle that saw the Italian hit the canvas no less than ten times. The referee finally brought the contest to a halt in the eleventh round.

Above: Carnera hits the deck and looks up to see Baer prowling around for the kill. The Italian got to know the canvas well and Baer became champion in the eleventh round.

Left and below: The two men slugged it out for fifteen rounds, before Braddock was awarded one of the most unlikely victories in ring history. No less a reporter than Damon Runyon christened Braddock 'The Cinderella Man' for his fairytale good fortune. In truth, this was more a question of Baer losing his crown than Braddock winning it. It was a typical example of Baer's lack of application, though in fairness he was fighting with seriously damaged hands.

MAX BAER V JIMMY BRADDOCK

June 13 1935
Long Island

Baer lost the world heavyweight title to the unfancied Braddock in his first defence. The fifteen-to-one outsider, who had been given virtually no chance of winning, became known as the 'Cinderella Man' after his shock points victory.

Left: The winner was as surprised by the result as the crowd. A stupefied Braddock salutes his victory with a clenched fist. Baer later said that he had not taken the fight seriously enough.

MAX BAER V JOE LOUIS

September 24 1935
New York

Soon after losing his heavyweight title to Jimmy Braddock, Baer fought the up-and-coming Joe Louis. It was a one-sided contest that ended in the fourth round and it placed Louis in line for a world championship challenge.

Above and left: Baer was no match for the classy Louis (below) who started as favourite and was younger and fitter.

Above: Portraits of Louis and Schmeling at the time, and a scene from early in the fight, as both boxers probe for an attacking opportunity.

JOE LOUIS V MAX SCHMELING

June 19 1936
New York

Louis, a rising star, met the former world champion Schmeling in a non-title fight in Yankee Stadium. He had been undefeated in twenty-seven fights, but the experienced German had detected a weakness in the American's defence and succeeded in knocking him out in the twelfth round.

Right and far right: The wily Schmeling, a good tactician, had studied hard, and worked out Louis' weaknesses. He was able to trade on these in the twelfth by breaking through the 'Brown Bomber's' defence and sinking him to the canvas.

Above: Britain's Tommy Farr.

Left, below and bottom: Tommy Farr was born in Tonypandy, Wales, and his first career was as a coalminer. In an era when British heavyweights earned little respect in the USA, he beat Tommy Loughran, Bob Olin and Max Baer on his way to meet Louis. Still given no chance, he took Louis all the way, and the bruising bout, which is still talked about with awe in the Welsh valleys, won him great acclaim.

JOE LOUIS V TOMMY FARR

August 30 1937
New York

Louis became heavyweight champion on beating James J Braddock in 1937. His first defence was supposed to be an easy contest, but Farr put up a spirited effort and took the new champion the distance before losing on points.

Right: Ambers plummets to the canvas in the fifth round after a combination of punches from Armstrong. Luckily, or possibly unluckily, he was saved by the bell.

Above: A left jab from Armstrong has Ambers in trouble towards the end of the fight. Armstrong was able to keep going non-stop throughout the contest because he had an abnormally slow heartbeat.

HENRY ARMSTRONG V LOU AMBERS

August 17 1938
New York

With the featherweight and welterweight titles already in his trophy cabinet, Armstrong wanted a third and so took on Ambers for the lightweight world championship. The fight ended in a points victory for Armstrong, who consequently became the first, and last, person to hold three world titles simultaneously.

Right: Henry Armstrong becomes the first man to hold three titles at the same time. Far right: Armstrong undoubtedly qualifies as an all-time great.

JOE LOUIS V BILLY CONN

June 18 1941
New York

Right: During the early rounds, Conn showed that he was not afraid of the champion and launched fast attacks that forced Louis on to the defensive.

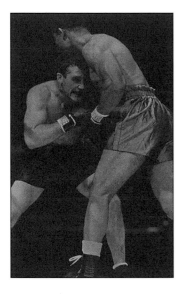

Above: As the fight wore on, Conn caught Louis in clinches and taunted the champion with verbal abuse.

Conn was the reigning light-heavyweight champion, and although the odds were against him, he was no 'Bum of the Month'. This challenger gave the heavyweight title holder a big surprise and nearly grabbed the championship for himself before being knocked out in the thirteenth round.

Left: Deciding enough was enough, Louis ended the fight in the thirteenth round with a series of punches that had Conn reeling.

Right: Beaten but unbowed, Conn manages a smile as he talks to reporters after the fight.

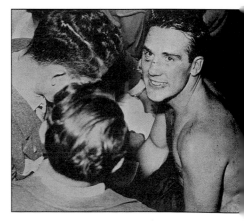

'SUGAR' RAY ROBINSON V JAKE LAMOTTA

February 23 1945
New York

Below: Jake LaMotta had come up the hard way: he later admitted that he was only allowed a championship fight because he agreed to throw a match for the gangsters who controlled the fight game in the 1940s – and that it cost him $20,000 on top of that. His world title fight against Cerdan was still four years ahead: many think that by the time he was allowed to challenge, his best years were past.

Above: The legendary 'Sugar' Ray Robinson. His first ever loss (after forty successive victories) was against LaMotta, on February 5 1943, and thereafter their rivalry became one of the greatest in ring history.

Jake LaMotta fought 'Sugar' Ray Robinson five times before he finally won the middleweight title in 1949. Robinson came out on top in four of the fights but each was a classic contest and the bout in 1945 was no exception. Robinson won the ten-round bout on points and went on to prove that he was still the superior boxer six years later when he beat LaMotta for the fifth time to wrest the middleweight crown from the 'Bronx Bull'.

Above: Robinson (right) catches LaMotta with a punishing left to the head on his way to a points decision.

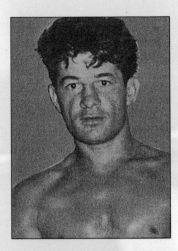

Tony Zale v Rocky Graziano

July 16 1947
Chicago

Zale and Graziano fought each other three times for the world middleweight title and this contest in 1947 was the only one in which Graziano emerged the victor. It was a tough, brawling battle and Zale later felt bitter that the referee had stopped the contest in the sixth round, claiming that he could have carried on and won.

Top left and top right: The two men who fought out a three-bout series in the 1940s that lives on in legend as one of the greatest ever: Tony Zale (left) and Rocky Graziano.

Above: A beautifully balanced and positioned Zale turns a left jab into a punch that stuns Graziano.

Left: Later, Zale, perhaps over-confident, let Graziano back into the fight. He always claimed that this scene, from the fifth round, was not nearly as bad as it looked, and that Graziano had pushed him into the ropes. The referee took a different view. In the sixth, the fight was stopped: again, Zale was outraged, feeling he could have gone on to win. To his eternal pride, Zale never went down.

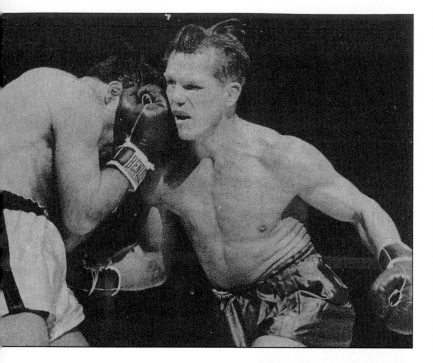

Cerdan (top right) dodges one of Zale's thrusting lefts. Zale concentrated on attacking Cerdan's body (above) in the hope that the Frenchman would lower his unusually high guard. This devastating right to Zale's head in the eighth round (right) marked the beginning of the end for the champion. Below: Marcel Cerdan.

TONY ZALE V MARCEL CERDAN

September 21 1948
Jersey City, New Jersey

Zale's reign as middleweight champion was brought to an end by Cerdan who became a French national hero. The Frenchman stopped the champion in the twelfth round.

Right: As if bowing in deference to the new champion, an exhausted Zale struggles to maintain an upright position after the fight has been halted.

Right: Joe 'Sandy' Saddler was born in Boston on June 25 1926, but raised in New York's Harlem district. On October 29 1948, in his ninety-fourth professional fight, he had taken the world featherweight title from Willie Pep in New York, and this was the first rematch in what was to become a famous series. He possessed a devastating punch, and it was this weapon that had caused the tremendous upset the year before, when he took the title against the odds with a fourth-round knockout.

Left: Willie Pep was born William Papaleo in Middletown, Connecticut, on September 19 1922, of Italian-American parents. He won the world featherweight title on November 20 1942 from Chalky Wright, and proceeded to hold the crown for nearly six years, before it was surprisingly taken from him by Saddler. Shocked into action, he was determined to get it back, and made no mistakes in this violent encounter.

SANDY SADDLER V
WILLIE PEP

February 11 1949
New York

Saddler had defeated Pep in October 1948 to take the featherweight world title. In the return fight Pep had to resort to unorthodox tactics to regain his crown. He won the contest on points but lost two subsequent fights to Saddler in 1950 and 1951.

Below: Pep (left) breaks free from the constraints of the boxing handbook and launches a two-fisted attack on Saddler, leaving his head and body wide open. His target was the scar tissue around the champion's eyes.

'SUGAR' RAY ROBINSON V KID GAVILAN

July 11 1949
Philadelphia

This fight was Robinson's fourth defence of his welterweight world title. The Cuban challenger was supremely confident and, although he was soundly beaten on points, he did provide a few surprises for the champion and the outcome was in the balance until the very end.

Above: 'Kid' Gavilan was born Gerardo Gonzalez, in Camaguey, Cuba, on January 6 1926. This fight came early in his career, although he had been boxing since he was seventeen. His first fight in the USA was in 1946, but at this stage he was still seeking international recognition. His great years were still ahead of him, and he was to become world champion in 1952. He is above all remembered for a remarkable series of bouts against Billy Graham.

Above: Robinson (left) keeps a wary eye on the challenger, who nearly floored him in the eighth round with a flurry of hooks.

Right: Robinson won on a unanimous verdict that outraged all the Cubans who witnessed the fight.

EZZARD CHARLES V JOE LOUIS

September 27 1950
New York

Desperately needing money, Louis attempted a comeback in 1950 and challenged Charles for the world heavyweight title. The result was an easy points victory for Charles for by this time Louis was long past his best. It was not a popular win as Joe Louis was a national hero.

Right: Charles lands a left jab smack on Louis' face. The American public would have been happier if their favourite had remained in retirement. Even Charles was sorry when he beat his long-time hero.

Left: This was the end of an era. Ezzard Charles, together with Joe Walcott and Marciano, can be viewed as the first of the modern champions.

'SUGAR' RAY ROBINSON V JAKE LAMOTTA

February 14 1951
Chicago

Robinson won the middleweight world title for the first time by stopping LaMotta in the thirteenth round. This was the sixth time the two boxers had met: previous results were Robinson, four; LaMotta, one.

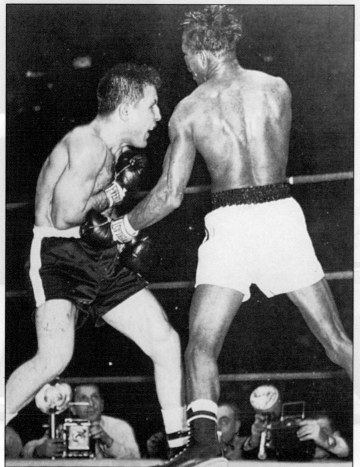

Left: The pain can be seen on LaMotta's face as he receives a savage blow in the midriff from Robinson. The referee stepped in to end the contest in the thirteenth round, awarding a knockout. Robinson's tactics had been to wear out the champion (albeit LaMotta was a year younger), and he effectively boxed 'The Bronx Bull' to a standstill. This fight brought to an end one of the greatest rivalries seen in the ring – their meetings were as follows: October 2 1942, Robinson wins on points in ten rounds; February 5 1943, LaMotta wins on points in ten rounds (this was the only defeat Robinson experienced in his first 133 professional fights); February 26 1943, Robinson wins on points in ten rounds; February 23 1945, Robinson wins on points in ten rounds; September 26 1945, Robinson wins on points in twelve rounds (split decision); final fight, as here.

'SUGAR' RAY ROBINSON V RANDOLPH TURPIN

July 10 1951
London

Turpin became the toast of England when he beat Robinson on points to relieve the champion of his recently won middleweight title. The Englishman only held the title until September of the same year, however, when Robinson stopped him in ten rounds to regain the crown.

Right: Turpin lunges with a left, and his aggression has the champion looking awkwardly unbalanced. Later in the fight, suddenly realising that Turpin had had the best of the early rounds and was ahead, Robinson started to attack and show better form, but he had left it too late, and the Englishman held on to win on points. Top: Robinson won the return match by stopping Turpin in the tenth round in September 1951.

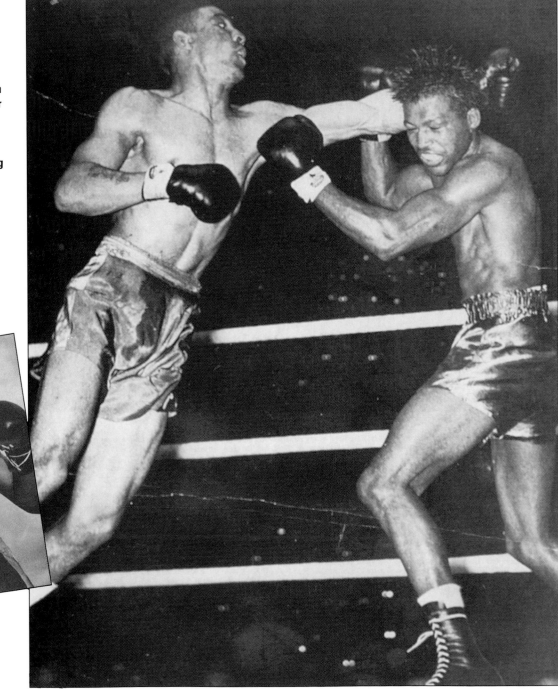

Above: England's Randolph Turpin.

EZZARD CHARLES V 'JERSEY' JOE WALCOTT

July 18 1951
Pittsburgh

Charles won the vacant world title over Walcott in 1949 on a points decision. In this second return fight, Walcott emerged as the better man and knocked the champion out in the seventh round. In a fourth meeting the following year, Walcott again proved his supremacy.

Top: Walcott had been given no chance in this fight, but they forgot to tell him that. This right was the beginning of the end for Charles, who moments later was finished completely by a powerhouse left hook. This was an emotional triumph for Walcott: he had lost four previous world title challenges – two to Louis, and two to Charles – but came good at thirty-seven to fulfil his dream.

Above: Charles is unable to stand up as referee Buck McTiernan kneels on the canvas to give the final count.

KID GAVILAN V
BILLY GRAHAM

August 29 1951
New York

In one of the most controversial fights on record, Gavilan retained his welterweight title in a split points decision. Many who saw the fight, reckoned that Graham had done enough to win.

Right: Gavilan (right) got the better of the early rounds with point-scoring jabs that kept the challenger at bay.

Far left: Billy Graham was born of Irish-American parents in New York City on September 9 1922. He never became world champion, but was a great fighter whose main claim to fame was the series of contests against Gavilan (below). Unfortunately for him, Graham lost all four fights. This 1951 fight was originally intended to be for the US championship only, but at its close, Gavilan was controversially awarded the world crown despite the claims of European champion, Frenchman Charley Humez.

Left: In the closing rounds, Graham went on an all-out attack that very nearly won him the championship and convinced many spectators that he had edged a victory.

SANDY SADDLER V WILLIE PEP

September 26 1951
New York

Saddler and Pep met each other four times for the featherweight world title, with Saddler coming out on top in three of the contests. In this, their fourth fight, Pep retired from the contest during the ninth round, claiming that Saddler had fought dirty.

Above: Pep shows off his eye after the fight, with the obvious implication that the injury was caused by his opponent's head rather than his glove.

Right: Pep sinks to his knees in the second round after being stung by a combination of blows.

Below: This scene is from the third fight in the Saddler v Pep series, which took place at Yankee Stadium on September 8 1950. Stung by his defeat in the second encounter, Saddler came out strongly, and had Pep on the floor, and nearly through the ropes, in the third round. The result, a knockout win for Saddler in eight rounds, set up the keenly anticipated 1951 fight, which was to be their last meeting.

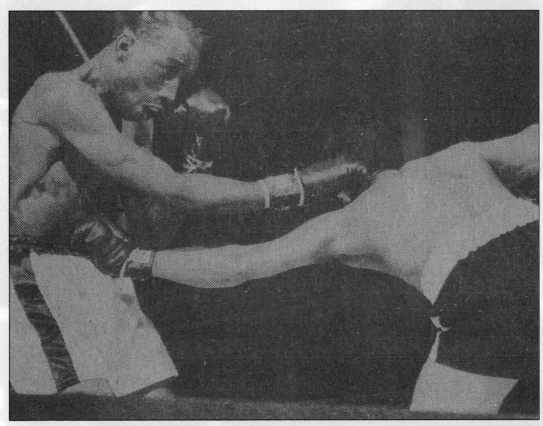

Left: Still early in the fight, and Pep (right) has Saddler bent double as he attacks his body. Things deteriorated after this, with less and less boxing taking place as the fight progressed. It was replaced by butting, gouging, tripping, and wrestling, and became a disgraceful brawl – one of the dirtiest contests in history. Pep was banned for life after the fight, and Saddler was suspended: Pep's ban was later lifted.

Right: Marciano pounded Louis to a humiliating defeat. The fight was stopped by the referee, Ruby Goldstein, in the eighth round.

JOE LOUIS V ROCKY MARCIANO

October 26 1951
New York

In a comeback attempt to regain the world heavyweight title, Louis met Marciano on the understanding that the winner would go on to meet Walcott for the championship. Louis was by this time only half the great boxer he had once been and was savaged by Marciano throughout the fight.

Above: Joe Louis probably took more punishment in these comeback fights than he did through the whole of his main career. Like many great modern fighters, he came out of retirement for the wrong reasons, and to some extent tarnished his reputation. He should be remembered in his prime (far left).

'JERSEY' JOE WALCOTT V ROCKY MARCIANO

September 23 1952
Philadelphia

Marciano knocked out Walcott in the thirteenth round but he did not have it all his own way: until that point the defending champion was ahead on points. Walcott also had the satisfaction of decking Marciano in the first round but it was not quite enough and he took a terrible beating towards the end of the fight. In a return fight in May the following year, Walcott was a truly beaten man and lasted just one round.

Top: Walcott about to receive a massive blow from the all-powerful Marciano. However the defending champion was ahead until the fateful thirteenth.

Below: A typical shot from a Marciano fight: it is difficult to recognize Walcott through the pain.

ROCKY MARCIANO V EZZARD CHARLES

June 17 1954
New York

Marciano started as hot favourite to retain his title, and no-one expected Charles to give him much of a fight. The courageous former champion, did, however, stay the distance and he severely hurt the champion before losing on points. In the return match in June the same year, Charles succumbed in eight rounds.

Top: Marciano was backed to win at more than 3–1: he came in to the fight with forty-five straight victories under his belt, and was looking invincible. But Charles, drawing deep into his experience and courage, stood up to Marciano throughout, and ended with a points loss that, given Marciano's form, was perhaps the finest result of his career.

Above: Charles clubs Marciano with a right but the durable 'Brockton Blockbuster' was able to take punishment as well as dish it out.

Right: With a cut eye and a bloodied nose of his own, Marciano leans into Charles with a right. At the end, both of the challenger's eyes were closed and his face was badly swollen and bruised.

ROCKY MARCIANO V ARCHIE MOORE

September 21 1955
New York

Marciano retired after this fight, an unbeaten champion with a record forty-nine professional victories to his credit. Moore was knocked out in the ninth round.

Above: Moore floored Marciano in the second round with a devastating right.

Above: The indefatigable Archie Moore. This fight only came about because of Moore's publicity campaign, but once it was set it was a winner. Moore was on a twenty-one fight winning streak, and although few truly believed that the light-heavyweight champion could beat Marciano, everyone wanted to see for themselves. The fight turned into the biggest boxing payday since Dempsey v Tunney.

Left: Referee Kessler helped Marciano to survive by forgetting that the mandatory standing count had been waived for this fight. When Marciano rose groggily to his feet after the second-round knock-down, the extra seconds Kessler gave him kept Moore at bay just long enough to allow Marciano to get his defences set. From then on Marciano piled on the pressure, finally knocking out Moore for good in the ninth. Far left: Marciano retired after this fight, a wealthy and happy man.

GENE FULLMER V 'SUGAR' RAY ROBINSON

May 1 1957
Chicago

Robinson lost his middleweight title to Fullmer in January 1957 but regained it three months later in a return contest that lasted just five rounds. Fullmer later avenged this defeat, however, drawing a fight in 1960 and winning their fourth battle in 1961.

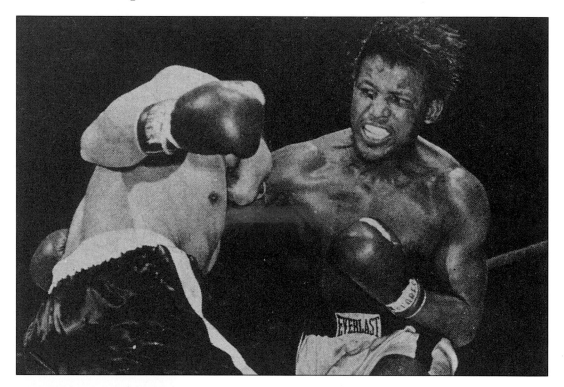

Above: Fullmer was so stunned by Robinson's flashing punches that he had to be told what had happened to him.

Right: In the fifth round Robinson was dominant and sent Fullmer to the canvas with a right-and-left combination.

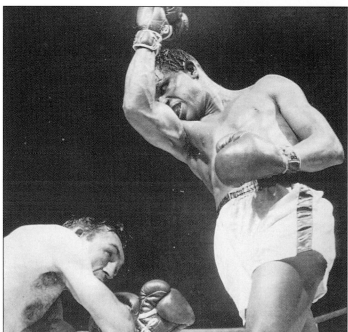

'SUGAR' RAY ROBINSON V CARMEN BASILIO

March 25 1958
Chicago

Robinson had two classic fights against Basilio when the middleweight championship was at stake. He lost the first, in 1957, on a split decision but won the second, also on a split decision.

Left: Basilio ducks a vicious right uppercut from Robinson. The split decision went against Basilio, cutting his championship reign short.

Right: Carmen Basilio.

FLOYD PATTERSON V INGEMAR JOHANSSON

June 20 1960
New York

Having lost his heavyweight title to Johansson the year before, Patterson was determined to regain it. He dominated the rematch and knocked out Johansson in the fifth round. A year later he proved his point again by knocking the Swede out in six rounds.

Right and below: Johansson's principal claim to fame is his series against Patterson. He surprised him in the first fight, but Patterson got his mark for the others. Below, he can be seen hitting the canvas in the second fight: he stayed so still that Patterson thought he had killed him.

Top: In their first fight, on June 26 1959, Johansson knocked Patterson down seven times before the referee stepped in.

Above: In the third fight, in 1961, the Swede knocked Patterson down early, but the American came back to win in six rounds.

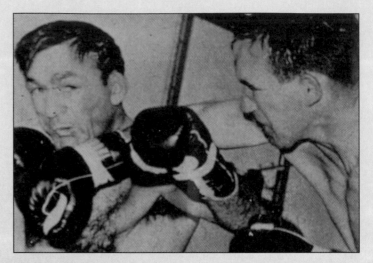

GENE FULLMER V CARMEN BASILIO

June 29 1960
Salt Lake City

With a 1959 knockout victory over Basilio already to his credit, Fullmer was confident of another success at this encounter. The National Boxing Association's world middleweight title was at stake and Fullmer succeeded in retaining the title by knocking out Basilio in the twelfth round.

Above, left, and below: Fullmer was a rugged fighter: nobody admired him as a boxer, but plenty of opponents respected him. In this rematch with Basilio – no slouch himself when it came to aggression – he simply took over the fight and pummelled the ex-champion to defeat. Above: Fullmer's right scorches through Basilio's defence to score a hit. Left: the reigning champion is about to land the killer blow. It goes into Basilio's right side and knocks him flat – and very nearly out of the ring (below). Some rank Fullmer as the toughest middleweight who ever fought.

Left: Gene Fullmer was a Mormon fighter, born in West Jordan, Utah, on July 21 1931. He won the vacant NBA middleweight title by defeating Carmen Basilio in 1959, and held it until he was beaten by Dick Tiger in San Francisco on October 23 1962. After two unsuccessful return fights against Tiger he retired on July 23 1964.

Left: Basilio takes to the canvas during the thirteenth round. He managed to climb to his feet, but lost the contest on points. This was the end of the line for the great man, who announced his retirement three days later. Basilio was born on April 2 1927 in Canastota, New York, and turned professional in 1948. His career spanned a golden age of middleweight and welterweight boxing, and during his fighting life he met such legends and fine fighters as Billy Graham (from whom he won the New York State welterweight title), 'Kid' Gavilan, Tony DeMarco (from whom he took the world welterweight crown), Johnny Saxton, 'Sugar' Ray Robinson, Gene Fullmer, and Paul Pender.

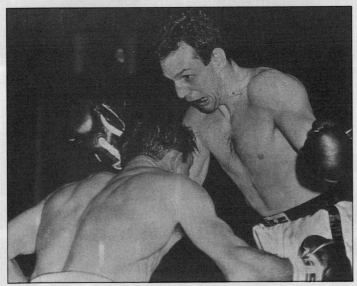

PAUL PENDER V
CARMEN BASILIO

April 22 1961
Boston

Pender had taken the middleweight world title from 'Sugar' Ray Robinson in January 1960 and this was his third defence. He beat the former champion on points in a fifteen-round contest.

Left: With his head low, Basilio attacks the champion's midriff early in the fight.

Right and below: Benny Paret was born in Cuba on March 14 1937, and turned professional in 1955. He won the world welterweight title from Don Jordan in 1960, and held it until it was taken from him by Griffith on April 1 1961 in Miami. He regained it from Griffith, and then agreed to this rematch, which went terribly wrong when his head was knocked back against a ringpost in the twelfth.

BENNY PARET V EMILE GRIFFITH

March 24 1962
New York

In this tragic fight, Emile Griffith won the world welterweight title but the hapless Cuban defender died of injuries sustained when his head was battered against a steel ringpost in the twelfth round.

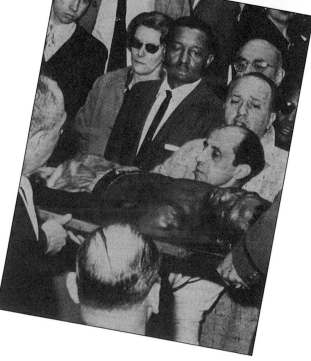

Right: Paret is eased onto a stretcher, oblivious of what is going on around him. He was taken to Roosevelt Hospital, but never recovered from his injuries, and died on April 3 1962. Griffith was distraught, especially when his attempts to visit Paret in hospital were interpreted by the **media as publicity seeking: he was eventually able to put the memory behind him, and went on to win many championships. The fight had been shown live on American TV, and the effect on the image of professional boxing was understandably disastrous.**

FLOYD PATTERSON V
SONNY LISTON

September 25 1962
Chicago

Liston had to wait a long time to challenge Patterson for the world heavyweight title. He didn't waste a second when his chance came, and he flattened Patterson in the first round.

Right: After a nine-year wait for a shot at the title, Liston finished the champion in two minutes six seconds. Liston had an awesome reputation at this time: most professional boxers were frankly afraid of him. Patterson was brave enough to enforce the return fight clause in their contract, though most critics wondered why. In the event, on July 22 1963, he was again the loser: floored three times in the first, the knockout blow was timed at two minutes ten seconds.

Above: Liston (right) smacks Patterson on the jaw two minutes into the opening round. The challenger followed up with a left hook that put the champion flat on his back.

CASSIUS CLAY V HENRY COOPER

June 18 1963
London

The up-and-coming Cassius Clay, who later changed his name to Muhammad Ali, fought Cooper at Wembley Stadium in a non-title fight to decide who should be allowed a crack at the new heavyweight world champion, Sonny Liston. Cooper unleashed his fabled left hook at the end of the fourth round and put Clay on the canvas. All of Britain held its breath.

But Clay beat the count, and just as Cooper was about to finish off the groggy American, the bell rang. In the fifth round a cut above Cooper's left eye streamed blood and the fight was stopped. These seconds in the fourth when Clay was decked transformed Cooper, already a popular favourite, into a national hero.

Right: A legendary moment for British sport. If it hadn't been for the bell, and some between-the-rounds tactics by Clay's shrewd manager, Angelo Dundee, who knows what might have been? The break between the fourth and fifth round was timed at 90 seconds, as Dundee insisted on replacing a glove that Clay had split on his fall to the canvas. When he came out for the fifth, Clay was immediately back in action.

Above: With a badly cut left eye, Cooper launches a final attack at Clay in the fifth round; but it was not enough and the referee was obliged to call a halt.

Right: Clay (left), infinitely more agile than the ponderous Liston, leans back to avoid a slow punch from the champion. He was as wary as the rest of the professional fraternity of Liston's iron fists and enormous power, but knew that he could out-box and out-manoeuvre him. In the end, Liston, controversially, failed to get off of his stool for the seventh round. This dubious end to their encounter was as nothing to the controversy surrounding the rematch. In the least satisfactory heavyweight title fight of all time, Liston went down heavily after only a minute and a half of the first round – and very few people could see why. A short right-hander was thrown, but no punch was seen or filmed that could genuinely explain the despatch of a man of Liston's enormous strength, and rumour still abounds as to what really happened.

Below: Clay makes Liston's eyes squint with a left hook. By the fourth round, Clay was dominating the fight which ended when the defending champion refused to come out for the seventh round.

SONNY LISTON V CASSIUS CLAY

February 25 1964
Miami

The arrogant and brash Clay taunted Liston before, during and after this, their first fight for the world heavyweight championship. Liston was thought to be unbeatable but Clay survived the champion's initial onslaught and then took the initiative. Notoriously, Liston refused to come out of his corner at the start of the seventh round, and the greatest career in boxing history reached its first major peak.

NINO BENVENUTI V
CARLOS MONZON

November 7 1970
Rome

Monzon was almost unheard of outside his native Argentina when he first fought Benvenuti for the middleweight world championship. Yet against the odds, and in a staggering performance, he knocked the Italian out in the twelfth round.

Right: The great Carlos Monzon stands like a colossus over a stricken Nino Benvenuti at the end of their world middleweight title fight. Born in Santa Fe, Argentina, on August 7 1942, Monzon became one of the finest boxers ever to emerge from South America. He travelled to Europe in 1970 for the Benvenuti fight with a phenomenal record of eighty-two wins and only three losses in his homeland: yet most critics, presuming his wins had been against sub-standard opposition, gave him no chance against the Italian. His prospects were seen as particularly difficult, as Benvenuti was fighting in front of a home crowd in the hotbed of Rome: they felt that a knockout was the only sure way to get a result, and doubted that Monzon could despatch the strong Italian. But Monzon did just that, and then confirmed his superiority in the return match a year later. His next defence was against Emile Griffith, whom he stopped in the fourteenth round, and he then proceeded to defend twelve times more over the next six years before retiring. After retirement, his life deteriorated, and he was jailed for murdering his wife. While on bail in 1995, he was killed in a car accident near Santa Fe. He was only 52.

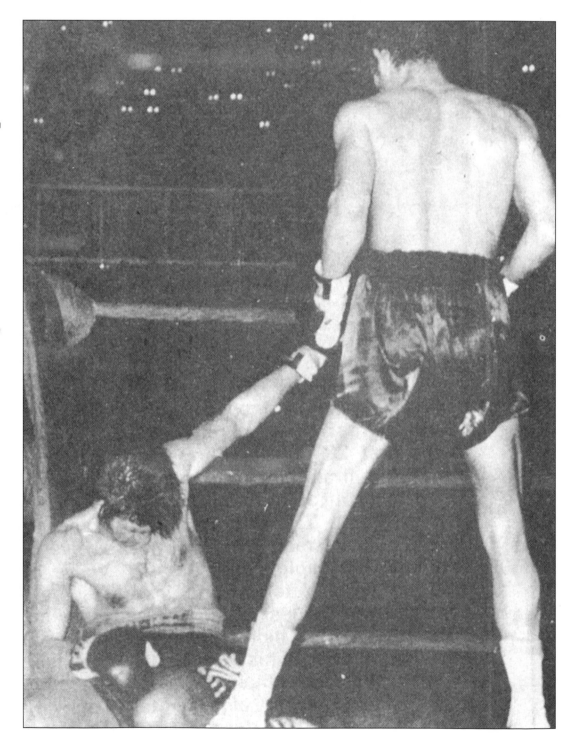

MUHAMMAD ALI V JERRY QUARRY

September 10 1970
Atlanta

After his enforced retirement from the ring following government legal action over his refusal – on religious and moral grounds – to be drafted into the United States Army, Ali announced his comeback in no uncertain fashion with a three-round victory over Quarry.

Left: Pain distorts Quarry's face as Ali hits him with a right to the head. The world had been waiting to see how Ali would perform after his lay-off.

Below: Ali catches Quarry with a swinging right to the head. It opened a bad cut above Quarry's left eye that led to the fight being stopped.

Right: This bout – the first of the modern 'superfights' – was hyped as an encounter between beauty and the beast. 'Ugly' Joe Frazier and 'pretty' Muhammad Ali obligingly posed for publicity shots – not surprisingly, as each of them was guaranteed around $5 million for the fight. Ali had forfeited the championship in 1967, and Frazier had unified the heavyweight succession by beating Buster Mathis for the WBC title in 1968, and Jimmy Ellis for the WBA belt in 1970. Ali, returning to the ring after a three-year absence, had fought his way up to challenge legitimately for the title he never lost.

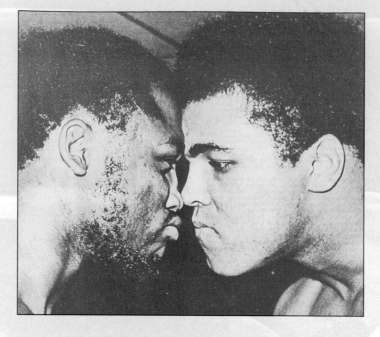

JOE FRAZIER V MUHAMMAD ALI

March 8 1971
New York

In one of the greatest heavyweight title fights of all time, Joe Frazier saw off the challenge of the former champion with a points victory. Both men proved their strength, courage and stamina and both had to be hospitalized after the contest.

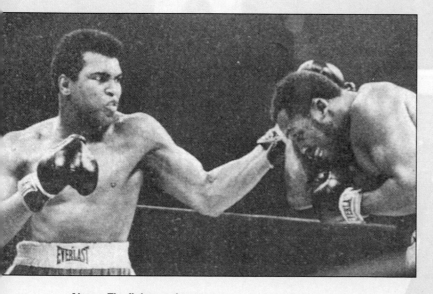

Above: The fight was by no means one-sided and the result was in doubt until the last round.

Above: Frazier thumps Ali's jaw with his favourite punch. It was the champion's left hook that did Ali the most damage.

Above: Ali's knees can no longer keep him up and he crumples to the canvas in the fifteenth round after Frazier has caught him with a hook. With a swollen jaw, Ali got up to finish the fight but lost the contest on points.

Right: The blow in the thirteenth round that Buchanan claimed cost him the title. It is clearly below the belt.

Above: Buchanan grimaces in agony after the illegal blow. The Scotsman claimed it was just one of several such punches, but the referee's decision is final, and he saw it differently.

KEN BUCHANAN V
ROBERTO DURAN

June 26 1972
New York

Buchanan lost the WBA lightweight title to Duran after being hit by a foul blow in the thirteenth round. Although few would say that Duran was an undeserving champion, there was nevertheless an enormous amount of sympathy for the circumstances of Buchanan's loss.

Above: Buchanan leans backwards through the ropes a few seconds before the referee calls a halt.

JOE FRAZIER V GEORGE FOREMAN

January 22 1973
Kingston, Jamaica

Foreman had a reputation for being a knockout specialist when he met Frazier for the world heavyweight crown, but, even so, nobody dreamed he would take the title in the second round.

Left: In the opening round, Foreman forced Frazier on to one knee but the breather did the champion little good.

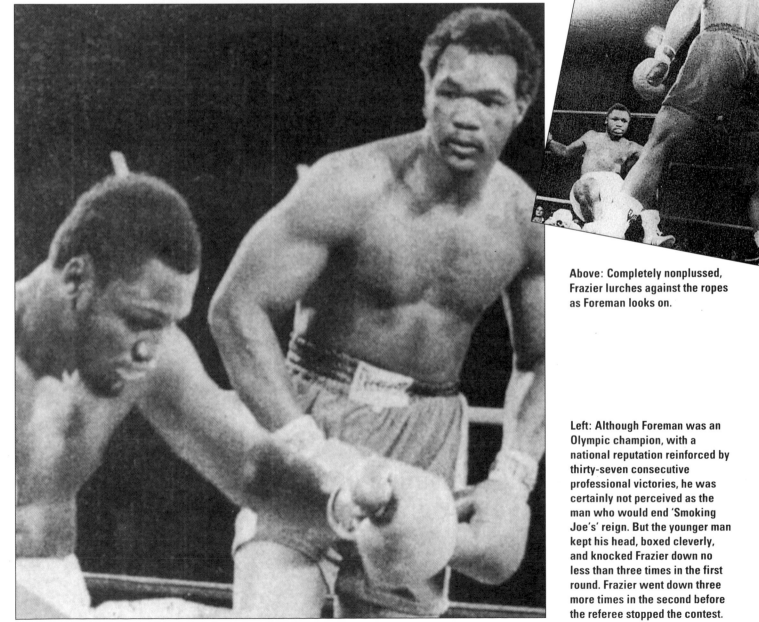

Above: Completely nonplussed, Frazier lurches against the ropes as Foreman looks on.

Left: Although Foreman was an Olympic champion, with a national reputation reinforced by thirty-seven consecutive professional victories, he was certainly not perceived as the man who would end 'Smoking Joe's' reign. But the younger man kept his head, boxed cleverly, and knocked Frazier down no less than three times in the first round. Frazier went down three more times in the second before the referee stopped the contest.

MUHAMMAD ALI V JOE FRAZIER

January 28 1974
New York

In a non-title bout that was billed as 'Superfight II', the two former world heavyweight champions slugged out a gruelling twelve-round contest. Ali was this time declared the points winner on a unanimous decision.

Right: Both men fought their hearts out as both had a lot to prove. Some experts reckoned that Frazier's loss of fire power gave Ali an advantage.

Left: Though never billed as such, perhaps in deference to the reputations and dignity of the two participants, this fight was essentially an eliminator to see who would take on the increasingly fearsome Foreman for the heavyweight title. Of course there was enormous hype, and the two men received gigantic fees, but the event did not quite live up to its billing. It was, nevertheless, a hard-fought and genuine battle, with Ali taking the fight on a narrow, but unanimous, decision. Here he unleashes an uppercut, with Frazier ducking low. Ali was not his former, fleet-footed self, but he still had great stamina and courage.

Left: Ahumada ducks under a right-cross from Conteh. Both men were fast movers as well as powerful strikers.

Below: Conteh had a win-at-all-costs style and attitude that did not earn sporting admiration, but brought great respect. This fight was the highlight of a career which did not go on to fulfil all of its promise.

JORGE AHUMADA V
JOHN CONTEH

October 1 1974
London

In this contest Ahumada and Conteh fought for the WBC light-heavyweight title which had been stripped from Bob Foster. Although both men were cunning, strong boxers, Conteh came out the winner on points on this occasion.

Left: In the twelfth round the Argentinian's eye began to close, but he gamely fought on to the finish, only to be edged out on points.

Right: In the early rounds, Ali rested on the ropes and allowed Foreman to wear himself out. It was a dangerous tactic but, well executed, it paid off.

Below: Against all predictions, the referee intones the count as Foreman lies flat on his back in the eighth round, barely able to raise his head. Bottom: Foreman struggles in vain to get to his feet, and Ali becomes world champion for the second time.

GEORGE FOREMAN V MUHAMMAD ALI

October 30 1974
Kinshasa, Zaïre

Ali, the challenger for the world heavyweight title, called this fight the 'Rumble in the Jungle'. He boxed a clever fight, absorbing Foreman's attacks while resting on the ropes, and allowing the champion to exhaust himself by pummelling away at a carefully constructed defence. Then, in the eighth round, he cracked the tired champion on the chin and sent him plummeting to the canvas.

MUHAMMAD ALI V
JOE FRAZIER

October 1 1975
Manila

'Superfight III' or the 'Thriller in Manila' lived up to all expectation and has been cited as one of the greatest heavyweight contests of the century. Both men were extremely brave and it was not until the twelfth round, when Frazier's left eye began to close, that either man had a worthwhile advantage. In the end Frazier retired in the fourteenth round, 'or else somebody would have got killed' as he put it.

Above: The punch that did the damage. Frazier's eye began to close up in the twelfth round and he began to take a great deal of punishment until the fight ended after the fourteenth round.

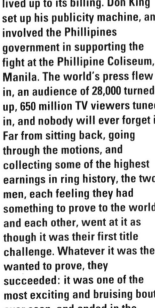

Right: For once a 'superfight' lived up to its billing. Don King set up his publicity machine, and involved the Phillipines government in supporting the fight at the Phillipine Coliseum, Manila. The world's press flew in, an audience of 28,000 turned up, 650 million TV viewers tuned in, and nobody will ever forget it. Far from sitting back, going through the motions, and collecting some of the highest earnings in ring history, the two men, each feeling they had something to prove to the world and each other, went at it as though it was their first title challenge. Whatever it was they wanted to prove, they succeeded: it was one of the most exciting and bruising bouts ever seen, and ended in the fourteenth, when the referee led a battered Frazier to his corner.

CARLOS MONZON V RODRIGO VALDEZ

June 26 1976
Monte Carlo

Monzon retired undefeated after fifteen world middle-weight title bouts. His last two fights were amongst his toughest – both were against Valdez. This was his first encounter with the Colombian and he won the contest on a points decision.

Right: Monzon dumps Valdez on to the canvas in the fourteenth round but the plucky Colombian got up to complete the scheduled fifteen.

MUHAMMAD ALI V LEON SPINKS

Above: Trapped in a corner, Ali turns his back on Spinks who was much more aggressive than the ageing champion.

February 15 1978
Las Vegas

Ali lost his world heavyweight title for the second time in this fight. The younger man was stronger and more aggressive and eventually won on points. However the incredible Ali won a rematch in September the same year.

**Above: The decision is announced and Spinks shows his joy at gaining the championship by flinging his arms in the air.
Top: The young Spinks.**

'SUGAR' RAY LEONARD V WILFRED BENITEZ

November 30 1979
Las Vegas

'Sugar' Ray Leonard relieved Benitez of the WBC welterweight title in this contest, but it was not an easy victory. Both fighters gave their all and it was not until the fifteenth round that a stoppage made Leonard the eventual winner.

Left: Benitez rocked Leonard with this left hook but the master technician came through to win in the end. It was a classic contest between two stylish boxers.

Above: The return fight proved to be one of the most controversial in recent history. On November 25 1980 Duran gave up his hard-won crown when he turned his back on Leonard (above) crying 'No mas' ('No more'). He was almost certainly frustrated by Leonard's style, but it took years for him to recover from the damage to his reputation.

'SUGAR' RAY LEONARD V ROBERTO DURAN

June 20 1980
Montreal

Roberto Duran took the WBC welterweight title from Leonard in this remarkable fight in which style was matched against slugging power. On the day, power won through, and Duran won on a points decision. Leonard, however, regained the title from the Panamanian five months later.

Above: Duran (left) succeeded in drawing the normally cagey Leonard into a toe-to-toe fist fight. His tactics proved successful.

MUHAMMAD ALI V LARRY HOLMES

October 2 1980
Las Vegas

This was Ali's penultimate fight and he was comprehensively out-boxed by the younger, fitter Holmes who was then the reigning WBC heavyweight champion. It was a sad defeat for the most famous sportsman in the world and even Holmes was sorry to see his hero beaten so easily. Ali quit at the end of the tenth round.

Right: This was a fight that should never have taken place, and, in retrospect, and seeing Ali today, it is obvious that the great ex-champion should never have been allowed to keep coming back into the ring. The fight was humiliatingly one-sided, and there was no credit to either boxer, nor to the managers, promoters, or the authority that sanctioned the bout. Ali tried one more fight, against Trevor Berbick, before retiring for good.

Above: The two boxers pose for a publicity picture before the fight (Hearns on right).

Right: In the fourteenth round Leonard launched an attack which had Hearns in so much trouble that the referee had to step in and call a halt.

'SUGAR' RAY LEONARD V THOMAS HEARNS

September 16 1981
Las Vegas

This fight was for the undisputed welterweight title of the world; Leonard held the WBC version of the title and Hearns the WBA version. It was a tough, evenly fought contest between two of the best boxers of the era. It ended when the referee stopped the contest in the fourteenth in Leonard's favour.

ROBERTO DURAN V THOMAS HEARNS

June 15 1984
Las Vegas

In this fight to unify the junior-middleweight world championship (Duran held the WBA version, Hearns the WBC version) Duran was overwhelmed and he was knocked cold and counted out in the second.

Right: Hearns (right) eyes his man warily, but it was Duran who was in for a shock. In the second round Hearns stepped in and knocked him out cold. Duran was in his seventeenth year as a professional boxer, and this was the first time that he had suffered such an indignity.

Below: This fight took place when Hearns was at his prime. His first title, the WBA welterweight, was won from Pipino Cuevas in 1980, but lost a year later to Leonard. Hearns had captured the WBC junior-middleweight world title from Wilfred Benitez in 1982, and this victory unified the division. He soon relinquished the title to move up to middleweight and challenge the likes of Marvin Hagler.

Right: Hagler (right) was the aggressor, continually moving forward to pressurize Hearns. The challenger had taken on a huge task: not only was he moving up in weight, but Hagler had by this time been middleweight champion for nearly five years, and had defended successfully ten times against the best in the division.

Above: Hagler unleashes a mighty right that knocks Hearns groggy. Shortly after this punch in the third round the referee stopped the fight.

Above: The two champions pose before the bout wearing their championship belts.

MARVIN HAGLER V THOMAS HEARNS

April 15 1985
Las Vegas

This contest was for the undisputed middleweight world championship. 'Hit Man' Hearns was the younger and taller boxer, but he was no match for the power of 'Marvelous' Marvin who dispatched the challenger in three rounds.

EUSEBIO PEDROZA V BARRY McGUIGAN

June 8 1985
London

In front of a partisan crowd at London's Queen's Park Rangers football ground, the Irishman McGuigan took the WBA featherweight title from the veteran Panamanian. McGuigan won the contest on points.

Left: McGuigan (left) appears tired towards the end of the fight, but the tenacious Irishman went on to win a famous points victory.

Above: Eusebio Pedroza, seen between rounds, was born in Panama City on March 2 1953. After turning professional in 1973 he quickly moved up through the ranks, winning the WBA world featherweight crown in April 1978 from Cecilio Lastra. He successfully defended the title nineteen times before meeting McGuigan in London, and came into the fight with an enormous reputation for durability.

Left: Pedroza (left) and McGuigan trade punches in the centre of the ring during their emotionally-charged contest.

MIKE TYSON V JAMES SMITH

March 7 1987
Las Vegas

In the first defence of his recently won heavyweight title, Tyson beat 'Bonecrusher' Smith on points in a twelve-round contest.

Below: The previous year Mike Tyson had become the youngest ever holder of the heavyweight crown, when, at the age of twenty years and five months, he crushed Trevor Berbick on November 22 1986.

Below: Tyson hits Smith with a right. 'Bonecrusher' failed to live up to his ring-name: he showed little aggression, and only lasted twelve rounds by alternately moving away from the champion and holding him.

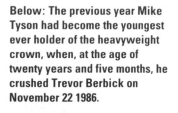

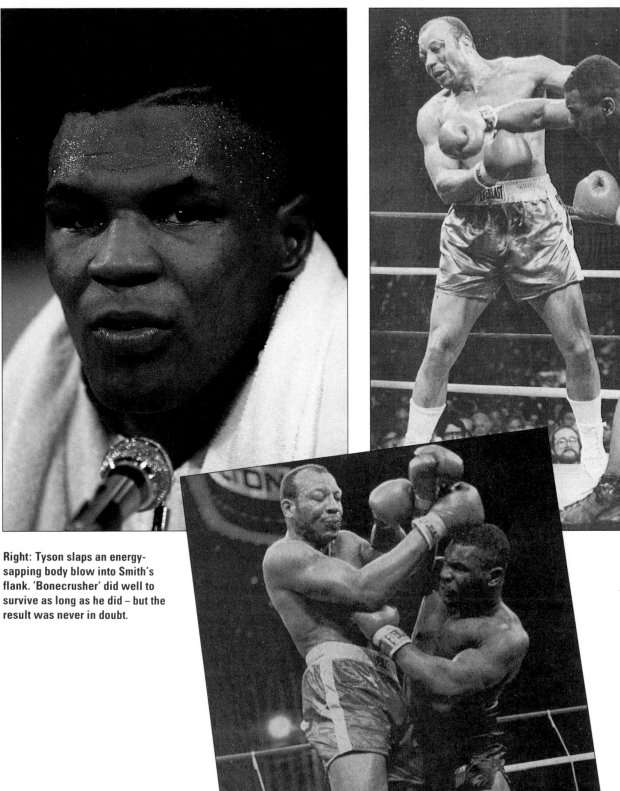

Right: Tyson slaps an energy-sapping body blow into Smith's flank. 'Bonecrusher' did well to survive as long as he did – but the result was never in doubt.

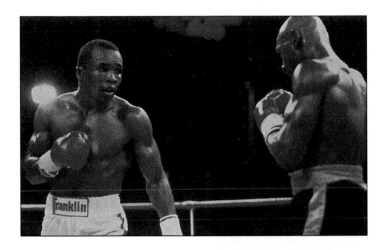

Left: Leonard (left) often boxed on the retreat, fully aware that if he tangled with Hagler he would get hurt.

Right: The more mobile Leonard (left) looks for an opening in Hagler's defensive guard.

Right: Hagler was the more aggressive of the two, and his intention was to end the contest with a knockout. Leonard defended well on the move, all the while scoring valuable points.

Below: In the ninth round, Hagler drew Leonard into a brawl which boosted his chances of success, but in the end Leonard's skill, and the points he had already accumulated, won the day.

MARVIN HAGLER V 'SUGAR' RAY LEONARD

April 6 1987
Las Vegas

Leonard recorded an astonishing points victory over Hagler after a lay-off of three years during which he did not box a single contest. The fight was for the WBC version of the middleweight world championship and became the richest contest in boxing history. Leonard won on a controversial split decision – many observers reckoned that Hagler had done enough to win.

FIDEL BASSA V DAVE MCAULEY

April 25 1987
Belfast

In front of his home crowd in Northern Ireland, McAuley put in a magnificent effort in his attempt to wrest the WBA flyweight title from Bassa. He floored the Colombian several times before he himself was stopped in the thirteenth round. In a return match the following year, Bassa again came out on top.

Right: McAuley (left) fought valiantly and skilfully, putting the champion on the canvas several times. However the champion retained his title when the referee saved the Irishman from taking a terrible hammering in the thirteenth.

MIKE TYSON V LARRY HOLMES

January 22 1988
Atlantic City

Holmes, the man who had beaten Muhammad Ali, was past his best and no match for the sheer strength and aggression of Tyson. The contest ended in the fourth round.

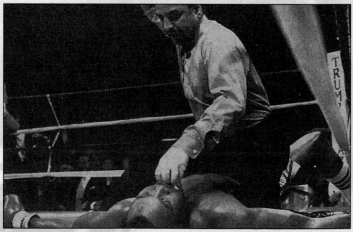

Left: The sluggish Holmes was completely overwhelmed by Tyson's non-stop assault.

Above: The referee takes the shield from Holmes' mouth as he lies flat on his back in the fourth round.

JORGE VACA V LLOYD HONEYGHAN

March 28 1988
London

Vaca had beaten Honeyghan on a technical decision the previous year to take away the Britisher's WBC welterweight title. Feeling that he had something to prove, Honeyghan came out strongly, and knocked the Mexican out in the third round.

Above: Fighting on his home turf, Honeyghan (left) went on the offensive and settled it quickly with a knockout.

Above: The formidable Mike Tyson, victorious in the fifth round against the British challenger. This was Tyson's seventh defence: his other wins had been against 'Bonecrusher' Smith in March 1987; Pinklon Thomas in May 1987; Tony Tucker in August 1987; Larry Holmes in January 1988; Tony Tubbs in March 1988; and Michael Spinks in June 1988.

Above: Bruno started well, and at one point in the first round the champion was clearly shaken. But thereafter, Tyson found his form, and battered the Englishman to a fifth-round defeat.

MIKE TYSON V FRANK BRUNO

February 25 1989
Las Vegas

Bruno, England's favourite heavyweight, rocked Tyson in the first round which surprised everybody, not least the champion. However there was no major upset and Bruno had to be saved by the referee in the fifth round.

'SUGAR' RAY LEONARD V THOMAS HEARNS

June 12 1989
Las Vegas

This classic contest for the WBC super-middleweight title ended in a draw. Both men were past their best but they fought tenaciously and fortunes fluctuated both ways. It was the fight of the year.

Right: Hearns on the attack. Some experts reckoned that Leonard was lucky to get away with a draw as he was knocked to the canvas on two occasions.

DENNIS ANDRIES V JEFF HARDING

June 24 1989
Atlantic City

Andries lost his WBC light-heavyweight title to the Australian in this contest after dominating most of the fight. He was rescued by the referee from a punishing last ditch attack in the last round. Andries regained the title from Harding the following year with a knockout victory.

Right: Andries and Harding exchange jabs. The champion used his experience and technique to edge ahead in the early rounds, but, as he admitted afterwards, he knew little about the Australian (who was a late replacement for Donny Lalonde), and was shocked when Harding seemed to get stronger and stronger.

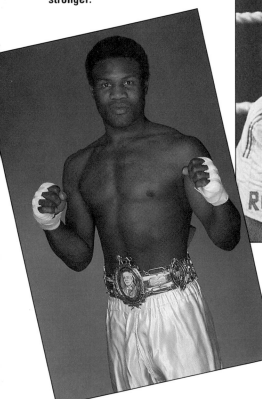

Above: This was Andries' first defence. He had picked up the vacant WBC title only months before by defeating Tony Willis on February 21 in Arizona.

Left: Jeff 'Hit Man' Harding resting between rounds. Together with Jeff Fenech, he is rated as the best boxer to emerge from Australia in decades. Virtually unknown outside his homeland, he got his shot at Andries as a late substitute, and was little fancied. His fantastic courage, and non-stop aggression, saw him home in an upset victory.

Left: Tyson slumps to the canvas after being whacked by a heavy left from Douglas.

MIKE TYSON V JAMES DOUGLAS

February 11 1990
Tokyo

Tyson was thought to be invincible until 'Buster' Douglas knocked him cold in the tenth round. Douglas was not considered to be a major threat – or any threat at all – to the champion but he did the 'impossible'. He subsequently lost the world heavyweight title to Evander Holyfield in his first defence. His performance against Holyfield was so lame, and he had prepared for it so poorly, that most critics' view that his victory in the Tyson contest was a fluke and a flash-in-the-pan was convincingly confirmed.

There was some controversy over whether the referee gave a long count earlier in the fight but the final knockout decision was upheld. It later emerged that most of the confusion was, according to some sources, deliberately caused by Tyson's manager Don King, in an attempt to get his boxer's loss overturned. The conspiracy theory alleges that, to their shame, the authorities nearly went along with this, perhaps having it in mind that Tyson as champion was better for boxing than the unknown Douglas. Certainly there was chaos after the fight, and the result was not finally confirmed for several hours. In the end justice, and conscience, were served.

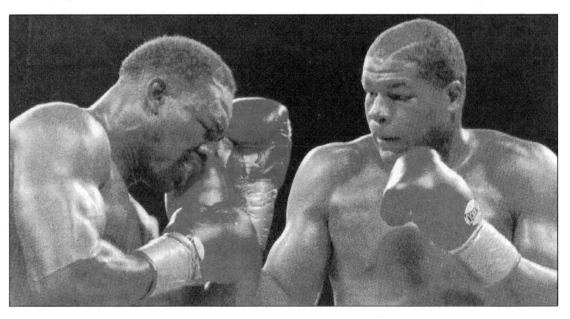

Right: Bowe lands a punishing right jab to the head of Evander Holyfield. The latter's attempt to trade punches with his bigger and stronger opponent proved ill-fated. He lasted the twelve rounds, having been knocked to the canvas in the eleventh, but by then the decision was in no doubt.

Right: A young man from the same Brownsville area of Brooklyn as Mike Tyson, Riddick Bowe's ability and determination look set to earn him an equally fabled position in the history of world boxing.

RIDDICK BOWE V EVANDER HOLYFIELD

November 13 1992 at Las Vegas
November 6 1993 at Las Vegas

In two of the hardest-fought heavyweight fights for years, Evander Holyfield and Riddick Bowe exchanged their tenure of the championship. Holyfield said of their 1992 clash: "Everything I did, he did better." In the return, Holyfield boxed and counterpunched with accuracy to regain his former title.

FRANKIE RANDALL V JULIO CESAR CHAVEZ

January 29 1994
Las Vegas

15–1 outsider Frankie Randall spoiled the hitherto unbeaten record of WBC light welterweight champion Julio Cesar Chavez by taking a 12 round points decision. To add insult to injury, Randall put Chavez down for a count of eight in the eleventh round.

Above: It was a thrilling and extremely closely-contested encounter, largely decided by the two points that referee Richard Steele ordered to be deducted from Chavez for low blows.

Right: Boxing's longest unbeaten record draws to an end, as Randall soaks up a little punishment and wears down the champion to a 12-round points defeat. Chavez lost his composure after the bout, and his post-fight behaviour and comments were felt by some to have tarnished a great career.

GEORGE FOREMAN V MICHAEL MOORER

November 5 1994
Las Vegas

Evergreen George Foreman became heavyweight champion for the second time when, at the advanced age of 45, he knocked out WBA and IBF title holder Michael Moorer in the tenth round.

Right: Moorer was born in the year of Foreman's first great triumph – the Olympic Gold Medal win of 1968. As the fight went on past the fifth and sixth rounds the assumption from fans and gamblers was that youth would tell – no-one realistically backed Foreman to last the pace.

Right: Foreman took punishment throughout the fight, then surprised everyone by going on to the attack. Most experts feel he would have lost the decision if the fight had gone the full twelve rounds – and maybe it was this feeling that spurred Foreman forward.

Left: Moorer always had a suspect chin, and Foreman's main hope was to find this target. As the crowd chanted his name – some forlornly – Big George finally put together a pinpoint combination in the tenth that hit the spot, flooring Moorer to grab the title.

ROY JONES V JAMES TONEY

November 18 1994
Las Vegas

One of the most eagerly awaited clashes in the super middleweight division took place when these two unbeaten men fought for Toney's IBF championship. Jones showed superb skills and dazzling speed to win clearly on points and to establish himself as one of the greatest fighters of his era.

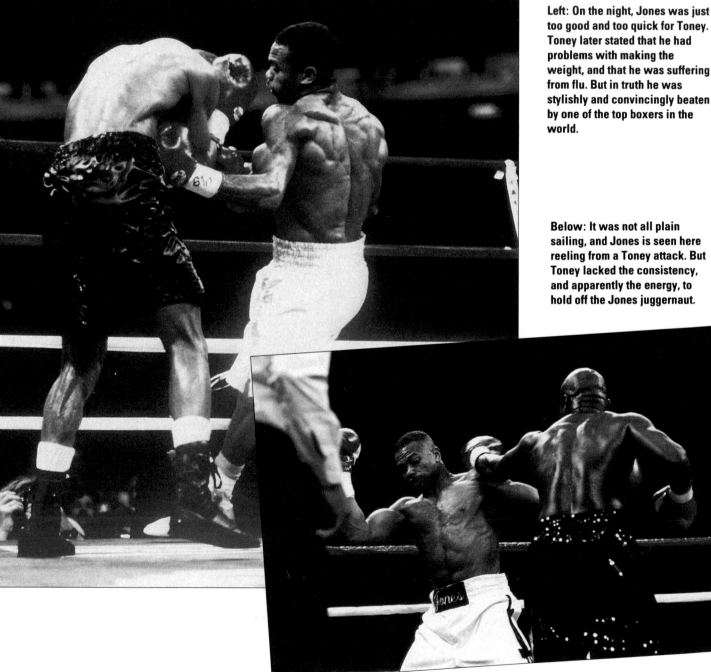

Left: On the night, Jones was just too good and too quick for Toney. Toney later stated that he had problems with making the weight, and that he was suffering from flu. But in truth he was stylishly and convincingly beaten by one of the top boxers in the world.

Below: It was not all plain sailing, and Jones is seen here reeling from a Toney attack. But Toney lacked the consistency, and apparently the energy, to hold off the Jones juggernaut.

NIGEL BENN V GERALD McCLELLAN

February 25 1995
London Docklands Arena

A stirring but brutal encounter at London Docklands Arena ended in near tragedy when Gerald McClellan collapsed after being counted out in the tenth round. Benn, defending his WBC super-middleweight title, barely survived a first round knockdown and then came from behind to outlast and outpunch a brave challenger who required brain surgery following the surprise ending.

Left: Something went seriously wrong for McClellan in the tenth round. Going in to it he looked fit and strong, then suddenly he was down, with many at the ringside left wondering why. Later debate questioned whether he had over-trained, over-fasted, or whether he had just taken a bad beating because he had under-estimated the strength and skill of his opponent. He took a slow road to recovery after post-fight surgery.

Right: It was a much different story earlier, as McClellan knocked Benn down in both the first and eighth rounds. Benn showed incredible resilience and determination in coming back to a victory which, though clouded by McClellan's predicament, was nevertheless well earned.

THE WORLD OF BOXING

The most important people in boxing are obviously enough the boxers themselves, but no history of the sport is complete if it fails to take account of the 'backroom boys', the managers, promoters and trainers who are as much a part of the game as the main protagonists. Nor can important venues, influential magazines, and the all-important trophies be ignored, for without them boxing would not be the popular sport that it undoubtedly is.

Over the years boxing has had a magnetic pull for people from all walks of life, catching the imagination of an enormous variety, from poets to blacksmiths, and from the rich and famous to ordinary working people. These fans have also added to the folklore and legend of boxing. Such is the wide attraction of the sport that if such differing characters as George Bernard Shaw, Norman Mailer, Sylvester Stallone, and Lord Byron could all sit down at a table together they would at least have one thing in common – an interest in boxing.

Above: 'A Mill Dispersed' by Charles Robinson which shows ninteenth-century pugilists and spectators fleeing the scene of the contest after the bout had been broken up by police.

Left: Boxing ephemera is perennially fascinating. In an era before photography was common, artists' impressions were usually the only long-distance view a fan could get of a fight: yet they were often hopelessly inaccurate. This drawing, of the Fitzsimmons v Jeffries heavyweight title fight at Coney Island in 1899, is wrong in almost every significant detail, including the colour of their shorts, but it still somehow captures the excitement of the event.

AMATEUR BOXING

The Amateur Boxing Association (ABA) was established in 1880 with the specific aim of promoting and developing amateur boxing in England. It was the forerunner of numerous similar organizations, such as the Amateur Boxing Federation (ABF) of the United States, which organize national contests for amateurs. Most of these organizations regulate boxing clubs where boys first learn the basics of the sport and where they are free to enter age-group competitions. Success in such competitions can lead to regional, national and international finals. In Britain, the ABA National Championships are the most important annual amateur contests in the country. In the United States, the Golden Gloves of America organizes annual competitions for amateurs and there are also competitions sponsored by the ABF every year. The premier international amateur competitions are the World Amateur Championships and, of course, the Olympic Games.

Nearly all professional boxers started as amateurs but amateur boxing is in fact very different from the professional game. Bouts only last for three rounds and it is the aim of every amateur boxer to land as

Above: The great Cuban heavyweight, Teofilio Stevenson, who abided by his Socialist beliefs, and the wishes of the Cuban government, and turned down all offers to turn professional.

Left: Laszlo Papp, the great Hungarian amateur, would almost certainly have figured prominently on the professional world championship scene if politics had allowed. He won three Olympic gold medals between 1948 and 1956; one at middleweight and two at light-middleweight.

many skilful, scoring punches as possible rather than to end a contest with one mighty blow. It is the busiest boxers who win amateur contests and not necessarily those who pack the heaviest punch. Mike Tyson had mixed success as an amateur because his all-or-nothing style won him few points with the judges.

Two of the most remarkable amateur fighters were Laszlo Papp of Hungary and Teofilio Stevenson of Cuba. Papp became the first man to win three Olympic gold medals (middleweight 1948, light-middleweight 1952 and 1956) and was subsequently allowed to turn professional by the Hungarian administrators. He became European middleweight champion in 1962 and was being groomed for a world championship fight against the title holder

Joey Giardello: then the Communist Hungarian government stepped in and forbade him to do so on the grounds that he would make too much money. Papp retired at the age of thirty-eight, having been unbeaten in his professional career.

Teofilio Stevenson also won three Olympic gold medals (1972, 1976 and 1980, all at heavyweight) as well as three World Amateur Championship titles. He had such a formidable reputation that when Istvan Levai met him in a semi-final bout in 1980, the Hungarian was prompted to run around the edge of the ring for the three rounds, thus becoming the first Olympic boxer to go the distance with the Cuban. Stevenson was once offered two million dollars to turn professional, but he turned the money down.

Left: Stevenson on his way to another victory in the Olympic Games. He won three Olympic gold medals, in 1972, 1976 and 1980, and three World Amateur Championship titles.

Right: 'Boxeurs', a lithograph by
the famous French Romantic
painter, Théodore Géricault. It
gives a somewhat fanciful view
of the match between Tom
Molineaux and Tom Cribb in 1810,
and was in fact drawn some
eight years after the event.

Above: A print showing George
Gordon (1788–1824), otherwise
known as Lord Byron, sparring
with the former champion, John
Jackson, in Jackson's Rooms in
London. Byron idolized Jackson
and in his poem, *Hints from
Horace*, mentions his name:
>   And men unpractised in
>   exchanging knocks
>   Must go to Jackson ere they
>   dare to box.

BOXING AND THE ARTS

Since its earliest days as a bare-knuckle sport, boxing has held a fascination for certain artists and writers. Possibly the most fanatical of them all was the famous Romantic poet, Lord Byron, who was a close friend of the bare-knuckle champion John Jackson. Byron, who occasionally chanced his arm in the ring, was so entranced by boxing that in the interval between 1812 and 1816 he pasted newspaper cuttings and copies of prints on to a screen much as a contemporary teenager would hang posters on a wall or stick pictures of pop-stars into a scrap-book.

Both Charles Dickens and Sir Arthur Conan Doyle, author of the Sherlock Holmes stories, had more than a passing interest in pugilism, and in more recent times two very different Nobel laureates have been fascinated by boxing. The Irish dramatist, pacifist, socialist and vegetarian George Bernard Shaw was, somewhat surprisingly, a boxing fan and wrote a novel, *Cashel Byron's Profession* on the subject. The

Opposite: A coloured engraving
by the famous English
caricaturist, Thomas
Rowlandson, entitled
'Description of a Boxing Match'.
The print is dated 1812 but the
bout between the two
protagonists, Ward and Quick,
actually took place in 1806 and it
is likely that Rowlandson never
in person saw the contest.

Lord Byron's Screen

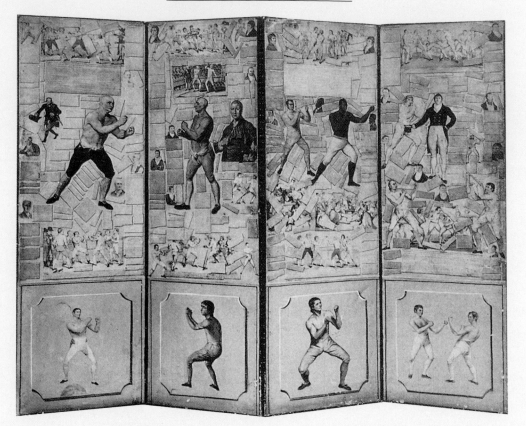

Above: Byron had a mania for boxing and created this famous screen between 1812 and 1816 by pasting cuttings taken from newspapers and *Boxiana* onto a canvas backing.

Above: Detail from Byron's Screen: Richard Humphries.

Above: Detail from Byron's Screen: the fight between John Gully (left) and Henry 'Game Chicken' Pearce who won in sixty-four rounds.

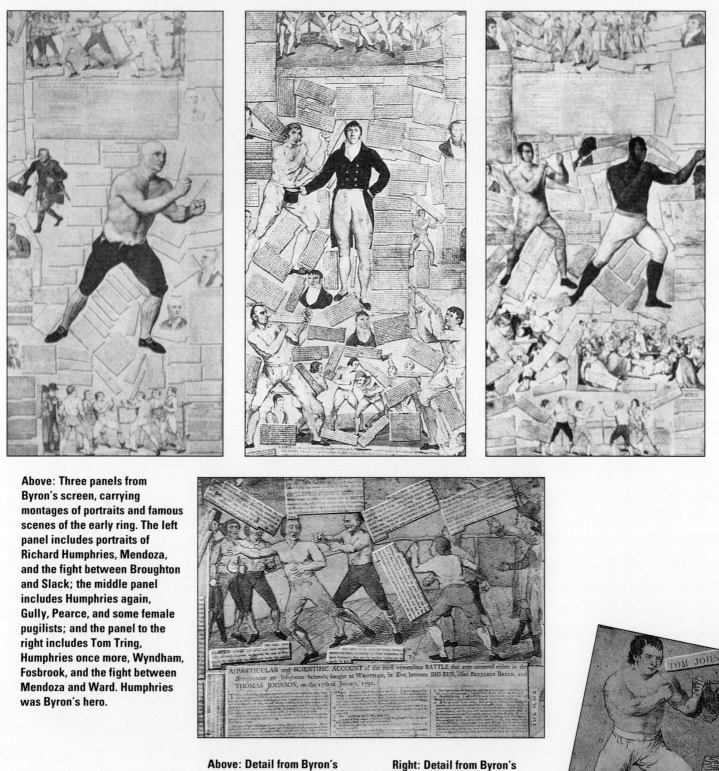

Above: Three panels from Byron's screen, carrying montages of portraits and famous scenes of the early ring. The left panel includes portraits of Richard Humphries, Mendoza, and the fight between Broughton and Slack; the middle panel includes Humphries again, Gully, Pearce, and some female pugilists; and the panel to the right includes Tom Tring, Humphries once more, Wyndham, Fosbrook, and the fight between Mendoza and Ward. Humphries was Byron's hero.

Above: Detail from Byron's Screen: the contest between Tom Johnson and 'Big' Ben Brian (right) who has had his hair cut short because Johnson kept tugging at it.

Right: Detail from Byron's Screen: Tom Johnson.

Above: A print of the fight between Jack Randall and Martin the Baker of 1821. It shows stage-coaches in the background which have stopped to let passengers view the fight, and also two seconds clutching bottles of water. The phrase 'to have a lot of bottle', meaning to have courage, is an old boxing term. Randall, incidentally, won the fight.

other Nobel Prize-winning author to have a deep interest in the sport was, more predictably, Ernest Hemingway, who by all accounts fancied he had a good right hand and once had a friendly sparring session with Gene Tunney. Jack London, author of *Call of the Wild*, was also a fight fan and is reputed to have instigated the search for a 'Great White Hope' to challenge Jack Johnson when the 'Galveston Giant' beat Tommy Burns for the world championship in 1908.

In the days before photography, print-makers were called upon to record fights and fighters. Some of their works are now considered classics and,

Above: The frontispiece of a rather fanciful biography of the black heavyweight, Peter Jackson. In the 1890s, drawings and engravings were the norm, rather than photographs, and boxing art became quite a speciality. Seen, left, is a photograph of the same boxer, taken when he was coloured champion of the world, and overall champion of Australia, where there was no boxing colour bar.

Boxing and photography have always been kind to each other. Technical advances in film speeds and camera actions have allowed extraordinary moments in famous fights to be recorded in breathtaking detail, while the sport has provided the photographers of ten decades with some of their most exciting, stunning and moving images. The developments in the art of photography have enabled shots to be taken that show exactly what happens when a punch lands on its target. In the photograph to the right, Willie Vaughan is having his nose flattened by 'Tiger' Jones, while in the photograph below it is Art Persley who is having his features rearranged.

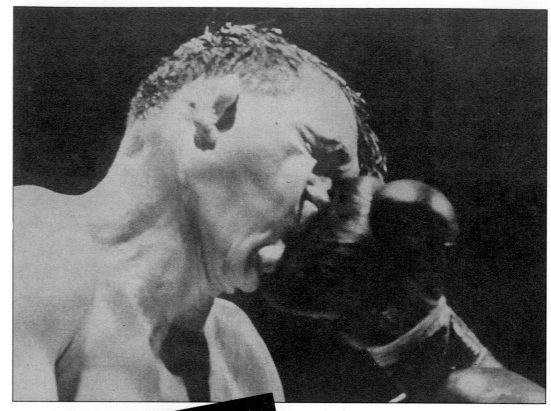

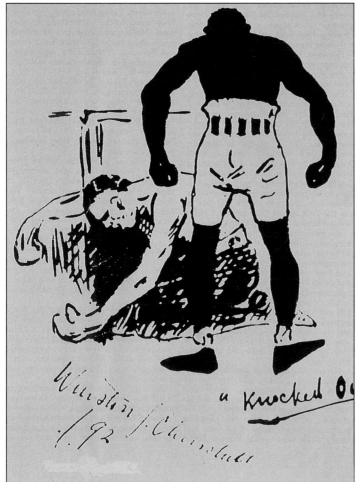

Above and left: Sketches of the fight between Peter Jackson and the Australian British Empire champion, Frank Slavin, which the American won in ten rounds. in 1892. Although the drawing on the left is signed by Winston Churchill, it's of doubtful authenticity. The top drawing is by Harry Furniss.

indeed, many great artists have created pictures of pugilists and their battles. The famous English artist William Hogarth painted a well-known portrait of his friend James Figg and did numerous sketches of boxers and boxing matches. In the nineteenth century one of the greatest of all Romantic painters, the Frenchman Théodore Géricault, was drawn to the subject and executed a fanciful etching of the Tom Cribb versus Tom Molineux contest. The one boxer to have excelled at painting was the middleweight world champion, Mickey Walker, who held several well-received exhibitions of his 'primitive' work.

Many boxers have found acting to be a lucrative career after they have hung up their gloves. Some even appeared on stage before their boxing days were over: John L Sullivan appeared in *Honest Hearts and Willing Hands* in 1890 some two years before he met

Boxing In Print

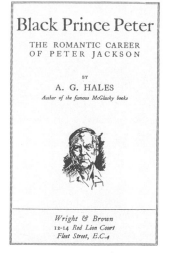

Above: The title page from A G Hales' biography of the great champion Peter Jackson. Like so many boxing biographies, it is more fantasy than fact.

Right: Schmeling gives the Nazi salute during the playing of the national anthem before a fight in Germany. He later claimed that he was against Nazism and all it stood for, and said that he was obliged to go along with it to save his career. Schmeling was never really a fascist, but was trapped like so many Germans at the time into obeying Hitler's wishes.

Below: The title page of Gene Tunney's autobiography. Before taking up boxing, Tunney contemplated a career as a writer and in later life he was friendly with George Bernard Shaw and Ernest Hemingway.

Below: The memorial gravestone of Tom Sayers in Highgate Cemetery, London. Sayers rivalled the Duke of Wellington as Britain's greatest hero, and William Thackeray wrote a poem about him. The sculptured dog, a mastiff, out-lived his master. He was a loyal friend and his collar bore the inscription:
I am Tom Sayer's dog Whose dog are you?

Above: The title page of Max Schmeling's autobiography (*My Life – My Struggle*). Adolf Hitler had great hopes for Schmeling but when the German heavyweight was defeated by Joe Louis in 1938, the dictator's dreams of proving that white was superior to black, already deflated by Jesse Owens at the 1936 Berlin Olympics, were further shaken.

Above: Many ring greats of different eras toyed with careers in entertainment, including Rocky Graziano, James J Corbett, Muhammad Ali, Bob Fitzsimmons, and Joe Frazier. Seen above in 1928 is a vaudeville act created by two great sluggers, Tom Sharkey and James J Jeffries, who toured the halls re-enacting their most famous bout.

James J Corbett for the title. Both Bob Fitzsimmons and Corbett appeared in money-spinning stage acts and, in the modern era, Muhammad Ali both trod the boards and appeared in films. Ali's great foe, Joe Frazier, attempted to become a rock singer with a band called the Knockouts but it was only a brief flirtation with show business and most who heard him sing wished they hadn't.

The first filmed boxing match was between James J Corbett and Peter Courtney in 1894. The films used in the giant Kinetoscope were only about one and a half minutes long and they consequently determined the length of the rounds. Two minutes were required to reload the camera so the boxers had extended breaks. Corbett won in the sixth round and the films that recorded the contest are available to the modern fan on video.

Many former boxers have attempted to become film stars, Rocky Graziano and Rocky Marciano amongst them, but the best movies on boxing have all had professional actors playing the leading roles.

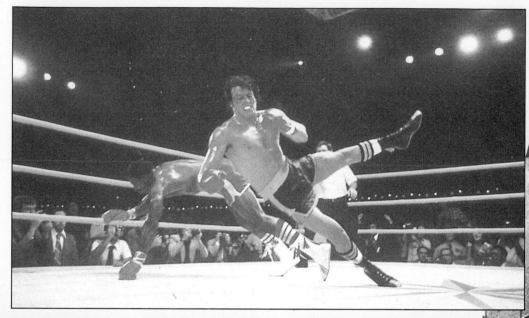

Picturegoer

THE NATIONAL **FILM** AND ENTERTAINMENT WEEKLY ★ NOVEMBER 17, 1956 ★ NO. 1,124 ★ VOL. 32

7

STOP MOONING ABOUT DEAN

This boy's better — he beats even Brando

EVEN in Hollywood, tragedy has its own kind of cockeyed justice. James Dean's car crash last year killed-off one brilliant screen career. But, ironically, it virtually gave birth to another. For Dean was scheduled to play Rocky Graziano, the ex-juvenile delinquent who became middle-weight boxing champion of the world.

And, even as Hollywood was mourning the death in *Somebody Up There Likes Me.*

And, even as Hollywood was mourning the loss of Dean, a new actor was picked to fill the gap. It was a break in a million.

American newcomer, the actor on Broadway, he met the real Graziano. That's how he picked up a lot of his walk and talk," And he adds a trifle bitterly: "Now I've got to play Graziano and they'll say: "I'm just like Brando."

Just how important *Somebody Up There Likes Me* is to Newman can be judged by his inauspicious beginnings in Hollywood. In *The Silver Chalice* he had little to do but stand around and gape at Jack Palance. In *The Rack* he showed promise. But as one character in *Somebody Up There Likes Me* says: "All youngsters are promising."

We should sue the young for breach of promise."

We can't sue Newman, though. His performance, here, comes as a staggering surprise. Even now Hollywood is talking about this portrayal as Oscar material. Whether Brando is, or Dean was. But off-set, is a far more manageable and honesty about his he talked

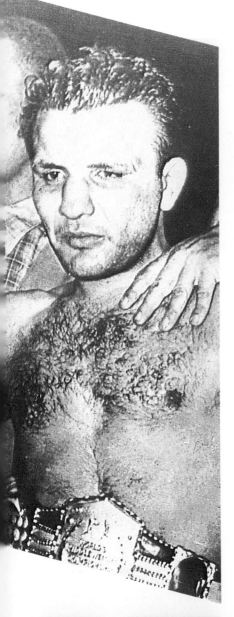

MAJOR BOXING MOVIES

Left: Boxing has always supplied the movies with a rich vein of inspiration, as shown here. Paul Newman's first big break came in Somebody Up There Likes Me: his portrayal of Rocky Graziano earned him comparison with James Dean and Marlon Brando. Seen also: Sylvester Stallone in the Rocky films; Jake LaMotta and the man who won an Oscar for playing him in Raging Bull, Robert De Niro; and Ali as himself in The Greatest.

Below: Three world heavyweight champions posing for a still during the making of *The Prizefighter and the Lady* in 1933. Max Baer (left) was the hero of the film but the current holder of the title, Primo Carnera (right), refused to be shown losing to the man who would eventually take the title from him, so they agreed upon a draw. The referee in the centre is the great Jack Dempsey.

Raging Bull – the story of Jake LaMotta, directed by Martin Scorsese and starring Robert DeNiro, who won an Oscar for his performance.

Somebody Up There Likes Me – a bio-pic of Rocky Graziano who was played by Paul Newman.

Fat City – the fictitious story of a comeback champion who struggles with his success.

Champion – the fictional tale of a character, played by Kirk Douglas, who rises to become world champion.

Rocky – the fictional story of a boxer named Rocky Balboa who becomes heavyweight champion against all the odds. It was written by Sylvester Stallone who also played the hero. (In all, five Rocky movies have been released at the time of going to press: but who knows . . .)

MANAGERS
AND
PROMOTERS

Above: Ted Broadribb shakes hands with Georges Carpentier long after their fighting days were over. Broadribb, known as 'Young Snowball', was one of only two Englishmen to stop Carpentier and he had a successful second career as a manager.

Left: A manager has to be prepared to give his charge all sorts of help. Here Jack Doyle, the Irish heavyweight, is shown flanked by advisers. He had the audacity to sue the British Boxing Board of Control when he was denied his purse after being disqualified in a contest against Jack Petersen in 1933.

MANAGERS

The most important and often the most influential figure in a professional boxer's career is his manager. It is the manager's task to look after the well-being of a fighter, to negotiate his fight contracts, and to oversee his training and preparation for a contest.

Managers first came into their own at the turn of the century. During the days of bare-knuckle fighting, the best pugilists had patrons who took care of their financial interests, but as the sport began to lose favour with the landed gentry, boxers turned to hiring professionals who not only took care of financial matters but also selected suitable opposition – still one of a manager's chief functions.

A good manager will nurse a protégé carefully towards the top, and his reward for doing a good job will be to take a percentage cut of the boxer's earnings. Often flamboyant and extrovert, some managers have become almost as famous as their charges.

Right: Gene Tunney admiring the cheque that has just been handed to him by Tex Rickard (left) after his defeat of Jack Dempsey in 1927. Billy Gibson (right), Tunney's manager, looks on, probably awaiting the opportunity to get the money into the bank.

Above: Barney Eastwood, a bookmaker from Belfast, who managed Barry McGuigan to fame and fortune before an acrimonious split over money.

Above: Mickey Walker (right) and 'Doc' Kearns relish another pay-day. As well as managing Walker and Dempsey, Kearns also looked after world champions Joey Maxim, Abe Attell, Benny Leonard and Archie Moore.

Left: The late Al Weill who managed four world champions: Rocky Marciano, Marty Servo, Joey Archibald and Lou Ambers.

Left: The late Cus D'Amato who managed world champions Floyd Patterson and José Torres. He also discovered Mike Tyson whom he rescued from a penal institution when the tearaway was just fourteen. He was possibly the only person able to harness Tyson's formidable aggression, and certainly the only man to have gained the respect and trust of the wayward champion. The positive effect of good management is sadly illustrated by the events in Tyson's life after his mentor's death.

FAMOUS MANAGERS AND THEIR BOXERS

Right: The most successful manager of them all, Jack 'Doc' Kearns (right), stands beside Jack Dempsey whom he started to manage in 1917.

Below: Ted Broadribb (left) and Dan Sullivan. Broadribb, a former fighter, managed such champions as Tommy Farr and Freddie Mills while Sullivan ran London's famous Blackfriars Ring arena after its founder Dick Burge died in World War One.

William A Brady (USA)
James J Corbett and James J Jeffries (heavyweight world champions)

Cus D'Amato (USA)
Floyd Patterson (heavyweight world champion) and José Torres (light-heavyweight world champion). D'Amato was also mentor to Mike Tyson (heavyweight world champion)

François Descamps (Fr)
Georges Carpentier (light-heavyweight world champion)

Mickey Duff (Eng)
Lloyd Honeyghan (welterweight world champion)

Billy Gibson (USA)
Benny Leonard (welterweight world champion), Gene Tunney (heavyweight world champion) and Louis 'Kid' Kaplan (featherweight world champion)

Jack 'Doc' Kearns (USA)
Jack Dempsey (heavyweight world champion), Mickey Walker (welterweight and middleweight world champion), Joey Maxim and Archie Moore (light-heavyweight world champions)

Al Weill (USA)
Rocky Marciano (heavyweight world champion), Joey Archibald (featherweight world champion) and Lou Ambers (lightweight world champion)

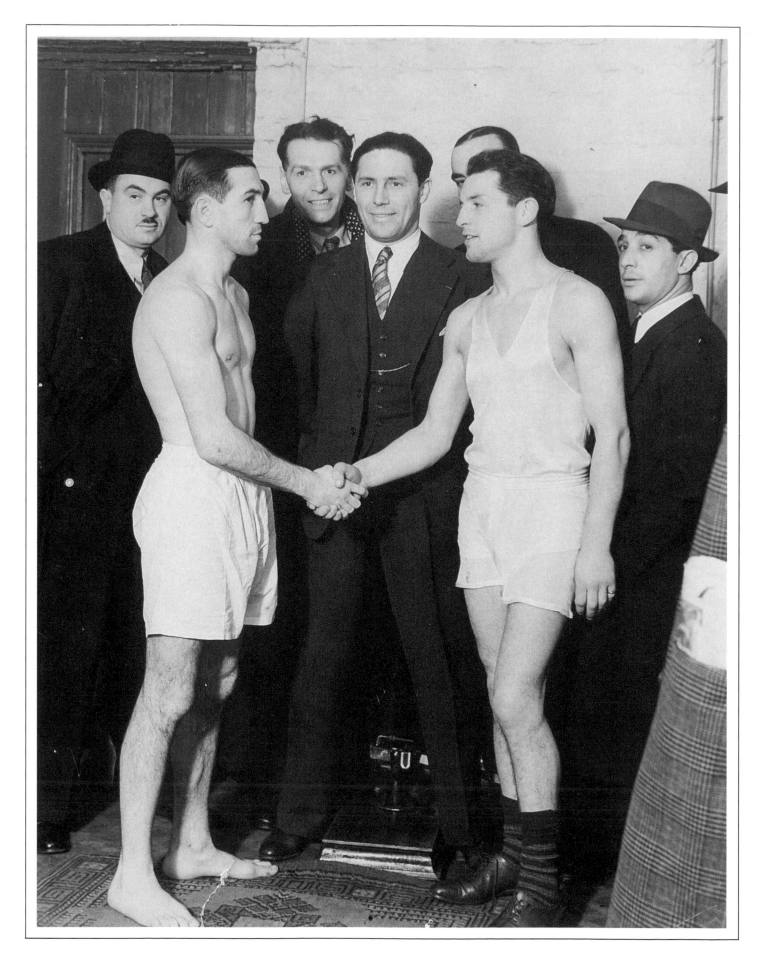

Right: Rickard's first major promotion was the Joe Gans v 'Battling' Nelson lightweight title fight in 1906. Before the contest, he introduced John L Sullivan (left) to Stanley Ketchel.

PROMOTERS

Promoters, the men who plan and organize fights and attract the boxers into the ring, are quite probably the most powerful men behind the scenes. It is they who arrange matches and often stand to win or lose vast fortunes. The most famous and, incidentally, most trusted, promoter of all time was Tex Rickard: he staged the first fight to gross more than a million dollars at the gate (Jack Dempsey versus Georges Carpentier) in 1921.

The English promoter, Jack Solomons, did much to boost the flagging fortunes of British boxing after World War Two and he managed to persuade many leading American boxers to cross the Atlantic when they would probably much rather have stayed at home. A number of notable English promoters have followed in Solomons' wake, including Harry Levene, Mickey Duff, Mike Barrett and Barry Hearn (who was also one of the first men to help snooker become recognized as a worthy international sport).

In recent times, boxing promoters have often been suspected of dubious associations, and the dealings of the two men who have dominated recent boxing promotions in America, Don King and Bob Arum, have allegedly been scrutinized by the FBI. The mysterious shooting of the English promoter Frank Warren in 1990 also did little to dispel fears that the sport of professional boxing was not as squeaky clean as it might be.

Above: The great Tex Rickard was born in 1871. He made a fortune in the Klondike gold rush and then lost it all gambling. He was the first big-time promoter and he orchestrated the Dempsey v Carpentier fight of 1921, the first to gross more than a million dollars at the gate.

Opposite: Gustave Humery (left), the French lightweight who became world champion in 1937, shakes hands with England's Jack 'Kid' Berg at the weigh-in before their bout which Humery won. Standing between them is the American promoter, Jeff Dickson, who ironically made his name promoting fights in Europe.

Above: Bob Arum (left) and Don King, the two most powerful promoters in the USA. Both men have come under fire for wheeling and dealing which many believe has done little to enhance boxing's image.

Left: King is one of the most controversial figures in modern boxing, and his career epitomizes some of its dilemmas. He has done an enormous amount to bring the sport to a massive public, and he has made many of his boxers, including Tyson and Chavez, rich beyond dreams. But at the same time his methods and style have made as many headlines as the fights he has organized, and many critics have speculated as to whether King's dominance as a promoter has been in the interest of the sport as a whole.

Left: Jack Solomons, famous cigar smoker and promoter, who salvaged British boxing from the doldrums after World War Two.

Below: Harry Levene who followed in Solomons' footsteps and did British boxing great service during the 1960s.

Left: Barry Hearn, one of a new breed of energetic English promoters, whose Matchroom empire is well known for managing some of the world's greatest snooker players.

Above: Mickey Duff, who took up the reins after Solomons and Levene, and is currently one of England's most powerful promoters.

Earl's Court Exhibition,

ON

Monday, October 2.

JAMES WHITE

WILL PRESENT **TWO** OF THE

Greatest Boxing Contests ever held in England.

The First Contest, timed to start at 9 p.m. sharp,

BETWEEN

SID BURNS

(of Aldgate)

AND

GEORGES CARPENTIER

(The Welter-Weight Champion of France).

These men will box fifteen rounds, and the winner will be matched against **Young Josephs** *for the Welter-Weight Championship of Europe.*

The Second Contest, timed to start at 10 p.m. sharp,

BETWEEN

JACK JOHNSON

(Champion of the World)

AND

Bombardier

BILLY WELLS

(Champion of England),

Who will box 20 Rounds for the World's Championship.

SEATS CAN BE BOOKED AT ALL THE PRINCIPAL HOTELS AND LIBRARIES.

Prices from 5 guineas to 10/6.

Bomb. Wells can be seen in action on Thursdays and Saturdays only, at 5 p.m. each day.

BOXING PUBLICITY
AND EPHEMERA

Above: Letters from the bare-knuckle fighter, Nat Langham. In the middle of the last century, fight locations were kept secret to avoid interference from the police: Langham's couplet 'if you intend to see the Fight you must be in town on Monday night' (in the letter on the right) shows how the word got around.

Opposite: A beautiful poster advertising an encounter between Britain's heavyweight champion and the great Jack Johnson. It is particularly rare – the fight never took place.

The first man actively to publicize boxing by handing out his own leaflets was the origina-tor of it all, James Figg. He was lucky enough to have William Hogarth as a friend and the famous painter produced an illustrated pamphlet for him which was handed out at fairs and public gatherings. The illustration was especially important to Figg as at the time not many people could read.

Many of the earliest fights were publicized by broadsheets which were distributed in the cities, towns and villages of England. Vivid accounts of past fights, often in verse, were written on the broadsheets which also advertised coming attractions at fairs. Newspapers like the *Gentleman's Magazine* also re-ported important contests and *The Times* of London, which was first published in 1785, is said to have had a surge in sales when it first carried accounts of prize fights.

The first notable book on boxing was *A Treatise on the Useful Art of Self-Defence* by one Captain Godfrey,

ERNIE JARVIS.

LEN JOHNSON.

FIDEL LA BARBA.

PHIL LOLOSKY.

TOMMY McINNES.

ALF MANCINI.

HARRY MASON.

CHARLIE SMITH

KID SOCKS.

BOB SPILLER.

JACK STANLEY.

A great gallery of boxing heroes could be assembled by collecting the cards given away in cigarette packs. Cigarette cards came into their own during the interval between the two World Wars when smoking was considered an acceptable habit. As well as promoting boxing, and other sports, such cards guaranteed sales of cigarettes as complete collections became prized possessions. Today, rare collections can be extremely valuable. These cards, issued free by the Imperial Tobacco Company, carried a portrait on one side and a short biography on the reverse.

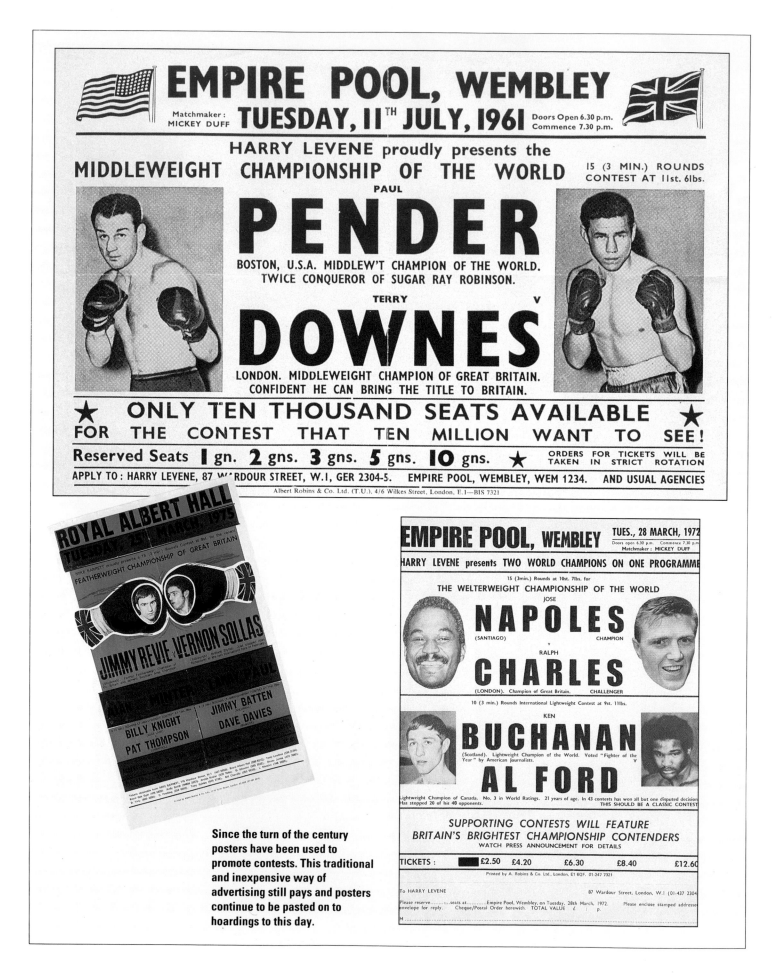

Since the turn of the century posters have been used to promote contests. This traditional and inexpensive way of advertising still pays and posters continue to be pasted on to hoardings to this day.

PANCRATIA,

OR A

HISTORY OF PUGILISM.

CONTAINING A FULL ACCOUNT OF

EVERY BATTLE OF NOTE FROM THE TIME OF

BROUGHTON AND SLACK,

DOWN TO THE PRESENT DAY.

INTERSPERSED

WITH ANECDOTES OF ALL THE CELEBRATED
PUGILISTS OF THIS COUNTRY;

With an argumentative Proof, that Pugilism, considered as a Gymnic Exercise, demands the Admiration, and Patronage of every free State, being calculated to inspire manly Courage, and a Spirit of Independence—enabling us to resist Slavery at Home and Enemies from Abroad.

EMBELLISHED WITH A CORRECT AND ELEGANT ENGRAVED

PORTRAIT

OF THE

CHAMPION, CRIB.

LONDON:
(PRINTED BY W. HILDYARD, POPPIN'S COURT.)
PUBLISHED AND SOLD BY W. OXBERRY, 11, CLARENDON SQUARE, SOMER'S-TOWN, ALSO BY SHERWOOD, NEELY, AND JONES, PATERNOSTER-ROW.

1812.

Left: The title page of *Pancratia, or a History of Pugilism* which was credited to the author William Oxberry. It is one of the first and most important books on boxing and is much sought after by collectors.

Above and top: *Famous Fights* was a popular magazine in England at the turn of the century and gave vivid accounts of gruesome encounters. However both the illustrators and the journalists took liberties with the truth, and many of the tales, while exciting, are woefully inaccurate.

which described many gruesome contests in gory detail. *Pancratia, or a History of Pugilism* was published in 1811 and much of the information in this book was incorporated into the first boxing best-seller, *Boxiana: or Sketches of Ancient and Modern Pugilism* by Pierce Egan who became one of the prize ring's greatest chroniclers. In 1824 *Egan's Life in London and Sporting Guide* was first produced and was soon taken over by *Bell's Life in London* which continued to be published until 1886. *Bell's Life* was one of the most important of all the papers that carried boxing reports as its accounts were scrupulously accurate – which is more than can be said for the reports in the *Famous Fights* periodical, which often carried fanciful descriptions that were next door to pure fiction.

In the United States, the most important newspaper to promote boxing was the *Police Gazette* which was first published by Richard K Fox in 1873. The earliest copies of the *Gazette* had illustrations of bouts drawn by highly imaginative artists but it soon began to carry photographs and became a hugely successful paper. It continued to be published until 1932. By that time, however, the most famous magazine of all, *The Ring*, had been produced by Nat Fleischer. There are today hundreds of papers and magazines wholly devoted to boxing but none has managed to match *The Ring* for its international sales.

Above: An invitation to watch a boxing match between women. The contest was a publicity gimmick, and the invitation was issued to ticket-holders of the Georges Carpentier v Jim Sullivan European middleweight championship fight which was held in Monte Carlo in 1912.

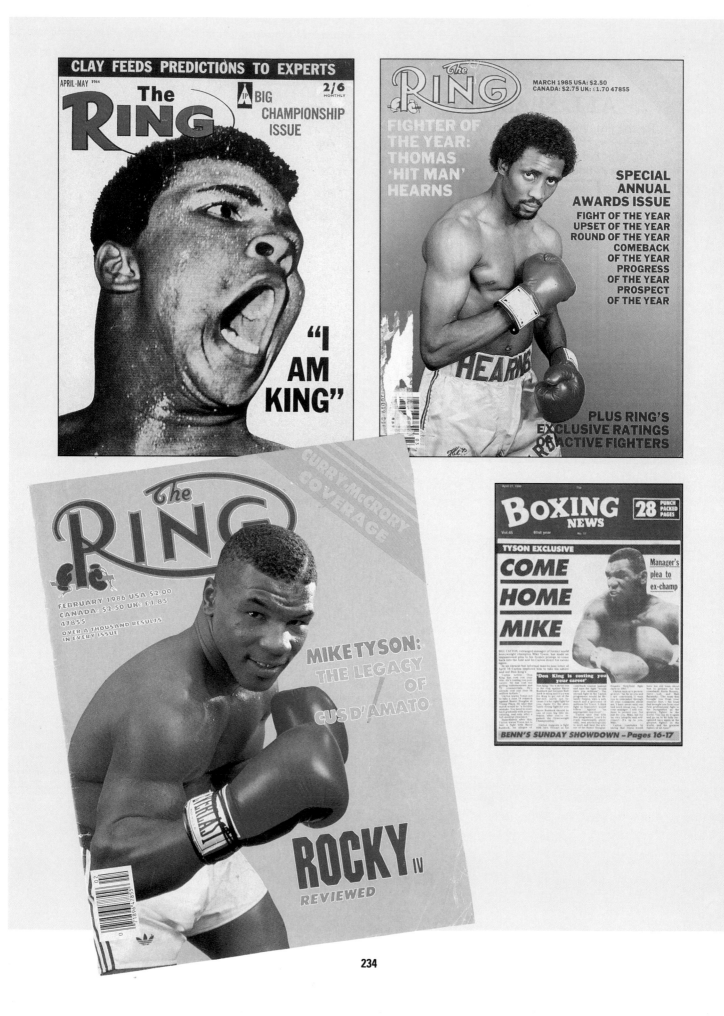

These pages show covers from eight of the most popular boxing journals. Boxing magazines continue to flourish on both sides of the Atlantic. The most famous monthly magazine is *The Ring* which was first published in 1922 by Nat Fleischer, a former sports editor of the *New York Telegraph*. Britain's longest-serving magazine is *Boxing News* (formerly called *Boxing*) which was first published in 1909.

BOXING
TROPHIES

Above: The 'colours' of John Heenan and Tom Sayers. Such colours were placed on diagonally opposing posts in the days of the prize ring, and the winner of a contest had the right to keep his opponent's colours. As Heenan and Sayers drew their fight in 1860, each man kept his colours.

Left: The first person to be permitted to keep a Lonsdale Belt on successfully defending his British title twice was the flyweight champion Benny Lynch in 1936.

The traditional boxing trophy is a belt. The first one ever awarded went to the English champion Tom Cribb after he had beaten the black American Tom Molineaux in 1810. Cribb was presented with the belt by none other than King George III, and a year later he was also given a silver cup for his achievements in the ring. A belt was also given to Jem 'Black Diamond' Ward in 1825 after he had won the championship from Tom Cannon. Ward picked up a second belt in 1831 on regaining the title from Simon Byrne, but he was obliged to hand this over to 'Bendigo' Thompson in 1835. Nobody knows exactly what 'Bendigo' did with the trophy but it is more than likely that he sold it for cash. Further belts were awarded to subsequent champions, including Ben Caunt, and lesser trophies were given to other pugilistic heroes by their admirers.

Before his epic confrontation with John Heenan in 1860, Tom Sayers put up his own personal belt as a trophy to be taken home by the winner. This first international championship contest ended in a draw so Sayers hung on to his belt, but after the fight both

Above: John L Sullivan's magnificent belt. It was presented to him by the people of Boston in 1887. The belt cost $10,000 and was encrusted with 397 diamonds. Portraits of the champion himself (left) and his manager, Pat Sheedy, were enamelled onto panels on each side of the buckle. Irish and American symbols on further panels show where Sullivan's loyalties lay.

Right: This cup was presented to Tom Cribb in 1811 after he had beaten Tom Molineaux. On it are inscribed a list of all his victories and a fanciful coat of arms. The cup was later presented to Tom Sayers.

boxers were presented with silver belts at a specially convened reception at the Alhambra Theatre in London.

Towards the end of the nineteenth century, Richard K Fox, owner of the prestigious American sporting paper the *Police Gazette*, had a special belt made. This, he suggested, should be awarded to the world heavyweight champion. John L Sullivan, who claimed he was the world champion, refused to fight Jem Smith for the trophy, so it was then given to Jake Kilrain. In 1887 the people of Boston were infuriated at this and clubbed together to give their hero, Sullivan, a magnificent $10,000 gold belt which was studded with 397 diamonds. When James J Corbett beat Sullivan for the world championship he was given the original *Police Gazette* belt, but it was subsequently stolen never to surface again.

In 1909 the National Sporting Club decided to issue belts to British champions in each of the weight divisions. The NSC hoped that by issuing these belts it would tighten its control of British boxing and it announced that only the men who had such belts should be considered genuine champions. The first belt was presented to the lightweight, Freddie Welsh, by the Fifth Earl of Lonsdale and the belts became known as 'Lonsdale Belts'. These belts are still

Above: The first Lonsdale Belt was awarded by the National Sporting Club to Freddie Welsh in 1909 when he became the British lightweight champion. Ever since then a belt has been awarded to British champions in each of the weight divisions. The central image is of the NSC's first president, the Fifth Earl of Lonsdale.

Left: Henry Cooper, the great British heavyweight, dons his Lonsdale Belts. Cooper is the only man ever to have won three belts outright.

Above: The front and reverse of a commemorative medal struck in honour of Joe Louis who successfully defended his world heavyweight title twenty-five times from 1937 to 1948.

Left: Gus Lesnevich wearing his *Ring* magazine belt after becoming world light-heavyweight champion in 1941.

awarded today by the British Boxing Board of Control which assumed control of the sport in England on the demise of the NSC. Originally a boxer was allowed to keep his Lonsdale Belt if he successfully defended his title twice. This rule enabled the heavyweight Henry Cooper to own a record number of three belts after winning nine British Championship bouts. In 1978, however, the rules were changed, and it is now only possible to own one belt.

When *The Ring* magazine was established in 1922, its proprietor, Nat Fleischer, announced that he would award belts to world champions. The original

Ring Belts were valuable; however with the proliferation of weight divisions and the rising number of ruling bodies that sanction their own world championship bouts, the expense of handing over such trophies to each world champion became too expensive, so they were discontinued.

The four leading international boxing organizations still award belts to their various champions in each of the weight divisions. This means that an undisputed champion can possess four belts and, although they are no longer made out of precious metals, they are still coveted tokens.

Above: Lloyd Honeyghan, a British welterweight world champion who was born in Jamaica, displays his three world championship trophies: the IBF (top left), WBC (top right) and WBA belts.

Left: Dennis Andries, a British subject who was born in Guyana and trains in Detroit, became WBC light-heavyweight champion in 1986. Here, he proudly wears his WBC championship belt.

BOXING VENUES

Above: This rather fanciful image of a typical English fair of the ninteeenth century, shows a 'barker' desparately trying to persuade a country yokel that he could stay three or four rounds with one of his champions in the boxing booth. Fairs with such booths flourished from the start of the eighteenth century and it is still occasionally possible to find one today. The English poet Vernon Scannell has recounted how he used to earn a living boxing in booths after World War Two, and several champions, Freddie Mills and Jimmy Wilde amongst them, first made a name for themselves at fairgrounds.

Left: A photograph of a match at the NSC, taken when the club was enjoying its most prosperous years. In those days, the referee sat outside the ring.

At the beginning of the eighteenth century, boxing matches were usually held in booths at fairs, or in simple arenas bounded by boards at such places as James Figg's amphitheatre. Fights out in the English countryside were held in 'rings' which were created by onlookers who held up a rope to confine the boxers. By 1723 the sport had become so popular that King George I, to popular acclaim, was prompted to order a square 'ring' to be erected in London's Hyde Park for common use by the sporting fraternity.

King George's ring lasted for a hundred years and as the sport boomed a number of other venues were established in England, including an arena at the Fives Court in Little St Martin's Lane in the heart of London. The Fives Court became a favourite meeting place for boxers and their supporters (who were invariably aristocrats). The gentry called themselves the 'Corinthians' and dubbed the boxers the 'Fancy'.

After boxing was outlawed in the nineteenth century, most contests took place outside the cities in the countryside where they were usually, but not always, beyond the reach of the law. More often than

Above: The Fives Court in Little St Martin's Lane, London, which was a popular rendezvous for the Fancy until it was destroyed at the beginning of the nineteenth century. The print shows Jack Randall sparring with Ned Turner, and it supposedly contains portraits of a number of the leading fighters of the age in the foreground.

Right: The title of this print by I R Cruikshank is *A Set-to at the Fives Court for the benefit of "One of the Fancy"*. The location illustrated, however, is not thought to be the Fives Court in Little St Martin's Lane.

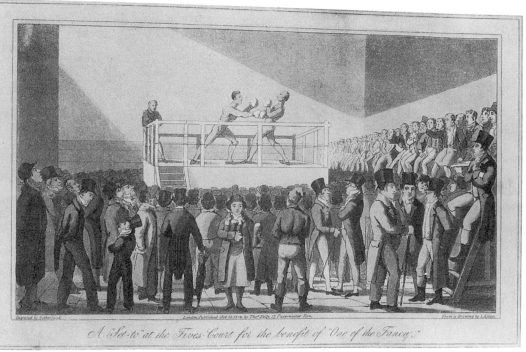

A Set-to at the Fives-Court for the benefit of "One of the Fancy"

Right: *The Art of Self-Defence* by I R and G Cruikshank. This print shows John Jackson sparring with 'Corinthian' Tom in Jackson's Rooms, which essentially comprised a gymnasium.

'TOM AND JERRY RECEIVING INSTRUCTIONS'
'Gentleman' Jackson's rooms in Bond Street
Coloured aquatint by R. I. and G. Cruickshank from Pierce Egan's *Life in London*, 1821

Below: A print, attributed to George Cruikshank, which shows a fight taking place either at a club or in a sporting inn. It was probably drawn *c*.1820 and it is worth noting the use of gloves.

Above: An illustration of the Daffy Club which met at the Castle public-house in London at the beginning of the nineteenth century. 'Daffy' was a slang term for gin, which says something about its members, and the club used to promote sporting dinners at which bouts took place.

not the rings for these fights were temporary affairs: four posts were hammered into the ground and a rope was hastily tied around. If the police did intervene it was a relatively simple matter to pull up the posts, wrap up the rope, and flee. With some of the major championship fights, of course, the police were at a loss: not only were the crowds huge, but the aristocracy turned out in numbers, and it was difficult for a humble policeman to arrest a duke or an earl.

Boxing was in a similar predicament in America, where some states sanctioned boxing while others did

not. Many fights took place on barges moored in the middle of rivers; if the police arrived, the ropes were cut and the barge was allowed to drift downstream. The celebrated fight between Bob Fitzsimmons and Peter Maher in 1896 was due to take place at Langtry in Texas; when the Texas Rangers arrived on the scene, however, the boxers, officials, spectators and a film crew were obliged to pick up their belongings and move over the Rio Grande into Mexico where the American lawmen had no jurisdiction.

When boxing started to become a legitimate and

Above: A F 'Peggy' Bettinson who, with John Fleming, founded London's National Sporting Club in 1891. Bettinson insisted on good behaviour from boxers and spectators alike and ruled the club with a rod of iron.

Left: The first premises of the National Sporting Club in King Street, Covent Garden. The club later moved to Holborn, then to Soho, and ultimately to the Café Royal in London's Regent Street.

Below: Jimmy Wilde, Britain's flyweight champion, shakes hands with the Prince of Wales, later to become King Edward VIII, before his fight against the American Joe Lynch at the NSC in 1919.

Left: From the outset, the National Sporting Club was exclusive. Members and their guests were expected to wear evening dress and bouts were held after dinner. No talking, let alone cheering, was permitted during rounds so the fights took place in an eerie silence. The NSC opened its doors to the public in 1928, but was forced to abandon its base in Covent Garden a year later.

Above: 'The Ring' at Blackfriars which was an octagonal chapel before being converted into a boxing arena by Dick Burge in 1910. It was one of London's most popular sporting venues until it was destroyed during the Blitz of World War Two.

recognized sport at the end of the nineteenth century, the National Sporting Club was created in England. This august and exclusive club was founded by A F 'Peggy' Bettinson in 1891, and Lord Lonsdale was its first president. Housed in a building in King Street in London's Covent Garden, the NSC had a massive influence on boxing worldwide and did much to make the sport more acceptable to a scathing public. Bouts took place after dinner at the NSC and both spectators and boxers were expected to behave themselves. No cheering was allowed, so the bouts took place in complete silence (except for the grunts of the contestants).

As boxing became more and more popular, other establishments came into being in England. One of the most famous of these was The Ring at Blackfriars in London. The building was formerly a Nonconformist chapel and was octagonal in shape so that no devils could hide in the corners. When it was no longer used as a place of worship, it was taken over by the former British lightweight champion Dick Burge and converted into a boxing arena where two or three shows were put on each week. These shows were

Above: One of Britain's most popular referees, Eugene Corri, who was also a stockbroker. He refereed over a thousand contests.

Above: The scene at the Jack Petersen v Jack Doyle fight for the heavyweight championship of Great Britain at London's White City Stadium in 1933. The contest ended controversially when Doyle was disqualified in the second round. The White City staged many famous bouts before being pulled down in the 1980s.

Left: The White House in Washington staged an exhibition match between Billy Grupp and the lightweight world champion, Benny Leonard (third from left), in 1917. Leonard's manager, Billy Gibson, stands between the two boxers and on the right is the former heavyweight world champion, James J Corbett. President Woodrow Wilson is said to have taken a keen interest in the contest.

immensely popular with London's East Enders but the building was destroyed in the Blitz of World War Two, and all that remains as an echo of its existence is a public-house opposite the original site.

Boxing blossomed in England after World War One, and places such as the NSC, which could only accommodate around 1,300 people, began to suffer. Promoters chose to stage fights at vast arenas like the Royal Albert Hall, Earls Court and even soccer stadiums which they managed to fill with ease. The NSC opened its doors to the public in 1928 but was forced to close down its Covent Garden establishment soon

afterwards. The club continues to exist today, but it has lost much of its former status.

If boxing began to take off in England after World War One, it positively boomed in the United States. The great Tex Rickard was the first to see its potential, and in 1919 he organized the construction of a $100,000 arena near Toledo for the fight between Jack Dempsey and Jess Willard. The stadium could seat an astonishing 80,000 people, but the amazing Rickard went bigger still in 1921 when a 91,000-seat arena was built in Jersey City for the Dempsey versus Carpentier fight.

Left: Yankee Stadium, the famous baseball ground in New York, has hosted numerous boxing contests, including the 1938 return match between Joe Louis and Max Schmeling.

Above left, above right, and left: Some of the sites and buildings that have housed the world's most famous boxing arena, Madison Square Garden. The original 1871 Garden was built, appropriately enough, in Madison Square and played host to circuses and other events. This structure was destroyed in 1889 and the second Garden was built a year later on Madison Avenue. The third Garden, built in 1925 and known as 'The House that Tex built', was sited on Eighth Avenue, nowhere near Madison Square. The current Garden stands at and over Pennsylvania Station, and is dwarfed by surrounding skyscrapers.

Right: Many great champions have fought at Madison Square Garden including Joe Louis, Rocky Marciano, 'Sugar' Ray Robinson, Muhammad Ali and Roberto Duran. The Garden has also played host to lesser mortals, however, and this illustration shows a packed audience enjoying a Golden Gloves contest during the 1960s.

Right: The venue for one of the most extraordinary fights in heavyweight boxing history: the '20 du Mai' Stadium in Kinshasa, Zaïre, where Muhammad Ali defeated George Foreman (at the 'Rumble in the Jungle') to regain the world title in 1974.

The most famous boxing arena in the world is undoubtedly Madison Square Garden in New York. The original Garden was built in 1871, but it did not stage a boxing contest until 1882 when John L Sullivan fought Tug Wilson. A new arena was built in 1890 and this second structure lasted until 1925 when none other than Tex Rickard constructed a new sports hall which was nicknamed 'The House that Tex Built'. The fourth Madison Square Garden was opened in 1968 and stands on Seventh Avenue. It holds 18,000 people but, although it has staged many great fights, it has proved too small for the blockbuster events of the current era. With the demand for bigger purses, promoters have turned to the rich gambling towns of Las Vegas and Atlantic City, where purpose-built stages are often built on tennis courts or in car parks. In recent times, national governments have even been drafted in to sponsor fights – Zaïre and the Philippines for example. Although the gate receipts for such fights have not been astronomical, the worldwide television coverage has guaranteed handsome rewards for the promoters.

Three tickets which illustrate the changing state of boxing. The Marciano v LaStarza fight (top left) was staged at New York's famous Polo Grounds in 1953. The Frazier v Foreman ticket (bottom left) is for a closed-circuit television broadcast; the fight itself was held in Zaïre and the promoters reaped their rewards by organizing such broadcasts in cinemas and licensed halls around the world. In recent times, the gambling-rich city of Las Vegas has promoted many fights and boxing extravaganzas. This ticket (right) was for a charity show hosted by the famous actor and boxing fan, John Wayne.

Left: The Mirage, Las Vegas, which is one of a clutch of hotels in the desert resort that regularly stages world championship fights.

The Ring

Above: The modern boxing ring is defined by three or four ropes strung between the corner posts. The only man allowed in the ring while the boxers fight is the referee, but time-keepers, seconds, judges, doctors and certain members of the press are allowed into the 'inner-sanctum' which immediately surrounds the raised stage.

The numbers indicate the officials and professionals who would be in attendance at a big fight, as follows: 1. the official doctor; 2. the steward or manager of the body under whose authority the fight is taking place – BBofC, WBC, etc; 3. time-keeper; 4. general secretary or chief officer of the authority concerned; 5. judge; 6. press; 7. TV commentator; 8. substitute referee; 9. master of ceremonies; Red Corner – 10. second/cuts man; 11. chief second/manager; Blue Corner – 12. chief second/manager; 13. second/cuts man; 14. referee; 15. boxers; 16. TV cameraman; 17. press photographer; 18. round boy.

Above: There is no finer sight than a beautifully set-up and illuminated ring, immaculately prepared for a big occasion. This dramatic setting was for the Bruno v Bugner fight at White Hart Lane, London.

BOXING TERMS IN ENGLISH

Up to scratch
a reference to the 'scratch' line marked in the centre of a ring at which bare-knuckle fighters had to stand before they started to fight.

Toe the line
similar to 'up to scratch' – each fighter had to place a toe on a 'scratch' line before a round commenced.

Whip round
unruly crowds at bare-knuckle contests were controlled by men who wielded whips and they consequently became known as Whips. Occasionally Whips would pass a hat around the spectators and the money would be donated to either or both of the gallant fighters.

Stake money
in the days of prize fighting, the money for which pugilists fought would be tied to a corner post, or stake.

Bottle
in prize fighting days, each boxer would have a 'bottle-man' in his corner who would supply him with sustenance between rounds. Today, a 'bottle-man' refers to a person who supports a cause and 'to have a lot of bottle' refers to a person who has courage and is prepared to go on against the odds.

Throw up the sponge
if a boxer had had enough, his second would throw the sponge used for mopping the brow into the ring to signify his retirement.

Throw in the towel
similar to 'throw up the sponge' – a second would throw a towel into the ring if his boxer had taken enough punishment. The action is still used today.

Below the belt
hitting below the belt has always been illegal: it has now come to mean any particularly nasty trick.

INDEX

ACKNOWLEDGEMENTS

The vast majority of the photographs in this volume are from the private collections of O F Snelling and Derek O'Dell. Additional material has been supplied by their many friends in the world of boxing, and is used with their approval. Mr Snelling wishes particularly to thank R A Hartley, bookseller and boxing bibliographer; Harry Mullan, editor of Boxing News, for the provision of material and permission to use it; Mrs Ethel Crome, widow of the late Tom Crome; Mr and Mrs Peter McInnes, dealers in boxing books and ephemera; and Charles Taylor. Mr O'Dell would like to express his special thanks to David Allen, boxing collector; George Zeleny and the staff of Boxing Outlook; and David Roake for allowing material from his extensive collection to be used.

The producers extend grateful thanks to Sporting Pictures of 7a Lambs Conduit Passage, London WC1R 4RG, for supplying many of the colour photographs of fights and boxers of the modern era.

The producers of the book have attempted where relevant and where possible to trace the original sources of archive and other materials used in the book, and to seek permissions and offer acknowledgements where appropriate. They apologize for any omissions, oversights, or occasions when efforts to make contact or trace sources have proved fruitless. The producers would be pleased to hear from any uncontacted sources so that these acknowledgements may be updated for future editions.